Locomotrix

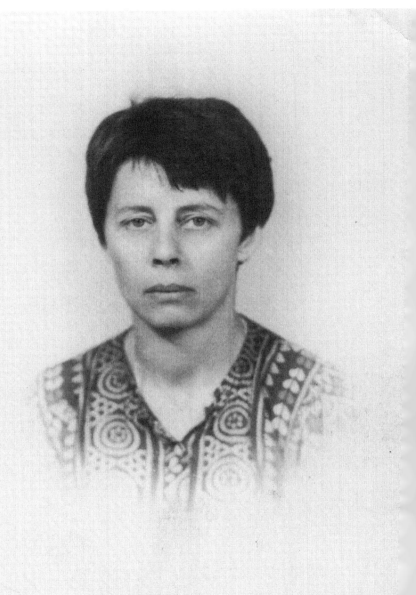

Locomotrix

Selected Poetry and Prose of Amelia Rosselli

A Bilingual Edition

Edited and translated by Jennifer Scappettone

THE UNIVERSITY OF CHICAGO PRESS ★ CHICAGO AND LONDON

JENNIFER SCAPPETTONE is assistant professor of English and creative writing and associate faculty of Romance languages and literatures at the University of Chicago, and was the Andrew W. Mellon Post-Doctoral Rome Prize Fellow in Modern Italian Studies for 2010–2011. Her poetry collections include *From Dame Quickly* and the bilingual *Thing Ode/Ode oggettuale*.

AMELIA ROSSELLI (1930–1996) was the author of eight volumes of poetry in Italian, English, and French and of other collected writings. She is widely considered one of the most important Italian poets of the second half of the twentieth century.

The University of Chicago Press, Chicago 60637
The University of Chicago Press, Ltd., London
© 2012 by The University of Chicago
All rights reserved. Published 2012.
Printed in the United States of America

Italian poems © Centro Manoscritti, University of Pavia. English translation, introduction, notes, selected bibliography, and compilation © The University of Chicago. All rights reserved.

21 20 19 18 17 16 15 14 13 12   1 2 3 4 5

ISBN-13: 978-0-226-72883-4 (paper)
ISBN-10: 0-226-72883-8 (paper)

The University of Chicago Press gratefully acknowledges the generous support of the Italian Ministry for Foreign Affairs, through the Italian Cultural Institute of Chicago, toward the publication of this book.

Library of Congress Cataloging-in-Publication Data
Rosselli, Amelia, 1930–1996.
  Locomotrix : selected poetry and prose of Amelia Rosselli / a bilingual edition edited and translated by Jennifer Scappettone.
     p. cm.
  Includes bibliographical references and index.
  ISBN-13: 978-0-226-72883-4 (pbk. : alkaline paper)
  ISBN-10: 0-226-72883-8 (pbk. : alkaline paper)
  I. Scappettone, Jennifer. II. Title.
  PQ4878.08L6313 2012
  851'.914—dc23

                          2011032210

♾ This paper meets the requirements of ANSI/NISO Z39.48-1992 (Permanence of Paper).

Frontispiece: Portrait of Amelia Rosselli (n.d.). Photograph reproduced by permission of Guglielmina Otter.

To the memory of
Raffaele Sirica,
Maria Michela Esposito,
Gregorio Tozzi,
Concetta del Ninno,
Filomena Ioacovino,
Isadore Del Gatto,
Concetta Pantano,
and Gaetano Scoppettone,
who made the journey courageously
and without an alphabet.

A nearness to Tremendousness—
An Agony procures—
Affliction ranges Boundlessness—
Vicinity to Laws

Contentment's quiet Suburb—
Affliction cannot stay
In Acres—Its Location
Is Illocality—

Emily Dickinson, Poem 963

Una vicinanza al Tremendo—
Un'Agonia procura—
Afflizione supera l'Illimitato—
L'Aderenza alle Leggi

Della Contentezza la quieta Periferia
Afflizione non può misurarsi
In Acri—la Sua Locazione
È l'Illocazione—

trans. Amelia Rosselli

Contents

Poems in Italian

Illustrations

Introduction

Stanza as "Homicile": The Poetry of Amelia Rosselli
(Paris 1930–Rome 1996)

Half a century after the searching start—across and between tongues—
of her uncompromising poetic practice, the poet Amelia Rosselli has
emerged in global literary discussions as exemplary: as both prophetic
and crucially contemporary. She has come to occupy a prominent posi-
tion in literary history as one of the twentieth century's most significant
and demanding poets of the Italian language and beyond, with a body
of work that concretizes in its agitation the postwar era's fallout and be-
quest. Her books of poetry and recently collected prose are testaments
to a uniquely multiform sincerity, and to a fiendishly restless mind, syn-
thesizing a literary tradition that stretches from the thirteenth-century
dolce stil novo through Rimbaud, Campana, Kafka, Joyce, and Pasternak
with the frankness of the news. The daughter of an assassinated hero of
the Italian Resistance who spent her childhood and adolescence in exile
between France, England, and the United States before settling in Rome,
Rosselli is esteemed for the idiolect she forged to voice the aftermath of
this experience while resisting both the confessional first person domi-
nating mainstream poetry during the years of her production and the
aesthetic conformities of vanguardist schools. Self-described "poeta della
ricerca" ("poet of research"), she regarded poetry as a sphere of activity
exceeding the narcissistic gamut of self-expression and constraint of gen-
teel intellectualism: language in Rosselli's handling is a site of innovation
with imperative philosophical and political consequences.[1] Never mere
linguistic exercise, her writing launches explicit and implicit structural
assaults on the authority of traditional poetic forms, as well as the social
and cognitive forms that gave rise to them.

1. Quote is from "Non mi chiedete
troppo, mi sono perduta in un bosco,"
an interview with Sandra Petrignani, in
Amelia Rosselli, *Una scrittura plurale: Saggi
e interventi critici,* ed. Francesca Caputo,
Biblioteca di "Autografo" (Novara: Inter-
linea, 2004), 290. Her use of the word
"poeta" here rather than "poetessa" (the
feminine form) is notable. All translations
into English in this volume are mine unless
otherwise noted.

She has fed me senseless small change, brought me to the bank, had
me counted and found the sum surplus.

—"My Clothes to the Wind" (1952)

To summarize her oeuvre, then, is but "an obligatory cruelty"; in its
errancies, this work draws into question the synthetic categories of post-
war poetry that have been forged thus far. In the early English prose piece
called "My Clothes to the Wind," the young author describes those who
would encompass her as "Biscuit-makers all, and I a crumb who'd not
coagulate," voicing an attitude of alienation from reigning forms that
would persist on many fronts. Rosselli's tumultuous upbringing in the
midst and aftermath of the Second World War as a victim of Fascism
fostered her estrangement from the Italian literary establishment for de-
cades. Being linguistically and culturally heterogeneous, her writing was
initially regarded as a key exception to the rule of this national literature,
even in the face of acclaim by prominent poet-critics and her historical
distinction as the first—and still one of few—female Italian authors in-
cluded in canon-defining anthologies of twentieth-century poetry.[2] Yet as
consciousness rises regarding the fundamental reciprocity between *itali-
anità* (Italianness), emigration, and immigration, her poetic output has
been subject to an explosion of attention. The impulses of Rosselli's work
in and against the Italian language are best appreciated when aligned with
aesthetic trends that are international, while her role in shaping the future
of this particular language and its literature is best grasped if we listen for
the way it articulates the Italian *patria,* or "fatherland," as itself a hybrid,
transnational cultural formation. Rosselli's is arguably the poetry most
vital to evolving understandings of global modernism and postmodernism
to have emerged from postwar Italy, testifying to the privations and hard-
won inheritance of cultures bound by colossal networks of commerce and
violence. Her poetic transmutes the war into which she was born into a

---

2. Rosselli's inclusion as the only fe-
male author in Pier Vincenzo Mengaldo's
Poeti italiani del Novecento was an event of
considerable consequence in modern Ital-
ian poetry. See Pier Vincenzo Mengaldo,
Poeti italiani del Novecento, "I Meridiani"
(Milano: A. Mondadori, 1987). For a sur-
vey of the critical trend casting Rosselli as
anomalous, and an argument laying out
the sociohistorical conflicts and economic
asymmetries that gave rise to Rosselli's
particularity (thereby undermining any

claim that she is not "representative"), see
Nelson Moe, "At the Margins of Domin-
ion: The Poetry of Amelia Rosselli," *Italica*
69, no. 2 (Summer 1992). Moe help-
fully distinguishes between biographism
and "bio-graphism," or what he calls the
writing of a life wherein "certain histori-
cally determined formations of personal
experience come to structure the field
of possibilities for the practice of writ-
ing" (185).

battle against every species of tyranny: literary, cultural, sexual, economic, and, congenitally, political.

Rosselli was born in Paris in 1930 into a prominently, ardently anti-totalitarian climate—into a family living in political exile.[3] Her paternal grandmother and namesake, Amelia Pincherle Rosselli, was a secular Jewish Venetian feminist and republican thinker from a family active in the unification of Italy; Amelia Pincherle was the celebrated author of plays, some in Venetian dialect, and of short stories, children's literature, political and literary essays, and translations.[4] Amelia's mother, Marion Catherine Cave, was a brilliant English activist of the Labour Party, from a family of Quaker and distant Irish Catholic heritage and modest means. Her father, Carlo Rosselli, was an intellectual leader and eventually a martyr of the anti-Fascist Resistance. Having been convicted—in a trial he exploited to critique Mussolini's regime—of facilitating socialist Filippo Turati's flight from Italy, Carlo himself escaped from the penal colony on the island of Lipari in 1929; Marion, pregnant with Amelia, was briefly arrested for complicity before the family was reunited in Paris. It was from the French capital that, with his brother Nello (who remained in Florence), Carlo launched Justice and Liberty, a prominent non-Marxist resistance movement based on principles of "liberal socialism," which included Primo Levi, Cesare Pavese, and Leone Ginzburg among its affiliates, and later became the influential if short-lived Action Party. Upon the outbreak of the Spanish Civil War, Carlo was among the first to mobilize an armed brigade of volunteers in the fight against Franco, articulating the importance of organizing resistance to Fascism

3. Many critical essays provide thumbnail sketches of Rosselli's life, but the most sustained biography published thus far, focusing on the period from the end of the war through 1958 (and followed by an analysis of verse from *Variazioni belliche* and *La libellula*), can be found in Silvia De March, *Amelia Rosselli tra poesia e storia* (Naples: L'ancora del Mediterraneo, 2006).

4. Amelia Pincherle Rosselli's previously unpublished *Memories* appeared in 2001 and recounts her childhood in Venice as well as the loss of her sons—including her first son, Aldo, who had been killed in combat in the Alps during World War I. See Amelia Pincherle Rosselli, *Memorie*, ed. Maria Calloni (Bologna: Il Mulino, 2001). Correspondence between Amelia Pincherle and her sons is contained in Carlo Rosselli et al., *Epistolario familiare: Carlo, Nello Rosselli, e la madre (1914–1937)* (Milano: SugarCo, 1979). Letters sent from her nephew, the prominent writer Alberto Moravia, were published in Alberto Moravia, *Lettere ad Amelia Rosselli, con altre lettere familiari e prime poesie (1915–1951)*, ed. Simone Casini (Milan: Bompiani, 2010). Aldo and Silvia Rosselli, children of Nello, are also writers. Aldo is the author of various narratives, including the history of his family, published as Aldo Rosselli, *La famiglia Rosselli: Una tragedia italiana. With a Foreword by Sandro Pertini and Preface by Alberto Moravia*, 1st ed. (Milano: Leonardo, 1992). Silvia's memoir was published as Silvia Rosselli, *Gli otto venti,* ed. Cristina Zaremba (Palermo: Sellerio, 2008).

"Melina" in a Paris garden (marked 1937). Photograph reproduced by permission of Guglielmina Otter.

across Europe with the rallying cry "Today in Spain, tomorrow in Italy." Identified as prime enemies of the regime, the Rosselli brothers were brutally murdered by the French Fascist terrorist organ La Cagoule in Bagnoles-de-l'Orne, Normandy, in June 1937.[5] The news was dealt to the

5. For the definitive account in English of Carlo Rosselli's life and thought, see Stanislao G. Pugliese, *Carlo Rosselli: Social-* *ist Heretic and Antifascist Exile* (Cambridge, MA: Harvard University Press, 1999).

Nello and Carlo Rosselli with Silvia and John Rosselli: the young cousins, living respectively in Florence and Paris, meet for the first time in a secret encounter between the brothers at Juan-les-Pins on the French Riviera (January 1934). Photograph reproduced by permission of Guglielmina Otter.

seven-year-old "Melina" and her younger brother Andrea by their mother as a problem of language: "Do you know what the word assassination means?" She recalled in a 1987 interview, "We answered yes."

The assassination of the Rosselli brothers was viewed as a blow not only to Italian, but to European democracy. Days before their monumental funeral in Paris, attended by an estimated 100,000–200,000 people, André Breton, Fernand Léger, Emmanuel Mounier, and Pablo Picasso were among those who signed a public statement declaring, "The assassination of Matteotti signaled the death of liberty in Italy; the assassination of the Rosselli brothers signals the death of liberty in Europe."[6] On a more intimate level, the consequences were severe: the assassination triggered a succession of cultural and linguistic displacements for the loved ones left behind. The families of Carlo and Nello were forced into a series of moves between Switzerland, England, France, and the United States.[7] Political and medical stress caused Marion and her chil-

6. Quoted in Pugliese, *Carlo Rosselli*, 229.

7. The initial flight to France had already been quite disruptive for Carlo's

Front page
of *Giustizia e Libertà*
(June 18, 1937)
announcing the
assassination
of Carlo and
Nello Rosselli.
Courtesy
Centro Studi
Piero Gobetti.

dren to move back and forth twice between the Continent and England; both families fled the occupation of France by the Nazis and then the bombardments of London, finally crossing the Atlantic from Liverpool to Montreal in August 1940 under the potential threat of Axis submarines. (They had managed to acquire visas for the United States with the help of Marion and Max Ascoli, who solicited the intervention of then first lady Eleanor Roosevelt.) The wives and children of Carlo and Nello and

---

family. Amelia's cousin Silvia Rosselli recalls that in 1935, Melina and her younger brother Andrea had been sent with their grandmother from France to the Rosselli home in Florence for nearly a year due to

Marion's ill health, and that the children spoke only French at first, which they proceeded to forget by the end of their stay. (Related in a conversation with the translator in February 2011.)

matriarch Amelia Pincherle eventually settled just off the Long Island Sound in the town of Larchmont, Westchester County, New York, where an important association of Italian anti-Fascists called the Mazzini Society had been established. It was in this relatively bucolic setting that Melina attended middle and high school. In the summer, she was sent to Quaker camps in Vermont, learning to fell trees and build bridges, and at thirteen, she worked on farms and in the fields at harvest time to fill in for the men at war—forming memories that remained precious throughout her life. These relatively blissful experiences of the Northeastern American countryside resonate through Rosselli's writings. An appeal to the natural landscape emerges forcefully at the midpoint of her career, most prominently in the second half of *Hospital Series,* and persists through the ominously overseen fields of wheat and linguistic *par terre* punctuating her final *poemetto, Impromptu* (1981). Her poetry is also suffused with an unruly democratic spirituality akin to that of the Quakers—expressing an irreverent attitude toward hieratic religious ideology, yet passionately seeking out a world beyond this one.

Though Amelia had spent her childhood in a French environment, and Italian continued to be the language of her American home (where Amelia Pincherle read to her grandchildren from classic Italian authors such as Dante every evening), she was educated largely in English, residing in New York State from 1939 through her graduation from Mamaroneck Public High School in 1945—an experience she valued for its direct education in democratic values and a sense of civic responsibility. Shortly after the end of the war, in 1946, the family returned to the Rosselli home in Florence. Though she wished to stay in Italy, Amelia's American diploma was not recognized there, and she found herself forced to return to London, finding at the last moment before the upcoming school year a private school in which to matriculate according to European standards: the prestigious, yet more academically oriented St. Paul's Girls' School. She lived alone in rented rooms while her mother, who had suffered from heart, rheumatic, and circulatory problems from a young age and was now quite ill, lived separately with her sons, John and Andrea. This unanticipated detour—which has been read as an additional period of exile—was ultimately fruitful insofar as it led Amelia to the musical study that would remain at the heart of her artistic practice.[8] In London she began private violin and piano lessons, studied classical

8. Lucia Re refers to the period as an "ulteriore esilio." Lucia Re, "Amelia Rosselli: Poesia e guerra," *Carte italiane* 3 (2007): 74.

harmony and counterpoint, and was exposed through concerts to the contemporary Viennese school of composers and to Bartók. She would continue these studies in Italy and elsewhere; musicology was to form a touchstone for the duration of her career.

We find a rare shard of direct autobiography charting Amelia's nomadic youth in a glaringly passive voice within her debut volume, *Variazioni belliche*, or *Bellicose Variations* (published in 1964), whose title bespeaks the ruthless fusion of beauty, music, and corporeality with war which courses through her work:

First Christmas in America, 1940, the year of FDR's reelection: the families of Carlo and Nello Rosselli at the home of the Ascolis, who had helped them acquire a visa to enter the United States through contact made with Eleanor Roosevelt. *Top, left to right:* Marion Cave, Maria Rosselli (wife of Nello), Amelia Pincherle Rosselli, Melina's elder brother John. *Middle:* Amelia's younger brother Andrea, Paola Rosselli (daughter of Nello), "Melina," Silvia Rosselli (daughter of Nello). *Bottom, left to right:* Alberto Rosselli, Aldo Rosselli (sons of Nello). Photograph reproduced by permission of Guglielmina Otter.

Born in Paris labored in the epic of our fallacious
generation. Laid in America amid the rich fields of landowners
and of the statal State. Experienced in Italy, barbarous country.
Fled from England country of sophisticates. Hopeful
in the West where nothing for the moment grows.

Such roots gave rise to lasting hardships that were cultural, but also
acutely physical, economic, and emotional. Marion's health was already
compromised by an embolus when the family returned to Florence,
and her death in Isleworth, west of London, in 1949 drove the sensitive
nineteen-year-old Amelia into a severe depression, while obliging her to
support herself financially. She moved from Florence to Rome, where
she worked half days as a translator for Adriano Olivetti's publishing ven-
ture, Edizioni di Comunità, with additional funding for her music lessons
provided by her grandmother until Amelia Pincherle's death in 1954.
During this period Amelia met her cousin, Alberto Moravia (born with
the Jewish surname Pincherle), who was married to Elsa Morante, and
whose books she began to translate and devour. Because Carlo Rosselli
had devoted all of his money to Giustizia e Libertà, the family had few
resources on which to survive other than their property, and Amelia lived
modestly, with the threat of economic hardship looming constantly, for
the remainder of her life. Money for study and research, medical and liv-
ing expenses came from translation and journalism commissions, work as
an interpreter and as a consultant to publishing houses, donations (often
disguised) from members of the Mazzini Society and sympathetic friends
such as Max Ascoli, and modest pensions from the Italian state for chil-
dren of those killed in war and, later, for distinguished cultural figures in
economic need.

Over the years, Amelia endured bouts of psychic trauma and waves
of treatment, ranging from Jungian and Freudian psychotherapy and
psychoanalysis to electroshock treatments for schizophrenia—a diag-
nosis she refused, referring to herself instead as afflicted with "nervous
exhaustion," meningitis, or Parkinson's disease. She suffered, during the
Cold War, from an obsession with being tracked by the CIA, the Italian
secret service, and the Mafia that could easily be regarded as a feasible
possibility as opposed to paranoid fantasy.[9] Her affliction culminated in

9. Amelia wrote famously about the
CIA as "disease" in a piece published in
Nuovi argomenti in 1977, reprinted as Ame-
lia Rosselli, "Storia di una malattia," in
Una scrittura plurale, 317–26. In this piece,
she criticizes the psychological establish-
ment for having dismissed her concerns
and effectively turns the language of illness
inside out, so that it reflects public as op-
posed to individual psychic ills.

Amelia Rosselli with her mother, Marion Cave, in England, before the flight to America (1939–1940). Photograph reproduced by permission of Guglielmina Otter.

her suicide—a notorious leap from the window of her loft apartment on the Via del Corallo in Rome's historic center on February 11, 1996, the thirty-third anniversary of Sylvia Plath's death.[10]

When she was well, Rosselli translated the unsettling repercussions of her experience into poetry—but it will not be my strategy here to prolong the trend of reading her work as a direct expression of individual suffering. We would be mistaken to conflate the difficulty of this poetry with psychic difficulty. In fact, despite her admiration for the verse of Plath, which she wrote about and translated, Rosselli repeatedly critiqued the kind of confessionalism she viewed as "a great defect of feminine or slightly

10. Her cousin Aldo writes about her mental condition and suicide in Aldo Rosselli, "Amelia, Sibilla e Gorgone," *Galleria* 48, nos. 1–2 (1998). For a reading of Rosselli's suicide as an act of "poetic prolepsis," see Elizabeth Leake, "'Nor Do I Want Your Interpretation': Suicide, Surrealism, and the Site of Illegibility in Amelia Rosselli's *Sleep*," *Romantic Review* 97, nos. 3–4 (May 2006).

feminist literature" by authors who "don't know how to escape from their private life"—so that the classification of her work alongside that of confessionally oriented poets, particularly female poets, as a reflection of personal difficulty and idiosyncrasy, is misleading.[11] Rosselli was outspoken in attacking the "absolute egotism" of "[t]he return to the private," recommending that writers subject themselves to analysis early on rather than passing confused individual neuroses off as art through confessionalism.[12] Her work, instead, seeks an "exit from the I" and eventually even from the rapport between the I and the thou.[13] She strove to transpose broader sociohistorical conditions in verse—but without ever divorcing those conditions from phenomena experienced on an intimate, corporeal scale. The extraordinary circumstances of her childhood and adolescence prompted her not to self-exceptionalizing, expressivist gestures, but to the search for a choral idiom that would address afflictions shared.

Having lived the first two decades of her life between three languages and four nations before settling in Italy, Rosselli crafted a "barbarous" idiolect plying its way between discursive systems. This idiolect distinguishes itself from both the modernism of her forebears and the more delirious and arguably more superficially derived polylingual experimentation of her contemporaries in the Neoavanguardia. She states in an interview that she regards each "linguistic order" as "a discipline of the mind," noting then that "[t]he multilingual work that has been fashionable from Pound forward does not interest me at all."[14] Though Rosselli pushed language to more extreme degrees of experimentation than her precursor Pier Paolo Pasolini did, she shared Pasolini's contention that

11. Rosselli speaks at length about the dominance of ego and the private confession in a 1979 interview with Mariella Bettarini, in Rosselli, *È vostra la vita che ho perso: Conversazioni e interviste, 1964–1995*, ed. Monica Venturini and Silvia De March, with a preface by Laura Barile (Florence: Le Lettere, 2010), 32–33. Mengaldo's preface to Rosselli's work in the definitive *Poeti italiani del Novecento* notoriously cast her as an exception to the rule of Italian letters due to her verse's "private" concerns. Successive critics have read Mengaldo's characterization of the single female author included in his anthology as a problematic gendering move: see, especially, Lucia Re, "Poetry and Madness," in *Shearsmen of Sorts: Italian Poetry 1975–1993. Forum Italicum*, Italian Poetry Supplement, ed.

Luigi Ballerini (Stony Brook: State University of New York at Stony Brook, 1992), 132–53. Re's argument surrounding Rosselli's reception as a "mad" poet of "free psychological fluctuation" was a crucial intervention; Re instead works to provide a reading of Rosselli's work as ideologically revolutionary, and *strategically* so, using the writing of Kristeva as a model. Despite such critical revision, this interpretative tendency is still common, even in sensitive accounts.

12. "Laboratorio di poesia," in Rosselli et al., *È vostra la vita che ho perso*, 239.

13. Interview with Mariella Bettarini, in ibid., 32–33.

14. "La poesia è un piacere privato," a 1977 interview with Gabriella Sica, in ibid., 15.

language is never a matter of form alone. Rosselli's "poetry of research" is also a search for a new content-bearing language: a new semantics. In a polemical report on the conference of the Gruppo 63 in Palermo to which she was invited, authored under the pseudonym "Xenaxis," but which she never succeeded in publishing, Rosselli speaks with skepticism of the prevailing opposition of (and attempt to synthesize) "stylistic avant-garde versus content-based realism."[15] Impatience with such antagonisms sheds light on her response to a 1977 interview question soliciting her formula for writing: "Post-neorealist or, better, post-realist."[16]

Living in Rome during the so-called economic boom of the postwar years, in a consumerist cultural atmosphere characterized by what Pasolini called a "loss of reality," Rosselli never lost sight of her early exposure to neorealism and Marxism.[17] She registered in the Communist Party in 1958 despite its ideological differences from her father's socialism, in light of the betrayal of the freedoms and equality imagined by Carlo and other martyrs of the Resistance—becoming an active member of the community who cleaned the meetinghouse as well as organizing cultural events.[18] Political engagement led her to more trenchant, if at times defeated, demands on literature's relation to life. In interviews she used the word *contenutistica* ("privileging content") to describe her work, distinguishing herself from formalists, and noted that her interlocutors rarely understood the term.[19] Still, she was never to abandon formal invention in the service of a greater political efficacy and transparency: her "post-neorealist" writing continues neorealism's efforts to tether the stylistic innovation of the historical avant-gardes to their apparent antithesis, socially engaged realism, without transfixing content or its interpretation—resisting the instrumentalization of language resulting from traditional hermeneutic operations. Rosselli's recurrent use of the term *oscuro* ("dark" or "obscure") thus also needs to be read

15. Reprinted as an appendix in Amelia Rosselli, *Lettere a Pasolini, 1962–1969*, ed. Stefano Giovannuzzi, Quaderni del Tempo (Genoa: San Marco dei Giustiniani, 2008), 78. This opposition came to a head in a notorious agon between Sanguineti and Pasolini.

16. "La poesia è un piacere privato," 14.

17. Pasolini writes that one must protect oneself from a "loss of reality" in "Dal Laboratorio." See Pier Paolo Pasolini, *Empirismo eretico* (Milan: Garzanti, 1995), 74.

18. Silvia De March discusses this decision at length in De March, *Amelia Rosselli tra poesia e storia*. Participation in the party's activities became a fundamental part of Rosselli's daily life. See "Vita e problemi alla base: Le sezioni un tabù?" in *Una scrittura plurale* (233–38) for Rosselli's 1968 polemic against the "eccessively symbolic-spiritual and *hedonistic*" (234) participation of contemporary party members.

19. See Silvio Perrella, "Per Amelia Rosselli," *Nuovi argomenti* 12 (1997): 13*n*.

as gesturing toward *that which is obscured,* the humble and unknown, as it was in her grandmother's stories about the lives of anonymous workers and the nonworking poor, collected under the title *Gente oscura* ("obscure people," or "people obscured").[20] Pier Vincenzo Mengaldo was keen early on to distinguish the "disaggregative aggression" of Rosselli's approach to language from the "controlled, technological experimentation of the neo-avant-garde," because her work commits to documenting a span of contingencies that are more deeply entrenched in history and more over-powering. The poetry ultimately leaves these contingencies unmastered, or as Pasolini put it, "imposseduta."[21]

Rosselli's use of multiple linguistic systems was thus no modish affectation, but an outcome of necessity. Her literary education differed from many of her peers in that she studied the French moderns—Baudelaire, Verlaine, Rimbaud, Breton—and an Anglo-American literary heritage extending from Shakespeare through Faulkner in their original languages. An upbringing between languages was the organic vehicle for her wide-ranging literary interests, which can be gleaned from the essays she wrote, on John Barth, Roberto Bazlen, John Berryman, Gregory Corso, José Craveirinha, T. S. Eliot, Thomas Kyd, Boris Pasternak, Sandro Penna, Virginia Woolf, and black writers of resistance in the United States, among others. But it is in her poetry that the ramifications of this back-ground find their unparalleled melding. Rosselli draws on the linguistic traditions of her formation to create a language of amalgamation that subjects the terms "mother tongue" and "fatherland" to battle and travail.

More macaronic than polylingual, Rosselli's poetic stages the recip-rocal interference of languages: roiling research of one linguistic system *within* another, far more disquieting than if it were to allow tongues to cohabit stanzas without contaminating one another. Time is as out of joint as geography in her universe, where archaic and courtly terms brush against neologisms and current speech patterns left startlingly un-adorned: in her youthful tour de force, *La libellula: Panegirico della libertà,* or *The Libellula: Panegyric to Liberty* (1958), Rosselli writes, "[. . .] I wash my / hands of it and rhyme antiquely with a modernity / I didn't suspect in my tangles."[22] The poet tangles classes and genders irreverently as well: she draws liberally on dialect and slang while borrowing terms from Dante, Leopardi, and D'Annunzio, and launches retorts to the phenom-

20. Amelia Rosselli, *Gente oscura* (Turin: Roux e Viarengo, 1903).

21. Pier Vincenzo Mengaldo, "Amelia Rosselli," in his 1978 anthology: *Poeti italiani del Novecento,* 993–97. See in par-ticular p. 994. Pasolini's neologism is from "A Note on Amelia Rosselli," included in this collection.

22. Amelia Rosselli, *Le poesie,* 2 ed. (Milan: Garzanti, 2007), 143.

enally male-dominated character of Italian letters (beginning with the Petrarchan tradition in particular) through transgendering maneuvers. Portmanteau words fusing syllables of sonically akin yet semantically distinct words coexist with prosodically driven elisions. Rosselli's deviations into error have plural effects: they can elicit the residual foreignness of an exiled speaker or a localizing strain of dialect, a hyperliterariness or, later in her career, what she strove to register more directly as a "grammar of the poor." Her departures from standard Italian into alien lexicons, syntax, and grammar were initially identified as "barbarisms." Yet closer study exposes this verse's conscious inversion of that term: the poetry produces *Italy* as the "barbarous country," alienating the linguistic progeny of Rome from itself, so that readers find themselves citizens of errancy.[23]

Rosselli's first poems were written in English, from 1953 to 1955, though she experimented with compositions in French and Italian as a young woman as well. She recorded a convoluted genealogy of relations between the several vernaculars of her experience in *Diario in tre lingue / Diary in Three Tongues* (dated 1955–1956, but with later revisions and perhaps with 1963 additions). This early plurilingual work of fifty pages cites Donne and Eliot, Joyce, Rimbaud, Montale, and Scipione, among others, and concepts from prosody and musicology, Eastern literature, and philosophy; its inventions cross French, Italian, and English. Pier Paolo Pasolini used the somewhat misleading Freudian term "lapsus" to introduce Rosselli's literary transgressions to the public in 1963, suggesting that lexical and grammatical error in this poetry takes shape of its own accord, provoked by unconscious desire. Yet the diary makes clear that Rosselli's mature poetic anomalies constitute not instances of the Freudian "slip," but the fruit of a strategy—grounded in the awareness of occupying an interstice, and come to fruition only after a protracted phase of study. In a 1963 letter written in English to her brother John, she writes, "I don't agree with his use of the word 'lapsus' (which is grammatically purely Freudian)—my 'mixtures,' linguistically, are rarely mixtures, at all, but refer to baroque or absurd turns of phrases or syllables, in use in Italy specially in the South, in the poetry of Campana, in dialect, or in

23. Rosselli plays with tropes of "barbarity" and "wildness" in her verse; in her personal copy of Claude Lévi-Strauss's *Race and Culture* (a 1967 Einaudi edition), she underlined a passage regarding the possible etymology of "barbarian" in the inarticulate songs of birds, and which stresses that this term contains within it a refusal to acknowledge inevitable cultural difference. The volume forms part of the Fondo Amelia Rosselli at the Università della Tuscia in Viterbo.

other languages . . . etc., etc."[24] However, Pasolini's term stuck. A quarter of a century after his essay was published, she would still be obliged to point out that "the lapsus would be a mnemonic forgetting, whereas linguistic invention is usually conscious."[25] A glance at Rosselli's capacious personal library, where the definitions and etymologies of unfamiliar words stud the margins of English, French, and Italian texts, provides additional insight into her lifelong exploration of interlingual relationships—and enjoins us to rethink linguistic identity in dynamic terms, as a process of research and construction.

contraption littéraire

contrazioni (cramps)

hystoire phonetik

—*Diary in Three Tongues*

The *Diary* is just one example of Rosselli's unrelenting inquiry across languages and literary traditions, and was later identified by the author as an exercise rather than a solution.[26] It was collected in *Primi scritti / First Writings* (1952–1963, published in 1980) alongside three texts in each of three alternating languages: prose poems and lyric sequences in French, Italian, and English.

Among these are a group of arresting lyrics written in a pseudo-Elizabethan idiom in 1956 under the title "October Elizabethans," so that—lest readers assume that exercises in archaism have no consequences for the twentieth century—"Elizabethan" rhymes with "Revolution." The revolution they enact may be said to be sexual before the letter, as well as more broadly cultural.

Come, come,
be though Brave, and Come to Mee,
a-Loaden with rich Jewelree. All Night long
shall we Curry the Milke 'f Innocenciee.

—"On Fatherish Men"

24. Letter of 25 October 1963, at the Fondo Rosselli of the Centro di ricerca della tradizione manoscritta di autori moderni and contemporanei, University of Pavia. Giovanni Giudici was perhaps the first prominent writer, besides Rosselli herself, to contest Pasolini's term, in his preface to Rosselli's *Impromptu* (Genoa: San Marco dei Giustiniani, 1981).

25. From "Fatti estremi," an interview with Giacinto Spagnoletti translated for this volume, reprinted in Rosselli, *È vostra la vita che ho perso*, 85.

26. See Rosselli's remarks about language choices in Andrea Cortellessa, ed., *La furia dei venti contrari: Variazioni Amelia Rosselli* (Florence: Le Lettere, 2007), 165.

More than 130 poems composed in English between 1953 and 1966 that remained relegated for years to a "private journal" equally "Curry the Milke 'f Innocenciee," cajoling, infusing presumptions of motherly and/or phallic purity with the taste of cultural otherness unvanquished. The English lyrics' solecisms remind us of the colonial origins of that term, recalling the corruption of Attic dialect among Athenian colonists in Cilicia. They are instantiations of what their translator, Emmanuela Tandello, calls Rosselli's "linguistic alter ego,"[27] but more broadly valuable for the work they do to stretch the English language in synchronic and diachronic terms. In the 1960s, when Rosselli was working adamantly to publish them outside of Italy, these poems found an impressive range of venues for publication abroad. Significantly, John Ashbery was the first to print a series of Rosselli's English lyrics, including six poems in the Summer 1966 issue of his Paris-based international quarterly, *Art and Literature*.[28] "What woke those tender heavy fat hands" appeared in *The Times Literary Supplement* under the title "Courage" on Bastille Day that same summer. Yet despite repeated attempts to publish them as a whole in the United States and England, the English poems were collected only decades later by Garzanti as *Sleep: Poesie in inglese,* alongside their Italian translations. The moment has come for a public of Anglo-American readers to grapple with these texts, just as Italians are beginning to confront the oddities of Ezra Pound's Italian prose and poetry as researched stylistic features in their own right.[29]

Amelia's sustained correspondence with her elder brother John, a gifted journalist, historian, and musicologist who spent most of his life in England, oscillates with remarkable facility between Italian and English, depending upon the siblings' circumstances. Their letters make it clear that Amelia's eventual choice to write in Italian would have been the result of substantial searching. Living in Italy from age nineteen forward more or less continuously, Rosselli traced her decision to compose in Italian to the untimely 1953 death of her companion Rocco Scotellaro, a poet, chronicler of *Contadini del sud / Farmworkers of the South* (1954),

27. Emmanuela Tandello, "La poesia inglese di Amelia Rosselli," in Amelia Rosselli and Emmanuela Tandello, *Sleep: Poesie in inglese* (Milan: Garzanti, 1992), 2. Tandello worked closely with Rosselli in translating this volume.

28. Ashbery printed "We had lit the world with our calling but," "slightly nauseated with all cry I fell," "Sleep," "radioactive confusion bit into my,"

"Worthless as was her itinerary to fame," and "impertinent with tears and impotent" in *Art and Literature: An International Quarterly* 9 (Summer 1966): 73–77.

29. See the prescient volume by Ann Snodgrass, *Knowing Noise: The English Poems of Amelia Rosselli*, Studies in Italian Culture: Literature in History (New York: Peter Lang, 2001).

and agitator for socialist reform in the Italian South, whom she had met several years before in Venice at the first conference on the legacy of the Resistance—and who had introduced her to Carlo Levi, a collaborator with Justice and Liberty, and paternal figure.

Lasciatemi
ho il battito al cuore
donna a cavallo di galli e di maiali

Leave me
I have beating in the heart
woman on horseback of roosters and hogs
  —"Cantilena (poems for Rocco Scotellaro)" (1953), in *First Writings*

The irresolvable conflict between an upbringing straddling disparate species of culture and the yearning for a localized, integral experience expressed in this "canticle" infuses all of her work. An undated letter to John sent from Rome elicits some of the specific tensions surrounding Amelia's choice of Italy as a *patria* both spiritual and practical. Composed in Italian, it demands information about the family papers and books from her father's library, though she does not have "what Abel calls *birthright*" (using the English term), since "Italian law is on my side." The letter also takes "Giovanni" to task for Anglicizing his name ("your sister won't have any regard for the word John which sounds antimusical to me"), teaches him "a bit of Roman dialect," and closes with the signature "your sister / (Amelia Rosselli of Genova / (Genevré) / Ginevra USA United / states of America and all that / it brings of prestige fame and / thousand-dollar bills."[30]

Mondo pollame divenuto malaticcio
duna di morti

Fowl world become sickly
dune of the dead
  —"Cantilena (poems for Rocco Scotellaro)"

Rosselli's choice to compose principally in a language that would voice the void left by two central male figures in her life suggests that she means to found in language a crucible for the work of mourning—or of melancholy, that less successfully elegiac affective force. Her poetry, everywhere yoking emotional to political experience, invokes the terms

---

30. Undated, unpublished letter to John Rosselli in the Fondo Rosselli at the archive of modern and contemporary authors at the University of Pavia.

Freud uses to draw the distinction between mourning and melancholy, whereby mourning constitutes "the reaction to the loss of a loved person, or to the loss of some abstraction which has taken the place of one, such as fatherland, liberty, an ideal," and melancholia the response to a loss "of a more ideal kind."[31] Melancholia takes root when such an abstraction has not succeeded in taking the place of the object gone, when a person knows "whom he has lost but not what it is he has lost in them."[32] Rosselli's implicit commemoration, through the choice of Italian, of loved ones who died while engaged in the struggle for freedom and equality in their country is also a revolt—wherein the poignant lack of fit between the ideal of the national language and a speaker displaced from her "birthright" by the state's constitutive violences is not only an expression of individual and collective trauma, but a challenge. Rosselli's "complaints are really 'plaints' in the legal sense of the word," part of what Freud calls the melancholic's "attitude of revolt."[33] "For the prohibition that prevents us from going on / perhaps I will lose you still and again," she conjectures in "For the singing that unwound in the air": through haunted repetition and metonymic drifting of signification, her variations on these perpetual losses track, suspend, and banish that prohibition in song.[34]

Ashore's the great servility
mobile on its two-legged carts
stripped-eased
by the road. A soldier wooden he
staked by the running homicile
flash-deep. Out your cross
out the bloody banner
and we shall fall stop. Oh the guards
do catch with us:
then hard-pressed time
cracks
rut.

—from *Sleep: Poems in English*

"Ashore's the great servility" is one of the poems Rosselli composed in the language of her deceased mother between her midtwenties and

---

31. Cf. Sigmund Freud, "Mourning and Melancholia," in *Collected Papers: Volume 4* (London: Hogarth Press, 1953), 153.

32. Ibid., 155.

33. Ibid., 158, 159.

34. For a discussion of the political subtext of melancholy and the antimetaphoric structure of melancholic texts, see Judith Butler, *The Psychic Life of Power* (Stanford: Stanford University Press, 1997), 190.

Above: Amelia Rosselli in Venice for the First Conference on the Resistance (April 1950). Photograph reproduced by permission of Guglielmina Otter.

Left: Amelia Rosselli and Rocco Scotellaro, Piazza del Popolo, Rome (1951). Photograph reproduced by permission of Guglielmina Otter.

Amelia Rosselli's *mansarda* (mansard apartment) on the Via del Corallo, Rome, with portrait of Carlo Rosselli above the desk. Photograph by Guglielmina Otter. Reproduced by permission.

midthirties, when she was living in Italy and publishing her first book of poetry in Italian. This lyric emblematizes a broader drive to express the dispersion of the mother('s) tongue in stanzas where Anglo-Saxon and Romance roots collide, where a deterritorialized "home" drifts from the English "domicile," deriving from the Latin *domus,* into "homicide" to produce the jolting neologistic "homicile"—forcing the sign and sound of "home" to coincide with brutality. Such impulses of *spaesamento* ("disorientation, displacement") balk at full stops, propelling the subjects and objects of Rosselli's embattled verse into detours. The "homicile" of "[T]he great servility," far from settled, is "running"; far from accommodating, it is merely "flash-deep." Placing us from the beginning "ashore," the poem still invokes a state of at-seaness as both a source of queasiness and a possible release from bondage. Servility is "mobile," though hobblingly, "on its two-legged carts," abjectly humanized.

The poem suggests that servility or its two-legged carts have been "stripped-eased" by the road; this alteration of English obeys Rosselli's ear for defamiliarizing puns. Perhaps that which servility carts is stripped or stolen, its burden thereby "eased." We cannot know, because the "homicile" is rendered so corporeal that we are forced to confront the "strip-tease" within the term "stripped-eased," which places emphasis on such an act's master/slave matrix, stressing the servility of its display. Rosselli's warping idiomatic phrase enforces that the one who "strips"—in this case, the vehicle itself—does not do so of his or her own will, is not teasing or easy by choice, but is both stripped and eased, transitively, by a master here underscored if unnamed, like the "he" who appears on the following line. The phrase following, "a soldier wooden," persists in inverting perception of power dynamics by deploying the syntax of Romance languages as opposed to the orders of perception familiar to English speakers. Reversing the term "wooden soldier" renders the woodenness of a harmless toy figurative, emotional—or physical, vulgar. Rosselli states in an interview that when *Sleep* was being written in the 1960s, she wished to insert the male body into poetry in addition to the female body that was being promoted in women's literature at the time—and that she wages throughout the text "a kind of war-love with man that is suited to the Anglo-American world," where feminism was more anchored historically and more advanced.[35]

The syntax that follows the "soldier wooden" keeps a general vertigo of agency in play, given that relations between phrases are open throughout, paratactic. It may be the "soldier wooden" who "stakes" an object ungiven, or it may be this member who is staked "by" the homicile, that troubled home in motion; the poem does not ultimately pin it down for us. This ambiguity surrounding the perpetrator and victim of the poem's overseen yet vague crusade persists so that ultimately readers understand "the great servility" of the opening line to pertain to all of us who are complicit in it.

Both of these linguistic improprieties, "stripped-eased" and "soldier wooden," accentuate gendered power dynamics by overturning the structures of linguistic expectation. Such inversions remain a core feature of Rosselli's poetry. A later poem composed in Italian dramatizes the switch in the hierarchy of sexual antagonism:

Il sesso violento come un oggetto (cava di marmo imbiancata)
(anfora di creta ricurva) e nascostissimo in forma
d'uovo assaltava il solitario, come se fosse la grandine
a tempestare, nel salotto. Non gaudente, non sapiente
serpentinamente influenzato da esempi illustri o illustrazioni

35. From "Paesaggio con figure," a 1992 radio broadcast from Rome with Gabriella Caramore and Emmanuela Tan- dello transcribed in Rosselli, *È vostra la vita che ho perso*, 279–80.

di candore, per la pace e per l'anima purulava. Non sapiente
non gaudente, ma sapiente e mercantile speronato come
il vascello contro rocce pipistrelle, cadeva di colpo
dall'alto del rigore e della danza, dal sol fa mi do di
un'altra giornata; non sapiente e non gaudente travestito
da soldato annaspando e arrischiando tra capanne di maiale
rovistando, come forma e come oggetto, il sesso si serviva
di lui.

Sex violent like an object (quarry of marble blanched)
(amphora of crooked clay) and most clandestine in the form
of an egg would assault the solitary one, as if it were hail
to storm, in the sitting-room. Not voluptuary, not wise
serpentinely influenced by illustrious exempla or illustrations
of candor, for peace and for the soul it purulated. Not wise
not voluptuary, but wise and mercantile rammed like
the vessel against rock bats, it fell of a sudden
from the heights of rigor and of dance, from the sol fa mi do of
another day; not wise and not voluptuary crossdressed
as a soldier groping and risking among huts of swine
rummaging, as form and as object, sex helped itself
to him.

—Hospital Series

This poem turns sex's conventional dynamic of mastery on its head.
Rather than taking an object, sex is itself likened to an object, echoing
gender norms insofar as this object is associated with a receptacle, and
therefore implicitly feminized (a blanched marble quarry or clay Grecian
jar; the form of an egg). Yet this object assaults the subject, *il solitario,* the
male-gendered solitary figure, rather than the other way around. Invert-
ing standard relations between figure and ground, the poem proposes
that (male-gendered) "sex" is a (female-gendered) hailstorm in a parlor,
falling from the "sol fa mi do" of another day, rammed "like a vessel"
against stone bats, though we are prone to picture the opposite: forms of
stone ramming against the vessel. Rather than being the instrument of
the male, sex is in this poetry a feminized force, crossdressed in soldier's
garb, which, groping and rummaging, "help[s] itself / to *him.*"

The reversals here, composed in the language of Rosselli's adopted
host country for the volume *Serie ospedaliera / Hospital Series* (composed
between 1963 and 1965, published in 1969), take place within the traf-
fic in feminine and masculine nouns; yet they are also lodged sufficiently
within the register of description, so as to be translatable into a more

gender-neutral language without colossal loss. But how would one translate the uncanny haunting of English by non-nativity in "Ashore's the great servility"—how would one translate the quirks of her poetry that most poignantly manifest linguistic roots lopped off and set into motion? How does translation shuttle awkwardness and impropriety responsibly into the target tongue as a poetic force rather than detraction?

> Cos'ha il mio cuore che batte sì soavemente
> ed egli fa disperato, ei
> più duri sondaggi? tu Quelle
> scolanze che vi imprissi pr'ia ch'eo
> si turmintussi sì
> fieramente, tutti gli sono dispariti! O sei muiei
> conigli correnti peri nervu ei per
> brimosi canali dei la mia linfa (o vita!)
> non stoppano, allora sì, c'io, my
> iavvicyno allae mortae! In tutta schiellezze mia anima
> tu ponigli rimedio, t'imbraccio, tu,—
> trova queia Parola Soave, tu ritorna
> alla compresa favella che fa sì che l'amore resta.

This short lyric from *Bellicose Variations,* which sets love in discomposing relation to "comprehended saying," is one of Rosselli's most daunting to translate. In a glossary provided to Pier Paolo Pasolini on the condition that it not be published, Rosselli identified the poem's "mixed—fused—and pseudoarchaic forms; species of language invented by students of philology."[36] Its lexical range reaches from the style of the medieval *dolce stil novo* in the first line and reverberating archaizing (or pseudoarchaizing) tendencies (the unconventional use of *egli,* for example), through stabs of startling—and neologistic—infiltrations of Italian by Latin (*mortae*) and English (the macaronic verb *stoppano; my*). It also encompasses departures into dialect (the Sardinian or Southern Italian tendency to end words with *u* rather than *o*—a vowel-shift that also recalls early Italian vulgate poetry, such as that of Saint Francis) and poetic or slanglike contractions that render univocal interpretation impossible (*tu Quelle* may be a contraction for *tutte Quelle* ("all those"), as Rosselli suggests, but *tu* continues nevertheless to indicate "you," rendering this "you" synonymous with "everything"—while *peri* (for *per* plus *i*)

36. She notes in particular the poem's "*stilismi 'novi'* [her quotation marks play upon the "new" in the term *dolce stil novo*], Provencalisms, Spanishisms, amorous Lat- inisms, with for ex. Southern or Sardinian *us.*" See her "Explicative Glossary" in Rosselli, *Una scrittura plurale,* 69.

is likely an attempt to increase the reading's velocity). The poem's semantic fusions include *brimosi,* made up of *brina* ("frost") and *bruma* ("mist," "haze") and *schiellezze,* a combination of *schiettezza* ("purity"), *scellerato* ("wicked"), and *celere* ("swift"), possibly a Roman-accented contraction of *scelerattezze.*[37] Perhaps the most difficult aspect of this lyric is its centrifugal treatment of personal, impersonal, and possessive pronouns, which are cast into archaic, elided, foreign, and improper forms (*ei,* for example, could be a contraction of *egli* ("he"), or *e* plus *i* ("and the"), or *ai* ("to the"), though Rosselli identifies it as the plural form of *e* ("and," which does not take a plural form); *eo* is an archaic form of *io,* though Rosselli claims that it refers to *egli* or *esso*; *sei muiei,* at first glance unidentifiable, is likely a quickening contraction of *se i miei* ("if my," deploying the Sardinian *u*). Only an English equally conglomerate, elided, and scarred could do such a lyric justice.

> What ails my heart which beats so suavely
> & maketh hee disconsolate, ese
> soundings quite steel? lle Those
> scomminglings therein 'mprinted fore Ille
> be harrowed so
> fiercely, alle hath evanished! O shhd mine
> hares rampant thru th'nerves &s thru
> channels rimed 'f thisse my lymph (o life!)
> not stopp, thus yes, th'I, mio
> nearyng unto mortae! In alle clandors soul of mine
> thou dost propose a cure, thee I imbrace, you,—
> find 'at Suave Word, you, return
> to the comprehended saying that makes sure love remains.

I have mimicked Rosselli's own mimicry of Elizabethan and Metaphysical diction and spelling, while finding equivalents wherever possible for her irregular elisions (*ei* becomes "ese"; *sei* becomes "shhd") and collisions (*scolanze,* from *mescolanze* ["mixtures"], *scolaro* ["pupil" or "student"], and *scolare* ["drain"] becomes "scomminglings," *brimosi* becomes "rimed," from "covered with hoarfrost" and echoing "rhyme"; *schiellezze* becomes "clandors," from "candor," "clan," "cloister," "launders," and

37. See the extended "Explicative Glossary" Rosselli provided to Pasolini in *Lettere a Pasolini, 1962–1969,* as transcribed from the Pasolini archive at the Gabinetto Vieusseux in Florence, 22. This glossary provides more details than the synthetic glossary at the Fondo Rosselli reprinted in *Una scrittura plurale,* 69–73, and at times divergent accounts of the poet's purposes.

"unders"). I have also sought to fissure the poem with the pressure of other linguistic systems: French, Italian, and Latin "remains." Rosselli's inappropriate usages, in rendering the properties of one language another's, gleefully transgress poetic decorum. In translating such work, to seek out that "fluency" sought by the dominant market in literary translation and well highlighted by Lawrence Venuti in *The Translator's Invisibility* would be heresy.[38] At the same time, the relative fluidity of her later verse, which favors spare, if everywhere lopped, verse architectonics and a semi-documentary endeavor to render the grammar of the oppressed, has to be translated differently from her early, more anarchic experiments.

In introducing the poetry of thirty-three-year-old Rosselli to the Italian literary public in 1963, Pasolini was obliged to confront the question of limits:

> [T]he avant-garde revival . . . has found in this sort of stateless person [*apolide*] from the great familial traditions of Cosmopolis, a terrain in which to explode with the fatal and marvelous fecundity of mushroom clouds in the act of their becoming forms, etc., etc. I will not go beyond the limits of the flyleaf.
>
> —"A Note on Amelia Rosselli"

It would have been difficult to contain any explication of this poetic force, who evolved a bellicose relation to limits that were national, literary and linguistic, geographical, corporeal, and finally historical. Rosselli occupied an implosive cultural state—but also rejected the terms Pasolini employed in his preface to her first publications. Her work refuses the prestige of the labels "exile" and "cosmopolitan" often tacked to an expatriated elite, the latter retaining traces of anti-Semitism. In a 1990 interview, she was still combating this posture as she declared,

> I am not a stateless person [*apolide*]. I have an Italian father and if I was born in Paris it is simply because he had fled. . . . My mother helped him flee and then reached him in Paris, my father was then killed with his brother. . . . Having learned English, in addition to French, is thus a consequence of the war. . . .
>
> The designation "cosmopolitan" goes back to an essay by Pasolini . . . , but I reject that epithet for us: we are children of the Second

38. *The Translator's Invisibility: A History of Translation*, 2nd ed. (London and New York: Routledge, 2008).

World War. . . . The cosmopolite is a person who chooses to be so. We were not cosmopolitans; we were refugees.[39]

"Children of the Second World War" are children for whom both mother and father are effaced. Such offspring would locate their forebears neither in a person nor in a place, nor certainly in the "liberal" institutions Pasolini accused the young poet of preserving through her linguistic deformations, but in a global phenomenon: in repercussions of aggression and retaliation. Indeed, such "children" inherit existence itself as repercussion. Alessandro Baldacci has compared Rosselli's resultant idiolect to that of Paul Celan, the Romanian Jewish poet of the German language—identifying in it "[u]na pronuncia orfana," or "an orphan speech," and a "familiarity with the void" as the origin of authorship.[40] The dissonance between mutually exclusive linguistic, sonic, and cognitive orders obliged to cohabit Rosselli's stanzas constitutes nothing less than an extension of these distressed origins, and the void's continual surfacing against the pyrotechnics of repetition and variation foregrounds the state of existential and epistemological crisis engendered by them. Baldacci writes elsewhere that Rosselli's poetic language "acts as a sort of *deux ex machina,* producing sense, meaning, yet overturning and displacing the plane of communication, depositing irreducible, fleeting material that is ever combating the limits of the amorphous inside a formally perfect apparatus."[41] In her stanzas even Christ drags an *informe materiale* of language behind him.

Following the publication of *Sleep,* Rosselli notes that upon having "chosen" Italian as a language of composition, she had to put her English poems aside, because, hailing from a different discipline of the mind, they required a different species of research—of the English language and literature. "It isn't a great advantage to think in three languages," she states with humility—foiling any assumption that her heritage would lead to mastery over multiple terrains.[42] Instead of mastery and fluency, the ef-

39. Interview with Paola Zacometti, "Ma la logica è il cibo degli artisti," *Il Giornale di Napoli,* 12 May 1990; reprinted in Cortellessa, ed., *La furia dei venti contrari,* 221.

40. Alessandro Baldacci, *Fra tragico e assurdo: Benn, Beckett e Celan nella poetica di Amelia Rosselli* (Cassino: Edizioni dell'Università degli studi di Cassino, 2006), 180.

41. Alessandro Baldacci, *Amelia Rosselli,* Universale Laterza (Roma: Laterza, 2007), 4.

42. In Cortellessa, *La furia dei venti contrari,* 166. Emmanuela Tandello emphasizes that Rosselli's interlingual contaminations do not lead to a facile, "happy hybridity," but tend to break up into nonsense, interfering with one another. See Tandello, "Doing the Splits: Language(s) in the Poetry of Amelia Rosselli," *Journal of the Institute of Romance Studies* 1 (1992).

fort of amalgamation confuses the Latinate and Anglo-Saxon roots of *heim* and *homo,* forcing "home" to coincide with "homicide." The effect is truly *unheimlich:* "unhomely," in a perceptual and philosophical as well as psychic sense.

Such effects of linguistic dislocation are accompanied, on the other hand, by Rosselli's compensatory utopian effort to forge poetic environments that would house an objective, total language: a search for the "formally perfect apparatus" to which Baldacci refers above. From *The Libellula* forward, Rosselli composed her poems within what she called a "cube-form" aimed at creating an "absolute time-space," where a dictated regularity of line length, in spatial and temporal terms, would harmonize the conflictual energies seething in each stanza. She lays these strategies out in a poetic tractate called "Metrical Spaces" ("Spazi metrici," 1962), written at Pasolini's behest, included as an appendix to *Variazioni belliche,* and glossed several times over the course of her career. The cube-form may be seen as a formal solution to the schisms of her experience, fruit of what she identified as an adolescent search for "universal forms" that would contain multiple vectors of expression—linguistic, rhythmic, and visual. We can grasp the urgency driving Rosselli's exploration of spatial form if we view the cube-form as a new poetic "homicile," recruiting the noise of cacophonous ambient life to the confined and intimate space of the stanza (a word whose architectonic quality is made explicit in Italian, as it literally means "room" or "chamber"). The poems of Rosselli's first and second books in particular lay out a field of subtle sonic and visual variation as a veritable climate to enter and scan, a new literalized "stanza" characterized by a narrative at-seaness like that of her "running homicile / flash-deep."

For contrast, we can return to the free-verse English lyric "Ashore's the great servility." Its breaching close, "then hard-pressed time / cracks / rut," transposes one of Rosselli's obsessions—rhythmical regularity and irregularity, fits and starts of cognitive and corporeal locomotion—into a quasi metaphor. What does it mean for time to be "hard-pressed"? Does it refer to time condensed to an anguishing degree? Time pursued? Time—and history—tamped down, squashed? We cannot contemplate the "pressure" in question without recalling the stress of futurist velocity upon the cultural landscape of an earlier moment. What happens when "time / cracks / rut"? A rut is itself a site of interruption, a channel or groove—presumably the structure into which "we shall fall stop." The poem's "Oh" laments that the guards "do catch with us"—a phrase that suggests more a game of catch than actual capture, not stillness but a deadening pattern. The guards may "catch" their booty by rendering us their instruments—carts of great servility. Time irrupts this scene to dislodge such paralysis by driving against it, cracking it—so that a historical landscape lies in chunks as irregular as these lines of free verse. As another English lyric from *Sleep* puts it, "Time / drags and breaks."

By contrast, the condensed stanza structure and metrical system Rosselli adopted in *The Libellula*, rigorously applied in the second section of *Bellicose Variations*, and never, as she affirms in late interviews, actually abandoned, enforce an evenness of verses, and therefore of spatiotemporal units: her compositional process fixes a spontaneous frame for each poem, requiring each line to be roughly the same length and duration as the one initially scored. The cube-form possesses an aural and, secondarily, a visual character. Lines are equivalent in terms of the duration of reading, a fact also signaled by subtle visual cues. The shorter poems are roughly square in shape, and longer poems columnar or "tubular"—an effect she achieved with type and managed to maintain by publishing her second volume, *Hospital Series*, in a monospaced font, placing each new poem on its own recto surrounded by empty space so as to cue readers to the regularity of characters and measures, as below:

```
settanta pezzenti e una camicia che si rompeva
nel nulla, per un capriccio io mi stendevo nel
nulla e tutto era alloro e beneficenza, benefatto
il re dei poveri, cammello che strisci. Una pioggia
dura, sottile, penetrava, per un bisogno d'assistenza
io penetravo in camere arredate ad una vera vita
che con le maiuscole si scostava dalla mia, gentilmente
servizievoli erano i condannati a morte. Inviti
strisciavano per i cardini piovosi d'una città
permeabile: nessuna bestia nascosta spolverava
le capre che marciavano estasiate per i monti della
Trinità: un cammello, due indiani e la gente maestra
di tutte le arti, musica e matematica, il furore
di sogni realizzabili. Perduta nella vasca d'ombre
le ragnatele bianche e la polvere per le ciglie,
granelli e piccole perle sotto una pioggia miserissima
decidevano per il meglio una vita chiusa.[43]
```

43. Mondadori agreed to publish the book in this format with the Il Saggiatore series, placing each new poem on its own A4-sized page. Original typescripts for *Hospital Series* contain notes regarding the approximate minimum and maximum measurement of each line. I have had largely to forfeit the visual effect by using what Rosselli called the "nineteenth-century characters" of mod-

Rosselli developed this rule over the course of years as a means of "eluding the banality of free verse, which seemed unhinged, without historical justification, and above all, exhausted":[44] spatiotemporal constraint grants a greater objectivity to the work, akin to the dynamic harmony of the first sonnets, yet without recurrence to classical prosodic structures. Ultimately the cube as concept is meant to establish a space rather than simply being adapted to one: as she prescribes in an Italian passage of *Diary in Three Tongues*, "[I]t is not the content that must *fit in* [underlined English in original] the space / but you who must mold the space / that is *your content must provoke the space*."[45]

In this space provoked by her clamorous transcriptions of reality, Rosselli hoped to exceed the egotism of the individual voice or tongue, to choreograph instead an unlikely commingling of voices with the capacity to exorcise ills: "the union of two souls / a *tarantella*." She notes in "Metrical Spaces" that "the language in which I write . . . is only one, while my sonic, logical, and associative experience is certainly that of many peoples, and reflectable in many languages." She elsewhere admits to the utopian character of such an effort; an Italian passage in *Diary in Three Tongues* confesses, "And I who discharge myself every day from the city council, 'ask myself if it wouldn't be possible, in an absurd effort, to forget how much surrounds to enclose me in the alchemies of a language good at every latitude.'"[46] The passage suggests an absurd oscillation between the desire to release oneself from the authority of the state and the desire to enclose oneself in a more capacious language of citizenship. Rosselli's search for a total idiom remains rigorously counterhierarchical, never asserting the supremacy of any one language or logic over the others; she declares elsewhere, "I aspire to panmusic, to the music of everyone, of the earth and of the universe, in which there is no longer an individual hand that regulates."[47] Florinda Fusco compares this process

---

ern publishing; printing all of her poetry as she had printed *Serie ospedaliera* would have been misleading in the current volume. Moreover, Rosselli did not consider herself a visual poet, and referred to the graphic equivalence as a "secondary" matter, which served merely to highlight the metric system she was deploying. It is important that we understand this system in conceptual terms, not as a superficial visual effect. See "La poesia è un piacere privato," 17. I have nonetheless attempted to be true to the length and duration of lines in translation where possible,

notwithstanding the substantial aural differences between Italian and English.

44. See the "Introduction to Metrical Spaces" included in this volume.

45. Rosselli, *Le poesie*, 114. Florinda Fusco writes convincingly of the cube-form's link to Platonic philosophy, wherein the cube is considered a stable and "moldable" form. Florinda Fusco, *Amelia Rosselli* (Palermo: Palumbo, 2008), 58.

46. Rosselli, *Le poesie*, 95.

47. "Musica e pittura," in Rosselli, *Una scrittura plurale*, 38.

to the forging of a *koiné,* or common dialect, which corresponds not to an effort of centralization, but to the tension inherent in creating a *"mobile site of language."*[48] We might view Rosselli's aspiration as a gesture of compensation for the fissuring of languages after Babel: the desire to forge an inspired space of xenoglossia, in which languages unlearned and unknown may be articulated.

Writing into the cube-form unexpectedly emphasizes filling over cropping, while continuing to generate disjunction. Rosselli regarded this process of replenishment as a fluid performance; though her work's foundations lie in intense literary and musicological study, she composed at high speed, at the typewriter, attempting to produce antirhetorical receptacles of sound and perception. In this regard, Rosselli's process reveals the influence of Charles Olson's seminal 1950 essay "Projective Verse," which laid out the new, improvisational technique of open-field composition enabled by the typewriter. But unlike her American male counterpart, Rosselli underscored this technique's utility for displacing the poetic I, evading contemporary poetic tendencies of privatization and egotism. Composing within cubes that dictate the length of each line and necessitate the total replenishment of space hampers the fits and starts of subjective judgment that are "courteously" obliged by free verse. Rosselli's revisionist interest in Olson is clarified by the script for a 1975 radio broadcast on American poets of the elite, in which she describes his "conception of metric spatiality":

> [I]n an attempt to abolish the I of the poet, he projects surrounding space, the totality of chaos, into the page—considering the poem as "transported energy" and the line as a vectorial unity in the field of the page. . . . Metaphors and images generate a sort of animated grid; the poetry in itself is not a space of separation from reality, but itself becomes a reality in which the world narrates itself and "enacts itself."[49]

Generative misreadings shed light on Rosselli's search for her own solutions; the constraint of her square, cube, or grid provides a stark contrast to the gestural liberation of Olson's open field. In her early experiments, the spatial emphasis generates a dense aural texture recalling the writing of poets such as Gertrude Stein, in which repetition reigns and all words, even articles and conjunctions, take on equal weight and

48. Fusco, *Amelia Rosselli,* 10.

49. The Olson discussion appears in "Poesia d'élite nell'America di oggi," in Rosselli, *Una scrittura plurale,* 158–61.

value, as she notes in "Metrical Spaces." The resultant texts possess the ambient quality of a meditative chant, though they stray from the candid mysticism of an early poem from *Palermo '63* called "Chiesa," or "Church":

. . . Rovinainfinitasimuove
romanzochiarificatoreunisce
Jesùnellemembratotali
Combinalarimanuovaiopregoilluminare

iquattromondi

Preghieradisperatarimuove
passionedisperataangoscia
Infernoimmobilesintetizza
Cantonidisintegratidella
miavita.

. . . Infiniteruinisstirred
Romanceclarifiereunites
Jesusinthelimbstotal
ArrangethenewrhymeIpraytoilluminate

thefourworlds

Desperateprayerremoves
Desperatepassionanguishes
Hellimmobilesynthesize
Disintegratedcantonsof
mylife.

—Palermo '63

This piece evokes the lived space of a church through the chanting that takes place within, linking Rosselli's poem to the continuum of thought in oral discourse; graphically it resembles ancient manuscripts lacking spaces between words, a tradition of *scriptio continua* to which she refers as a sign of the association between sonic and visual experience in archaic writing forms.[50] The "[d]isintegratedcantons" of this poem recall the cul-

50. In a 1988 workshop hosted by Elio Pagliarini, Rosselli points out that spaces between written words are an invention: "At one time sound was so close to the graphic text that one wrote absolutely without spaces between one word and the other." She adds that the interruptions of commas, semicolons, periods and the like in modern discourse are "psychological." "Laboratorio di Poesia," in Rosselli et al., *È vostra la vita che ho perso,* 237.

tural and linguistic subdivisions of nations—as well as the corners that, once imposed on language and sound, form cantons, or songs. Paradoxically, "Chiesa" consciously or unconsciously recalls the "fusedwords" of futurism—one of many signs that while she clearly departs from the antihistoricist rhetoric of the historical avant-gardes, Rosselli's belligerent leftist politics did not lead her to neglect the most radical stylistic gestures of modernism on ideological grounds, as many contemporaries did. Here modernist principles are recruited to the intimate scene of a prayer and to the evolving ambient forms of postwar literary, sonic, and visual arts. The cube-form stands at the juncture of modern and postmodern aesthetics: echoing an obsession with the square and grid by various factions of the historical avant-garde (Cubism, Suprematism, De Stijl) and its emanations in postwar abstraction and concrete poetry, the conceptual volume of Rosselli's cube also reflects a spatial turn in postwar European aesthetics that draws focus away from linear narrative and toward the creation of immersive environments, heightening awareness of the material installation of language. Futurist foci on kineticism and ambient noise had paved the way for such thinking in Italy, prompting a range of minimalist and spatialist movements in visual and sonic media throughout Europe and the Americas.

While a modernist fascination with pure geometry and structuralist fixation on the grid were clearly developing in the two- and three-dimensional visual arts of her day, Rosselli's metrical strategy is most directly an outgrowth of her musical training.[51] She studied violin, piano, and particularly organ seriously from the early 1950s on, later taking music lessons with Luigi Dallapiccola in Florence and with Guido Turchi and Goffredo Petrassi in Rome. Her performance work ranged from interpretation of contemporary composers to soundtracks for documentary films on the Italian South and performances of *Pinocchio* and of Mayakovsky and Esenin with the theater of Carmelo Bene. Rosselli's early exposure to Bartók in London would remain her principal point of reference in this field; her interest in ethnomusicology eventually super-

51. Rosselli's family was dedicated to music: her grandfather Joe was a pianist and composer in Mahler's Vienna, while Carlo Rosselli was a pianist and music lover. Though her mother discouraged Amelia from an impractical focus on music during her period of schooling in England, her grandmother supported her musical studies. Siriana Sgavicchia notes that the *Allegretto* of Beethoven's Seventh Symphony was played at the Rosselli brothers' funeral. See Siriana Sgavicchia, "In principio era la musica: Da Bartok a Cage passando per l'oriente," *Il caffè illustrato* 3, nos. 13–14 (2003): 54.

seded her aspirations as a composer, and she devoted years to developing a new system of notation for folk music, while commissioning the fabrication of instruments based on the laws of physics and acoustics rather than the tempered scale. Her critical study "The Harmonic Series," which seeks to reevaluate the untranscribed "substructures" of folk music and analyzes the liberation of notes outside of the tempered scale, was published before any of her poetry, in *Diapason* (1952–53) and *Civiltà delle macchine* 2 (1954). She continued to work on this essay for twenty-five years, sending it, translated, to interlocutors all over the world, before its final publication in *Il verri* in 1987.[52]

These studies were nourished by Rosselli's admission to the Darmstadt school for new music, where post-Webernism was being developed, for three summers from 1959 to 1961 (though a psychic breakdown prevented her from attending in 1960). At Darmstadt she entered into dialogue with the principal actors of the postwar avant-garde: Karlheinz Stockhausen, Pierre Boulez, and John Cage.[53] She also attended summer classes in contemporary electronic music with Luciano Berio at the Dartington College of Arts in 1962. In the same period, she did work at the RAI Phonology Studio founded by Berio and Bruno Maderna, the best-equipped forum for electronic music production in its day—exploring concrete music, the harmonic series, and, importantly for a poet, phoneme analysis.

Rosselli's musical education led her to experimentation with structure that is without parallel in postwar Italian poetics, swerving from both nostalgic recurrence to given forms and the free-verse tendencies of the Neoavanguardia. Serialism introduced her to the production of repetitive sonic climates that tap sound's estrangement from its point of origin; the result is a "closed" organization of poetic material that replaces linear with ambient form. Sonic replenishment relies heavily on the driving pulses enabled by serial echoing of similar phonemes and syntactical patterning, a phenomenon Lucia Re refers to as a "carpet of sound" that serves as a backdrop to the contrastive and polyphonic unfolding of variation in Rosselli's work, particularly in *Bellicose Variations* and *Hospital*

52. See "Paesaggio con figure," in Rosselli et al., *È vostra la vita che ho perso*, 284. "The Harmonic Series" is reprinted in Rosselli, *Una scrittura plurale*, 45–58.

53. In a 1992 interview, Rosselli relates a telling anecdote about her 1960 performance with Merce Cunningham and David Tudor, during which her less minimalist aleatory impulses led her to break into the anachronism of a Gregorian chant, until an audience member screamed "Amen!"—to Cage's distaste. "Partitura in versi," in Rosselli, *È vostra la vita che ho perso*, 145.

Series.[54] Rosselli highlights the relevance of this training to her prosodic experimentation and its relation to her vision of a total, universal language in "Metrical Spaces": "All possible imaginable rhythms filled my square meticulously to timbric depth, my rhythmics were musical in the sense developed by the latest experiments of post-Webernism; my regularity . . . came into contrast with a swarming of rhythms translatable . . . into microscopic durations."

Rosselli's method, which we might call "climatic," produced a substantial amount of misunderstanding in its day. Indeed, her first editor, Elio Vittorini, asked her to correct what he called—with unwitting clarity—"*le stonature*" or "off-key notes" in *Bellicose Variations*. In the first glossary provided to Garzanti upon Pasolini's suggestion, Rosselli explains anomalous linguistic additions in her poems such as "*contro* del *magazziniere*" ("against *of* the store-keeper") as "preferable" because of the poetic context, where each rhythmic or intensifying addition of a word is "licit": she notes that such elements of the poem are unchangeable due to her metrical rule—because "broken and incorrect language is born along with its squared form."[55] Rosselli thereby requires a new species of reading, less insistent on the linear unfolding of narration and more akin to absorption within each strategically framed environment/ instance; as she states elsewhere, such poems desire to cover the entire space of their *quadri* (pictures, frameworks) with a "geometric confusion of colors, vocalic timbres, without clarifying a central sense to the poem, but letting the ensemble speak for itself."[56] The cumulative serial quality of Rosselli's compositions also structures her books as wholes; she explained to Pasolini that the term "series" in *Hospital Series* refers to mathematical series and to the dodecaphonic series, but is also meant to highlight the composition of poems over a given period, ordered chronologically, and to render them a "neutrality" in the alternation of themes and forms.[57]

"Metrical Spaces" has challenged two generations of literary critics with its shuttling between sonic and graphic fact, between poetry's tem-

54. Lucia Re, "Amelia Rosselli and the Esthetics of Experimental Music," in *Amelia Rosselli*, ed. Daniela Attanasio and Emmanuela Tandello (Galleria: Rassegna Quadrimestrale di Cultura, 1997), 38. Snodgrass also highlights the influence of dodecaphonic music upon Rosselli's work in *Knowing Noise*.

55. Rosselli, *Lettere a Pasolini, 1962–1969*, 29.

56. "Musica e pittura: Dibattito su Dorazio," in Rosselli, *Una scrittura plurale*, 35.

57. Letter dated 28 November 1965, in *Lettere a Pasolini, 1962–1969*, 50–51.

poral and spatial expanse—by insisting that poetry, scored and scanned upon a page, is fundamentally both architecture and noise. Rosselli's poetic compositions manifest principles of *musique concrète* in striving to produce climates of sound recorded from the quotidian environment. In such work, an emergent ambience forms an aesthetic space less hermetic than "heterogeneous" in the sense Michel Foucault outlines in the essay "Of Other Spaces": "The space in which we live, which draws us out of ourselves, in which the erosion of our lives, our time and our history occurs, the space that claws and gnaws at us."[58]

The cube-form was emphasized by Rosselli's choice of cover art for *Hospital Series:* a series of receding squares, white on white, produced by Anita Klintz and Peter Gogel. The image spurs the vertigo of infinite regress, which can also be experienced as imprisonment; it resembles Max Bill's 1952 *Monument to the Unknown Political Prisoner.* This cover extends the walling tropes of Rosselli's earlier lyrics, such as the often-cited poem from *Bellicose Variations* that echoes T. S. Eliot's "Ash Wednesday":[59]

> Perché non spero tornare giammai nella città delle bellezze
> eccomi di ritorno in me stessa. Perché non spero mai ritrovare
> me stessa, eccomi di ritorno fra delle mura. Le mura pesanti
> e ignare rinchiudono il prigioniero.

> Because I don't hope ever to return within the city of beauties
> here I am returning to myself. Because I don't hope ever to find
> myself again, here I am returning amongst the walls. The walls heavy
> and ignorant enclose the prisoner.

Asked about the walls constantly appearing so as only to be undermined in her verse, Rosselli responded, "I detained the explosions that gathered in me. If I alternate, I mean to demonstrate the duality of the demonstration."[60] Fracture, arson, even urination and ejaculation versus ubiquitous walls: the revolt against persecution suffered by a person imprisoned before even entering the world persists in her poetry's paradoxical collusions of liberty and incarceration, union—whether sexual, spiritual, or political—and detachment. Her second published volume, which may

---

58. Michel Foucault, "Of Other Spaces," *Diacritics* 16.1 (Spring 1986): 23.

59. Critics have noted that this short poem cites the stammering that opens "Ash Wednesday": "Because I do not hope to turn again / Because I do not hope / Because I do not hope to turn. . . ." See T. S. Eliot, *The Complete Poems and Plays 1909–1950* (New York: Harcourt, Brace and Co., 1952), 60.

60. "La poesia è un piacere privato," 16.

Amelia Rosselli

**SERIE
OSPEDALIERA**

*il Saggiatore
di Alberto
Mondadori
Editore*

Front cover of the first edition of Amelia Rosselli's second printed volume, *Serie ospedaliera* (Mondadori: Il Saggiatore, 1969), featuring artwork by Anita Klintz and Peter Gogel.

be regarded as a revision of poetic hermeticism, continues to host alarming semantic vagrancy—tropological shifts and paranomasia—within a prevailing environment of enclosure that alternates in its effect between suffocation and reprieve.

This second book everywhere underscores the horizontal axis.[61] The title *Hospital Series* foregrounds a materialist urge to ground these latter-day *fleurs du mal* in order to confront a harsh collective history and undiagnosed corporeal ills—afflictions that cohabit the term for "evil," or *male*. Many of the poems were written as Rosselli was recovering from a serious bout of illness she later identified as meningitis or Parkinson's disease in the mountains of Abruzzo. The *Series* at hand is "hospital-like" in its "resignation to critically retrace one's own steps"—as Rosselli characterized its withdrawal from the battlefield of her first book—and in its attitude, "no longer bellicose in the face of more rare or even more rarefied sentiments or intuitions."[62] Yet accompanying this volume's relative hermeticism is her jackdaw's tongue, singing the splits of self and word in a style hostile, discomfiting, discomfited.

The second book addresses a state in which "guest" and "host" (invoked by *ospedaliera*: "hospitaler" or "hosteler," as well as "of the hospital") blur. Though experienced in aching solitude, this state is not confined to a domesticated subject. The modulations of Rosselli's *esile vocina* ("slight little voice," with a strong echo of "exile," or *esilio*) make palpable Theodor Adorno's 1966 assertion that "suffering is the objectivity that weighs the subject down."[63] Rosselli's subject lies down, wounded, abject, or dormant, confronting an undiagnosed malady and death, familiarizing herself with the low things; even in pointing to the sky she directs "your hands / full of mire."[64] The poetess's *suolo* ("ground," "soil," "land") inverts the Enlightened tyranny of Apollo's *sole*. Motion thus takes the form of linguistic and semantic travel along an often unforgiving ground. The *treno* ("train," "threnody"), a sign of this lateral drive and the trail it leaves behind, is ubiquitous in her poetry. The locomotive

---

61. For reflections on *cadere, giacere, scendere,* and *precipitare* (to fall, lie down, descend, precipitate) as verbs dear to Rosselli, see Tandello, "Il volo della 'Libellula'"; and Tatiana Bisanti, *L'opera plurilingue di Amelia Rosselli: Un "distorto, inesperto, espertissimo linguaggio,"* Letteratura Italiana (Pisa: ETS, 2007), 175.

62. See the interview with Giacinto Spagnoletti included in this volume.

63. Theodor Adorno, *Negative Dialectics,* as translated by Frederic Jameson in *Late Marxism* (London: Verso, 1990), 66.

64. "[A]lthough you afflicted, point your hands / full of mire to the sky." See "Se vuoi, non so, se puoi, riaccendere la miccia / If you want to, I don't know, if you can, relight the terribly," in *Le poesie,* 395.

(*locomotiva*)—or *locomotrice* ("locomotrix")—appears as a motif in her English verse as well:

> the lovely train of thought
> which had closest brought me farthest from
> your
> tight closet, returns, shivering
> with the lighted beacon of a distressed
> permit of pain. The lighted beacon which had
> furthest announced its rainbow
> joy, is delirious, soulfully
> singing rot
> into the crashed ears.
>
> —*Sleep: Poems in English*

Within an English context, the train also calls to mind the word's common Elizabethan meaning, to which her interest in sixteenth-century English lyric would have led her: "snare," with an echo of "threnody." Rosselli's repetition tempts us to anticipate an undeviating narrative or rhetorical route, but it functions as the site of displacement rather than encrustation; it lays the ground from which we grasp the departures of transposition and variation rather than paving the way toward some comfortable telos. In this universe of breakneck evolution, the "revolution" to which her generation clings leads implicitly, and quickly—even within the interval of a single line—to a stultifying vertigo or the threat of a revolver's shot. Attempts to avoid such disastrous trains of thought are signaled by the poems' accommodations of interruption: unpredictable uses and deletions of the comma, arrests of panoramic attentiveness within lines.

> . . . Rose coronavano
> le mie pezze e la luce brillava attraverso un
> occhio quasi crudele.
>
> . . . Roses crowned
> my patches and light gleamed across an
> eye nearly cruel.
>
> —*Bellicose Variations*

In *Hospital Series,* the mysticism of the rose emerges only after some eighty odd flowers of ill have been discomposed and recomposed. Restlessness ends in shelter and the less bellicose collision of dreams, in rest, as she had predicted in "My Clothes to the Wind" (1952): "I in the unreason of sleep came to the choosing and the mingling, and to the recognition."

Costruì corto-circuiti. . . .

She constructed short-circuits. . . .

—Obtuse Diary (1968)

While the influence of surrealism and expressionism upon the mutiny against "reason" staged by Rosselli's verse has been argued for persuasively, the poet's ambition to write "post-realist" verse suggests more complex foundations with regard to the mooring of representation and locus of subjecthood.[65] Subjectivity exposes itself as radically unstable across Rosselli's oeuvre, where the I/thou circuit is constantly and consciously reinscribed, rendered plural. "I tend toward the elimination of the I," she stated in a 1984 interview. "The I is no longer the expressive center, it is placed in the shadows, or to the side. I believe that it is only in this way that valid poetic and moral responses are reached, values useful to society."[66] With her third volume in Italian, *Documento / Document* (1976), which she considered her most architectonically rigorous, she attempts "to eliminate both the you and the I, this binarism, this little intimist alibi, . . . to ensure that the poem has the objectivity of a Pasternak in poetry, where the I is the public, where the I is things, where the I is the things that happen."[67] This goal hails from a period (1966–1973) that witnessed the culmination and dashing of many communal ideals; so the poet's insistence on the public character of her work is necessarily tempered by the awareness that she has committed herself to "the slow pilgrimage toward a public and also most private / debate."[68] The work's documentary impulse is mitigated by the understanding that poetry as a matter of record has always been imprecise, nonsynthetic, reliant on chance, subject to the limitations and exhaustion imposed by quotidian life. Documentary discipline and improvisation, publicly directed plaint and grievance that have been driven back to the private realm thereby co-conspire to produce these stanzas.

65. Pasolini was the first to invoke surrealism in describing Rosselli's verse, though he was quick to distinguish her from that movement between parentheses in "A Note on Amelia Rosselli"; Fortini follows up with a discussion of "simulated states of mental alteration" in Franco Fortini, *I poeti del Novecento* (Roma: Laterza, 1977), 208. A more recent reading of Rosselli's relation to the French surrealists appears in Leake, "'Nor Do I Want Your Interpretation." On Rosselli's relation to expressionism, see, for example, Francesco Carbognin, "Amelia Rosselli: Prove d'autore," *Strumenti critici* 19, no. 105 (2004): 245–72.

66. "Il dolore in una stanza," with Renato Minore, reproduced in Rosselli, *È vostra la vita che ho perso*, 64.

67. "Paesaggio con figure," printed in ibid., 276.

68. "Lo sdrucciolo cuore che in me è ribelle / The proparoxytone heart that is rebel in me," in *Le poesie*, 552.

The documentary urge exists in tandem with Rosselli's mature, self-imposed injunction to "translate what cannot be said by the illiterate, and what can be read . . . by the laborer who doesn't even have the time to read the newspaper."[69] Andrea Zanzotto notes that despite this change in sensibility, Rosselli's poetic does not contradict its initial intentions: even in her most politically explicit late poems, "the themes of an evident unequivocalness, brought to irregular intersections, grow and become real as they flee toward the most intense polysemy."[70] Ultimately, Rosselli's late politics and ethics prod her to reach for the most fundamental and challenging identifications. Giovanna Sicari writes of a 1985 trip with Amelia to the sea near Rome, during which a disfigured woman who tended the garden asked, "You are a poet, why don't you write a poem for me?" She recalls that Amelia replied simply, without emphasis, "All of my poems are dedicated to you."[71]

Rosselli's distressed claim to broader representativeness and Italian paternity, however destabilized by an accompanying claim to the phenomenon of global war as forebear, is one that I propose we take seriously. Rather than withdrawing into the social ambiguity of the interstice as so many vanguardist contemporaries did, Rosselli constructs an ardent relationship to the "barbarous" (implicitly heterogeneous) nation-state that gave rise both to Justice and Liberty and that movement's brutal termination. Her poetry traffics as much in hyperlocalizing uses of dialect and in "a grammar of the poor" as it does in a cosmopolitan literary heritage; she is as devoted to the distinct regions of Italy, rendered mobile in her handling, as she is to the formal constraint of the square or metrical space in containing a welter of experiences considered universal. In rebuking the privilege implicit in labels of cosmopolitanism attached to the avant-garde, and choosing Italian as her principal language of composition, she claims Italy as a *patria ideale* or "ideal fatherland," leaving the Italian language irrevocably changed in the process.[72]

---

69. Qtd. in Rosselli, *Una scrittura plurale*, 20.

70. See his essay included at the end of this volume.

71. "Grande, dolce Amelia," in Daniela Attanasio and Emmanuela Tandello, eds., *Amelia Rosselli, Galleria* 48, nos. 1–2 (1997), 165.

72. I draw the phrase "patria ideale" from Stefano Giovannuzzi's afterword in his edited volume of Rosselli's letters to Pier Paolo Pasolini, *Lettere a Pasolini,*

1962–1969, 116. For pathbreaking examples of an attempt to situate Italian literature within a transnational and migratory context, see Donna R. Gabaccia, *Italy's Many Diasporas*, Global Diasporas (Seattle: University of Washington Press, 2000); Graziella Parati, *Mediterranean Crossroads: Migration Literature in Italy* (Madison, NJ: Fairleigh Dickinson University Press; Associated University Presses, 1999); and Pasquale Verdicchio, *Bound by Distance: Rethinking Nationalism through the Italian*

Amelia Rosselli (*center*) with (*left to right*) unidentified friend, Carlo Nofri, Vito Riviello, cultural attaché of Frascati, and the young Lidia Riviello at the Riviello home in Frascati, outside of Rome, for the poetry festival "Il giusto verso" (1981). Photograph reproduced by permission of Daniela Rampa.

Her operations of estrangement, with their recalcitrant materiality, resistance to narrative, political saturation, and reach toward "collective assemblages of enunciation," resonate with the tactics of "minor litera-ture" as theorized in Gilles Deleuze and Félix Guattari's study of Kafka, an author Rosselli named among her primary influences.[73] Rosselli's poetry heaves the Italian tongue away from its naturalized usages, refram-ing, reconducting, reshaping, even perverting its form and contents, from a vantage point Pasolini identified in his "Note on Amelia Rosselli" as "the margins of dominion." Her literary occupation of the Italian national language could also be compared fruitfully to the work of what Jamaican

Diaspora (Madison, NJ: Fairleigh Dickin-son University Press, 1997).

73. Gilles Deleuze and Félix Guat-tari, *Kafka: Toward a Minor Literature*, trans. Dana Polan, Theory and History of Literature (Minneapolis: University of Minnesota Press, 1986), 18.

poet Kamau Brathwaite calls "nation language," appropriating the term "nation" to designate a creole of the colonized who transform the lexicon, syntax, and rhythm of a dominant tongue from within.[74] Rosselli described such play as an act of "molding one language with the other."[75]

Pasolini calls the younger poet's verse "a luxuriant, verdant oasis with the stupefying and random violence of the fait accompli"—but he traces its origins to "The Myth of Irrationality," in capital letters. In a 1963 letter to her brother John, she counters Pasolini's terminology: "As to 'Mystery' & 'neurosis' & 'Mito dell'Irrazionale'—some type of objection—I would have spoken rather of the 'Mito del Razionale'!"[76] It would be most accurate to identify Rosselli's generative oasis as the domain of post-Enlightenment poetics, wherein the violent unreason stemming from the world's programmatic disenchantment by way of "progress" is exposed.[77] The disturbances of her verse extend the formal experiments of the twentieth century's first avant-garde movement while composing a career-long riposte to futurist and positivist ideology.

Radically antinationalist in their innovations, Rosselli's ardently "Italian" poems provide a poignant introduction to the paradoxical phenomenon of Italian "modernism," while eliciting that Italy itself is a fundamentally transient, fundamentally clamorous form. By reading Rosselli as a legitimate representative of the Italian cultural landscape rather than an aberration, we can deprovincialize the framework of this national literature, and begin to find a vocabulary for the contributions of migrant, expatriated, and otherwise displaced authors of its past and future. As a mass of additional material surrounding Rosselli's oeuvre is published, and the constitutive bonds between Italy, immigration, and the plight of *extracomunitari* ("non-EU citizens") are recognized, she is emerging as an exemplary author as opposed to an anomalous female genius or tragically "sibylline" figure. It is time to find a critical language more attentive to the hybridity within Italian culture's discontinuous limits, with their necessary "etceteras"—limits that this poetry's implosive fecundity has the singular capacity to express.

74. Kamau Brathwaite, *History of the Voice: The Development of Nation Language in Anglophone Caribbean Poetry* (London: New Beacon Books, 1984).

75. She traced the poetic origins of such play to the verse of Ezra Pound. "Paesaggio con figure," in Rosselli, *È vostra la vita che ho perso*, 293.

76. Letter of 25 October 1963, at the Fondo Rosselli of the Centro di ricerca della tradizione manoscritta di autori moderni and contemporanei, University of Pavia. Original text is in English.

77. I have in mind the terms established by the classic study by Theodor W. Adorno and Max Horkheimer, *Dialectic of Enlightenment*, trans. John Cumming (New York: Continuum, 1999).

Portrait of Amelia (Rome, 1995). Photograph by Guglielmina Otter.
Reproduced by permission.

> . . . As slowly with circumvolution the notes spake out
> I sang slowly, slight nip
> into the beat of all multitudes.
>
> —*Sleep: Poems in English*

What deserves the attention of a global public is less the story of Rosselli's suffering than her extraordinary shaping of languages' responses to each particular corner—or to echo her term, "canton"—of experience. Her verse dramatizes our dwelling and flight in language, in languages, each of which constitutes a particular repository of instruments for sounding circumstance and erecting individual and collective prospects. Rosselli shows how *un*innate a fit language is to being, or statehood to personhood, while communicating how fervently one keeps battling to achieve such a match anyway, to render experience shareable. If her riotous idiom often dramatizes Wilhelm von Humboldt's dictum "All understanding is at the same time a misunderstanding, all agreement in thought and feeling is also a parting of the ways," it aims ultimately to exceed atomization, plumbing the word's "well of communication," to choreograph a cathartic convergence of voices.

O were I one in Three! Just like the Holy Ghost,
the Father and the Son, I'd reunite my scattered souls
and string them in from all the seas abroad;
no longer climb upon perdition's mast
and wave a banner crying God, at last!
—*October Elizabethans* (1956)

Although Rosselli has been anthologized outside Italian borders, few full-length translations of her poetry and prose have been produced. The heart of this volume offers a representative selection of Rosselli's Italian poems composed between 1953 and 1995, from *Primi scritti* through *Appunti sparsi e persi,* a later collection consisting of "notes" and "jottings" that did not find a place in *Documento.* The selection of Italian poetry tracks her trajectory from the more playful linguistic experimentation of *La libellula* and *Variazioni belliche* through the formal asylum of *Serie ospedaliera* and the sobriety of political consciousness in *Documento.* I close the selection of Italian poetry with extracts from Rosselli's final *poemetto* in thirteen sections, *Impromptu* (1981), composed after a seven-year silence, and—like Bernadette Mayer's *Midwinter Day* of the year prior—in a single sitting in the winter of 1979. Written against the backdrop of the "years of lead" in Italian politics, colored by the reign of Christian Democracy and the capture and murder of former prime minister Aldo Moro by the Red Brigades, this poem constitutes a final outcry against the injustices of a *voi* everywhere indexed but never named—and a final hunt for liberty and fecundity in a natural landscape everywhere hemmed in and surveilled. The work is a sort of Botticellian *Primavera* in a *jardinière,* patrolled by a plainclothes cop and a monotonous company of confraternity brothers, compared to stalks of wheat, who obscure the laid-out body of the poet; she lies against the earth and gazes at the sky recalling her youth through the "childhood's masonry of these verses." Written impromptu, this work was performed by Rosselli nearly as if it were Gregorian in a recording included with the Carlo Mancosu edition—chanted, even sung, contradicting musically the filth, terror, and currency of the scenes it sets.

This selection of poems, which aims to introduce the arc of Rosselli's career to an English-speaking audience, cannot replace the important Green Integer volume translated by Lucia Re and Paul Vangelisti as *War Variations,* which preserves with skill the serial integrity of Rosselli's first published work.[78] However, I have included poems from *Variazioni belliche*

78. Amelia Rosselli, *War Variations,*
trans. Lucia Re and Paul Vangelisti (Los
Angeles: Green Integer, 2005).

in the present collection that, due to their difficulty and interest, simply demand multiple interpretations. My selections and translations differ substantially from those contained in Giuseppe Leporace and Deborah Woodard's *The Dragonfly: A Selection of Poems, 1953–1981*. I strive closely to retain the sonic structure, linguistic seditiousness, and aperture to multiple interpretations of the original texts. I also provide a more robust understanding of Rosselli's intellectual and aesthetic motives through notes that clarify key moves on the poet's part, and hinges in translation.[79] The essays, interview, correspondence, and pivotal critical interpretations gathered here offer readers new to Rosselli further touchstones for exploration. Extracts from Rosselli's *Diario in tre lingue* and lyrics in English follow my translations; these are not intended as guides for reading the Italian verse, which operates differently, but instead as intertextual supplements and enrichment. With this context intact, I aim to be faithful in translation to Rosselli's "notes out of key," which the young poet herself, faced with editorial pressure, bravely refused to "correct."

> Questa grande differenza che ci pervade dopo: non credere alle parole ma invece stabilirle volta per volta.

> This great difference that pervades us afterwards: not to believe in words but instead to found them time at a time.
>
> —Obtuse Diary

It is reverie to translate Rosselli's poetry into one language of her background, imprinted in this oeuvre as the intimate but belligerent rhythm of "Lo sdrucciolo cuore che in me è ribelle," or "The proparoxytone heart that is rebel in me" (from *Document*)—a heart whose stress arrives on the antepenultimate syllable, as it does so often in English words, but not in Italian. It is a privilege to work these lines into the language of Donne through Berryman, authors Rosselli treasured, and to grasp her play of tongues from across a linguistic divide. This task reminds us again that "hospital" gestures back to a Greek root that indicates both "host" and "guest, foreigner, stranger." Engaged and engaging translation that speaks its own fatigue in crossing over and suturing a fundamental rift is, I am convinced, the only fitting expression of her poetic. Though I am not always able to reproduce the phonic or semantic effects of her lyrical improprieties and inversions within particular lines, I compensate for their occasional loss with parallel maneuvers elsewhere in a poem. This practice produces local differences between the original poem

---

79. Rosselli, *The Dragonfly: A Selection of Poems, 1953–1981*, trans. Deborah Woodard and Giuseppe Leporace (New York: Chelsea Editions, 2009).

Amelia Rosselli's grave at the Non-Catholic Cemetery for Foreigners in Rome, along the city walls in Testaccio, where Keats, Shelley, and Gramsci are buried. Photograph by Jennifer Scappettone. Reproduced by permission of David Rosselli and Mark Rosselli.

and the translation, but its global effect is, I hope, consistent with Rosselli's own sense of distortion. The I/thou gulf omnipresent in this oeuvre is more volatile than it at first seems to be—especially when rendered in English, which often cannot replicate her shifts between a masculine and feminine or singular and plural "you"; I provide cues to these shifts wherever possible without slowing down the verse. When the duplicity or figurative valence of an expression seems impossible to preserve I opt to keep the concrete surface of the original intact, to produce a text more glittering if more specked. I avoid the tempting alteration of Rosselli's eccentric punctuation, which is wielded more expressively and rhythmically than analytically or hypotactically.[80] Overall I choose to startle when

80. Textual cues alert us immediately to the most basic element of a potential strategy for fusing poetry and music, Rosselli's twin passions; errant commas and dashes should be read as akin to Shelley's rhetorical (rather than grammatical) punctuation, which was meant to serve as an aid in reading aloud—as a rhythmic and, additionally, an emotional "scoring" mechanism. For more on this aspect of the Romantic poet, see Donald H. Reiman and Sharon B. Powers' introduction to *Shelley's Poetry and Prose* (New York: Norton, 1977), xiv–xv.

Rosselli startles, and not to gloss. Doing so is a response to her own bid, authored in English and collected in *Sleep:*

> you might as well think one thing or another
> of me; I am not at mercy's chance, nor do
> I want your interpretation, having none
> myself to overpower me. You withdraw into
> your fevered cell, like a microscopic angel
> do engage battle with my thoughts, as if
> they were to my revolutionary heart, a promiscuous
> bell. Hell itself is what you
> want: a needle into necessity, foreseeing
> I shall not do better than you want.

I have attempted not to "needle" or pin down the verse according to my own need for exegesis or clarity. In the battle I have tried to respect the original's negative liberty. I want to keep it "dynamic and 'becoming' [*in divenire*]," as Rosselli directed in "Spazi metrici," so that my translation effects the sense of what Wang Wei would have called a mutual self.

For though Rosselli's evasion of the confessional "I" does away with the trappings of the individual subject, the self does emerge in this environment—fore-backwardly. In writing her mind, Rosselli composes by way of discomposure, faces herself through a pointed self-effacement: as if by spreading charcoal over a piece of paper, then depicting the figure by erasure. This figure remains as the hiatus in an ambience of ashes—one that conveys the hopes and dispossessions of the postwar epoch. Rosselli suspects the dazzle of crystal, even the solidity of coal; in her mind, coalitions have wrought the kinds of realizable dreams over which a war was *vinta*—that word's ambivalence registering the irrelevance of winning and losing in a context of global loss. She prefers ash: her supplication in "5 Poems for a Poetic" is "[R]educe to ash the rest of my days . . ."

We remain restless in Rosselli's "return / to the comprehended saying that makes sure love remains," or "rests" (*resta*), a resolve that is as sonic as it is semantic—pointing us to the need for poetry, and translation, to invent and *restore* an English as resonant as the languages being introduced to it in a global context. When we do, we are not annihilating "home," committing our own kind of homicide, but making way, as this poet did, for a new, more capacious linguistic domicile.

Poems in Italian

Da *Primi scritti* (1952–1963)

Prime prose italiane (1954)

Non so quale nuovo rigore m'abbia portato a voi, case del terreno nero. La stesura dei campi vi spinge sul limite dei viali appena inalberati. Tra i cespugli torti le case s'innalzano violente. Rompe il numero un fuoco d'erbe accese.

Ha le dita prese dal fastidio la luna, piena la notte, incomoda giù per i balconi nuovi. È tremante il quartiere d'ingiuria. La collina sciupa il nodo del sole.

★

Il ponte è perfettamente bianco e si stende perfetto sul fiume appena mosso. Le costruzioni pallide si rincorrono fino alla sponda. In là varca un ponte grigio.

Oltre lo squarcio della strada non andare, se questo è l'ultimo paesaggio.

★

Che strana trattoria possibile che anche qui sanno tutto? Mi accoglie l'oste grasso pericoloso con occhio sapiente. Era molto tempo sapeva. Mia esistenza dove m'hai buttata.

★

Bellissimo cameriere tu sei il re d'Italia tu che pazientisci e corri per le camomille.

★

From *First Writings* (1952–1963)

First Italian Prose (1954)

I don't know what new rigor brought me to you, houses of black terrain. The drafting of the fields pushes you on the edge of just-hoisted boulevards. Amidst the crooked cypresses the houses rise violent. A fire of grasses alight breaks the count.

The moon has fingers engrossed in distress, the night full, discomfortable down among the new balconies. The quarter of abuse is atremble. The hill spoils the node of the sun.

*

The bridge is perfectly white and stretches perfect upon the just-rough river. Pallid constructions chase each other up to the bank. Farther on a grey bridge crosses.

Do not go beyond the gash of the street, if this is the final landscape.

*

What strange kind of *trattoria* is this where even here they know everything? The fat dangerous host receives me with a knowing eye. It was much time he knew. My existence where have you thrown me.

*

Most gorgeous waiter you are the king of Italy you who patients and runs for chamomile.

*

Roma città eterna che silenziosamente di notte ti bevi il tuo splendore hai tu nulla da predire. Ti sei fatta principessa e languisci. Nulla ti vieta. Arrotonda pure i tuoi seni bianchi e lustri. Le massaie si sono stancate di portarti le acque piovane. Tu hai succhiato latte di volpe hai rubato hai saccheggiato e ora siedi riposi assestata.

★

L'acqua è una grande rana.
Il fiume si scioglie di carità. La carità scioglie i vizi l'acqua fiumara scioglie la città dondolante di incuria.
L'albero piange sottile armonioso di doglie.

Il fiume se ne va lentigginoso per via della brezza che non lo lascia più. È una pantera questo fiume brigante. Non chiede nessuna compagnia.
L'ombra dei tronchi duri piedistalli.

Ombre che vi rammaricate ombre fate scherno. Indicate che ho perduto le stagioni.
Lisciati acqua per l'arrivo del mare pettinati e sorvegliati grossolana.
Morti voi camminate lungo le rive a sfiorare le donne.

Mare, ti hanno proclamato. Sei una grande bestia lumaca. Hai la sordità nel fondo tufo. Mare mare hai la gioia e la misericordia con te. Sei un fiore trasparente una forte tomba.

★

Tu pioggia amica leggera tu cammini dolente tu cammini dolente e lenta e scendi i tetti per soccorrere.
Le acque scorrono con appena un suono.

★

Barocco bello tutt'impigliato Bianca ginestra con la solita Maria blu sul liquido cero nudo scandolosamente il Cristo attraente alle bambine. Cristo Jesù legno che non marcisci con lo cuore spinoso.

★

Rome eternal city who silently drinks yourself your splendor by night you have nothing to foretell. You made yourself a princess and languish. Nothing prohibits you. Go ahead and round off your white and lustrous breasts. The housewives have tired of bringing rainwaters to you. You have sucked wolfmilk have stolen have sacked and now you sit you rest orderly.

★

The water is a great frog.

The river dissolves its charity. Charity dissolves the vices the torrent dissolves the city rocking in negligence.

The tree cries tenuous harmonious with labor pangs.

The river goes ambling by way of the breeze that will not leave it alone. This bandit river is a panther. It does not ask for company.

The shadow of the trunks hard pedestals.

Shadows who regret shadows you mock. You point out that I have lost the seasons.

Preen yourself water for the sea's arrival comb and watch yourself coarse one.

Dead, you all walk the banks to graze the women.

Sea, they have promulgated you. You are a great snail beast. You have deafness in your tufa depths. Sea sea you have joy and mercy with you. You are a transparent flower a stalwart tomb.

★

You, rain, slight friend, you walk dolorous you walk dolorous and slow and go down the roofs to succor.

The waters surge with scarcely a sound.

★

Baroque beauty all ensnared white broomflower with the usual Maria navy blue on the liquid candle scandalously nude Christ alluring to the little girls. Christ Jesus wood that does not rot with thine thorny heart.

★

Erba nera che cresci segno nero tu vivi.

★

Il fiume delicatamente si torce. Bello che sei fiumincino cadaverino. Ti pescano. Siedi come un cane.

Da *Palermo '63* (1963)

Poesia dedicata a Gozzi

Come un sol uomo mi muovo impertinente
niente suspense nel giallo. Violento
cretino nel muoversi. Assassinio figlia di Grim
si violenta da non si sa chi che è da scoprire carino
Sistema in crisi perdita verginità trovare assassinatore
casualissimo. Nadia la figlia si muove liberamente
dopo le perdite casuali o no. Costruzioni allegoriche
scattano politiche. Moto insurrezionale sperde il
Dio traumaturgo. Poliziotto sempre Americano.
Grigioni i testi, la testa che si taglia, addirittura
manoscritta. Poliziotto scoglie dramma.

Poesia dedicata a Spatola

Il mare ha delle punte bianche ch'io non conosco e il tempo, che bravo
si dimena bravo nelle mie braccia, corrompo docilmente—
e sottile si lamenta per i dolori al ginocchio a me toccàti.
Senza livore io ti ricordo un immenso giorno di gioia
ma tu dimentichi la vera sapienza. Se la notte è una
veraconda scematura io rivorrei giocare con le belle

Black grass that grows black sign you live.

*

The river delicately twists. Gorgeous little cadaver riverlet that you are. They fish you out. You sit like a dog.

From *Palermo '63* (1963)

Poem dedicated to Gozzi

Like a lone man I move impertinent
no suspence in the thriller. Violent
fool in moving about. Assassination daughter of Grim
is violated by one knows not whom to be discovered cute
System in crisis virginity loss to locate most random
assassinant. Nadia the daughter moves freely
following the losses random or non. Allegorical constructions
spring political. Insurrectional movement disperses the
traumaturgic God. Ever-American cop.
Grisons, the texts, the head that gets cut, straightaway
manuscripted. Cop bluffs drama.

Poem dedicated to Spatola

The sea has white points that I don't know and tempo, so good
it wags good in my embrace, I corrupt sweetly—
and slight it laments the aches at the knee touched to me.
Without spite I remind you of an immense day of joy
but you forget true knowledge. If the night is a
trueful abature I would like again to play with the sweet

dolci signore che t'insegnavano che il dare o il vero, non
è vero.

Sentendo morire la dolce tirannia io ti richiamo
sirena volenterosa—ma il viso disfatto di un chiaro prevedere
altre colpe e docili obbedienze mi promuove cretine
speranze.

Gravi disgrazie sollecitano.

Il vero è una morte intera.

belles mister who taught you that giving or the true, is
not true.

Sensing sweet tyranny die I recall you,
eager siren—but the face stripped of a lucid prediction
of other faults and docile submissions promotes idiot
hopes in me.

Grave misfortunes solicit.

The truth is a death entire.

Da *La libellula: Panegirico della libertà* (1958)

La santità dei santi padri era un prodotto sì
cangiante ch'io decisi di allontanare ogni dubbio
dalla mia testa purtroppo troppo chiara e prendere
il salto per un addio più difficile. E fu allora
che la santa sede si prese la briga di saltare
i fossi, non so come, ma ne rimasi allucinata.
E fu allora che le misere salme dei nostri morti
rimarono per l'intero in un echeggiare violento,
oh io canto per le strade ma solo il santo padre
sa dove tutto ciò va a finire. E tu le tue sante
brighe porterai ginocchioni a quel tuo confessore
ed egli ti darà quella benedetta benedizione
ch'io vorrei fosse fatta di pane e olio. Dunque
come dicevamo io ero stesa sull'erba putrida
e le canzoni d'amore sorvolavano sulla mia testa
ammalata d'amore, e io biascicavo tempeste e
preghiere e tutti i lumi del santo padre erano
accesi. La santa sede infatti biascicava canzoni
puerili anche lei e tutte le automobili dei più
ricchi artisti erano accolte tra le sue mura;
o disdegno, nemmeno la cauta indagine fa sì che
noi possiamo nascondere i nostri più terrei difetti,
come per esempio il farneticare in malandati
versi, o lagrimare sulle mura storte delle nostre
ambizioni: colori odorosi, di cera, stagliati
nella odorante stalla dei buongustai. Ma nessun
odio ho in preparazione nella mia cucina solo
la stancata bestia nascosta. E se il mare che
fu quella lontana bestia nascosta mi dicesse
cos'è che fa quel gran ansare, gli risponderei

From *The Libellula: Panegyric to Liberty* (1958)

The holiness of the holy fathers was a product so
changeful that I decided to distance every doubt
from my all too lucid head and to take the leap
toward a more difficult adieu. And it was then
that the holy see took the trouble to leap across
the moat, I don't know how, but it appalled me.
And it was then that the wretched corpses of our dead
rhymed for the whole in a violent echoing,
oh I sing through the streets but only the holy father
knows where all that ends up. And you and your holy
troubles will bring kneelings to that confessor of yours
and he will give you that blessed blessing
that I wish were made of bread and oil. So
as we were saying I was laid out on the putrid grass
and the love songs soared over my head
afflicted with love, and I mumbled tempests and
prayers and all the lamps of the holy father were
lit. In fact the holy see herself mumbled puerile songs
as well and all the automobiles of the richest
artists were received within her walls;
o disdain, not even cautious inquiry ensures that
we can hide our sallowest defects,
as for example the raving in verse
malandante, o to weep upon the crooked walls of our
ambition: odorous colors, in wax, standing out
in the odorous stable of the epicures. But no
hatred do I have stewing in my kitchen only
the exhausted hidden beast. And if the sea that
was that distant hidden beast would tell me
what it is that's gasping so, I would say

ma lasciami tranquilla, non ne posso più della
tua lungaggine. Ma lui sa meglio di me quali
sono le virtù dell'uomo. Io gli dico che è più
felice la tarantola nel suo privato giardino,
lui risponde ma tu non sai prendere. Le redini
si staccano se non mi attengo al potere della
razionalità lo so tu lo sai lo sanno alcuni ma
ugualmente la cara tenda degli scontenti a volte
perfora anche i miei sogni. E tu lo sai. E io
lo so ma l'avanguardia è ancora cavalcioni su
de le mie spalle e ride e sputa come una vecchia
fattucchiera, e nemmeno io so dove è che debbo
prendere il tram per arricchire i tuoi sogni,
e le mie stelle. Ma tu vedi allora che ho perso
anche io le leggiadre risplendenti capacità di
chi sa fregarsene. Debbo mangiare. Tu devi correre.
Io debbo alzar. Tu devi correre con la coda penzoloni.
Io mi alzo, tu ti stiri le braccia in un lungo
penibile addio, col sorriso stretto e duro sulla
tua bocca non troppo ammirabile. E cos'è quel
lume della verità se tu ironizzi? Null'altro
che la povera pegna tu avesti dal mio cuore lacerato.
Io non saprò mai guardarti in faccia; quel che
desideravo dire se n'è andato per la finestra,
quel che tu eri era un altro battaglione che
io non so più guerrare; dunque quale nuova libertà
cerchi fra stancate parole? Non la soave tenerezza
di chi sta a casa ben ragguagliato dalle alte
mura e pensa a sé. Non la stancata oblivione
del gigante che sa di non poter rimare che entro
il cerchio chiuso dei suoi desolati conoscenti;
la luce è un premio di Dio, ed egli preferì vendersela
che vedersela sporcata dalle tue oblivionate mani.
Non so cosa dico, ma tu non sai cosa cerchi, io
non so cercarti. Nel mezzo di una luce che è
chiara e di un'altra che è la cattiveria in persona
cerco il ritornello. Nel mezzo d'un gracile cammino
fatto di piccole erbe trastullate e perse nella
sporca terra, io cerco, e tu ti muori presso
un albero infruttuoso, sterile come la tua mano.

just leave me alone, I've had it with your
prolixity. But he knows man's virtues
better than I. I tell him the tarantula
is happier in his private garden,
he responds but you don't know how to take. The reins
break off if I do not keep to the power of
rationality I know it you know it some know it but
still the dear curtain of the discontented punctures
even my dreams at times. And you know it. And I
know it but the avant-garde is still straddling
my shoulders and laughs and spits like an old
witch, and not even I know where it is I've got to
take the tram to enrich your dreams,
and my stars. But you see then that I too
have lost the graceful resplendent ability of
those who know not to give a damn. I've got to eat. You must run.
I've got to rise. You must run with dangling tail.
I get up, and you stretch out your arms in a long
onerable adieu, with a smile tight and hard upon
your hardly admirable mouth. And what is that
lamp of truth if you're being sarcastic? Nothing but
the poor pawning you had of my lacerated heart.
I will never know how to look you in the face; what
I wished to say took off through the window,
what you were was another battalion that
I no longer know how to war; so what new liberty
do you seek among exhausted words? Not the suave tenderness
of those who stay at home well balanced by the high
walls and think of themselves. Not the exhausted oblivion
of the giant who knows he cannot rhyme except within
the closed circle of his desolate acquaintances;
the light is God's prize, and he chose to sell it off
rather than seeing it dirtied by your oblivioned hands.
I don't know what I'm saying, you don't know what you're seeking, I
don't know how to seek you out. Midway between a light that's
lucid and another that is wickedness made flesh
I seek the refrain. Midway on a delicate journey
wrought of small grasses amused and lost in the
dirty earth, I seek, and you fade beside
a fruitless tree, sterile as your hand.

O vita breve tu ti sei sdraiata presso di me che
ero ragazzina e ti sei posta ad ascoltare su
la mia spalla, e non chiami per le rime. Io
allungo le gambe e vendo i parafanghi con un
color prezioso, tu ti stilli contento in un luccichio
di cattive abitudini. Io mordo la mela per sostenere
queste mie deboli vene al collo che scoppia di
pena, e la macchina urla più forte della mia
sensata voce. Io non so cosa voglio tu non sai
chi sei, e siamo quasi pari. Ma che ricerco io
se la canzone della debole pietà non è altro
che questa mia inventata invettiva. . . .

. . . .

Trovate Ortensia: la sua meccanica è la solitudine
eiaculatoria. La sua solitudine è la meccanica
eiaculatoria. Trovate i gesti mostruosi di Ortensia:
la sua solitudine è popolata di spettri, e gli
spettri la popolano di solitudine. E il suo amore
rumina e non può uscire dalla casa. E la sua
luce vibra pertanto fra le mura, con la luce,
con gli spettri, con l'amore che non esce di
casa. Con lo spettro solo dell'amore, con lo
rispecchiamento dell'amore, con il disincanto,
l'incanto e la frenesia. Cercate Ortensia: cercate
la sua vibrante umiltà che non si sa dar pace,
e che non trova l'addio a nessuno, e che dice
addio sempre e a nessuno, ed a tutti solleva
il cappellino estivo, col gesto inusitato della
pietà. Trovate Ortensia che nella sua solitudine
popola il mondo civile di selvaggi. E il canto
della chitarra a lei non basta più. E il condono
della chitarra a lei non basta più! Trovate Ortensia
che muore fra i lillà, fragile e dimenticata.
Sorridente e fragile fra i lillà della vallata
impietosita; impietrita. Trovate Ortensia che
muore sorridendo di tra i lillà della vallata,
trovatela che muore e sorride ed è stranamente

62

O brief life you laid yourself out beside me who
was a little girl and placed yourself on my shoulder
to listen, and you don't call out for the rhymes. I
stretch out my legs and and sell the fenders with a
precious color, you seep contented in a sparkling
of bad habits. I bite the apple to sustain
these frail veins at my neck which explodes with
sorrow, and the machine shrieks more powerfully than my
sensible voice. I don't know what I want you don't know
who you are, and we are almost equal. But what am I researching
if the song of weak piety is nothing other
than this invented invective of mine. . . .

. . . .

Find Hortense: her mechanism is ejaculatory
solitude. Her solitude is ejaculatory
mechanism. Find the monstrous gestures of Hortense:
her solitude is peopled with specters, and the
specters people her with solitude. And her love
ruminates and cannot leave the house. And her
light vibrates thus within the walls, with the light,
with the specters, with the love that doesn't leave
the house. With the lone specter of love, with the
mirroring of love, with disenchantment,
enchantment and frenzy. Seek Hortense: seek
her resonant humility that nobody knows how to pacify,
and that finds no adieu to anyone, and that says
adieu always and to no one, and lifts her summer hat
to everyone, with the uncommon gesture
of pity. Find Hortense who in her solitude
peoples the civil world with the wild. And the song
of the guitar is no longer enough for her. And the amnesty
of the guitar is no longer enough for her! Find Hortense
who dies amid the lilacs, frail and forgotten.
Smiling and frail amid the lilacs of the valley
made pitiless; petrified. Find Hortense who
dies smiling among the lilacs of the valley,
find her who dies and smiles and is strangely

felice, fra i lillà della villa, della vallata
che l'ignora. Popolata è la sua solitudine di
spettri e di fiabe, popolata è la sua gioia di
strana erba e strano fiore,—che non perde l'odore.

. . . .

Se i vent'anni ti minacciano Esterina porta
qualche filo d'erba a torcere anche a me, ed
io seria e pronta m'inchinerò alle tue gonne
di sapiente fanciulla, troppo stretto il passaggio
per il tuo corpo allegro. Dietro al tuo banco
degli usurai precisi e assurdi (i poveri con
la grinta sapiente nella loro inestetica differenza),
dietro ogni rimpianto di bellezza, dietro la
porta che non s'apre, dietro alla fontana secca
al sole, lanterne verdi e cupe e ingiallite portano
sino al monte della pietà, sino al castello miracolosamente
scolpito per i cattivi preti. I miei vent'anni
mi minacciano Esterina, con il loro verde disastro,
con la loro luce viola e verde chiara, soffusa
d'agonie; luci, nuvoli disfatti e incatenati,
incatenati dalla limpidità di Dio, scoloriscono
l'aria che non ha limite, il piccolo ruscello,
la grave spaccatura. Ma tu non sei di quelli
che s'incantano al paesaggio. Torna ai tuoi canti
del cavallo che sapeva lunga la storia della
razza della sua bisnonna. Esterina i tuoi vent'anni
ti misurano cavità orali ed auricolari Esterina
la tua bocca pendente dimostra che tu sei fra
le più stanche ragazze che servono al di dietro
dei banchi. E tu la zappa ti sei portata al collo,
s'infigge di mezze lune. Te cerco su di un altro
binario: io te cerco nella campagna deserta.
Il verde soppruso del tuo miracolo è per me la
prima linea incandescente del mio cuore, la mia
schiena infallibile. La morta collina, deserto
ingigantito dalla tua partenza—la luce che mi
folgora troppo dura l'occhio asciutto! Il pensiero

happy, among the lilacs of the villa, of the valley
that ignores her. Peopled is her solitude of
specters and fables, peopled is her joy of
strange grass and strange flower,—that does not lose its odor.

. . . .

If twenty years terrorize you Esterina bring
some blade of grass for wringing to me as well, and
serious and ready I will bow to your skirts
of a wise girl, the passage too tight
for your quick body. Behind your bank
of usurers painstaking and absurd (the poor with
wise grit in their unaesthetic difference),
behind every regret of beauty, behind the
door that doesn't open, behind the fountain dry
in the sun, green dim and yellowed lanterns lead
to the mountain of piety, to the castle miraculously
sculpted for bad priests. My twenty years
terrorize me Esterina, with their green disaster,
with their violet and lucid green light, suffused
with agonies; lights, sunlessness undone and fettered,
fettered by God's limpidness, discolor
the air that has no limit, the little brook,
the heavy breaking. But you are not one of those
enchanted by the landscape. Go back to your songs
of the horse who knows all about the history of its
great-grandmother's race. Esterina your twenty years
measure your oral and auricular cavities Esterina
your hanging mouth demonstrates that you are among
the most tired girls who serve from behind the counters
of banks. And you've worn the hoe around your neck,
imprinted with half moons. I seek you out upon another
platform: I seek you out in the deserted countryside.
To me the green abuse of your miracle is the
white-hot front line of my heart, my
infallible back. The dead hill, desert
your departure made colossal—the light that flashes
too hard against my dried eye! The thought

di te mi inveiva, il pensiero duro di te reale
mi smorzava la gioia di te irreale, più vera
della tua vera vissuta visione, più lucida della
tua vivida dimostrazione, più lucida della tua
lucida vita vera ch'io non vedo. Della solitudine
le trombe delle scale! Il tetro gingillo della
carità; il tubercolotico ansimare; la corta freccia
che avvelena.

Ben fortificata alla pioggia, ben sommessa
al dolore, ben recapitata fra i tanti filtri
delle esperienze—sapere che la luce è tua madre,
e il sole è quasi tuo padre, e le membra tue
tuoi figli. Sapere e tacere e parlare e vibrare
e scordare e ritrovare l'ombra di Jesù che seppe
torcersi fuori della miseria, in tempo giusto
per la carne di Dio, per lo spirito di Dio, per
la eccellenza delle sue battute, le sue risposte
accanitamente perfette, il suo spirito randagio.
Sapere che la veridica cima canta in un trasporto
che tu non sempre puoi toccare: sapere che ogni
pezzo di carne tua è bramata dai cani, dietro
la tenda degli addii, dietro la lacrima del solitario,
dietro l'importanza del nuovo sole che appena
appena porta compagnia se tu sei solo. Rovina
la casa che ti porta la guardia, rovina l'uccello
che non sogna di restare al tuo nido preparato,
rovina l'inchiostro che si fa beffa della tua
ingratitudine, rovina gli arcangioli che non
sanno dove tu hai nascosto gli angioli che non
sanno temere.

of you railed against me, the hard thought of a real
you dimming my joy of you unreal, more true
than your true & experienced vision, more lucid than your
vivid demonstration, more lucid than your
lucid true life that I don't see. From solitude
the conch-shafts of stairs! The tetric knick-knack of
charity; the tuberculotic panting; the squat arrow
that poisons.

Well fortified against the rain, submissive
to sorrow, well delivered through so many filters
of experience—to know that light is your mother,
and the sun almost your father, and your limbs your
children. To know and be silent and speak and quiver
and forget and find again the shade of Jesus who knew
to writhe his way outside of misery, in good time
for the flesh of God, for the spirit of God, for
the excellence of his quips, his answers
doggedly perfect, his spirit stray.
To know the veridical summit sings in a transposition
you cannot always touch: to know that every
piece of your flesh is craved by dogs, behind
the curtain of adieus, behind the single tear of the solitary,
behind the significance of the new sun that just
barely brings company if you are alone. Ruin
the home that guards you, ruin the bird
that doesn't dream of staying in the nest you've prepared,
ruin the ink that makes a mockery of your
ingratitude, ruin the archangels that don't
know where you have hidden the angels who don't
know how to fear.

Da *Variazioni belliche* (1964)

Da *Poesie* (1959)

Roberto, chiama la mamma, trastullantesi nel canapè
bianco. Io non so
quale vuole Iddio da me, serii
intenti strappanti eternità, o il franco riso
del pupazzo appeso alla
ringhiera, ringhiera sì, ringhiera no, oh
posponi la tua convinta orazione per
un babelare commosso; car le foglie secche e gialle rapiscono
il vento che le batte. Nera visione albero che tendi
a quel supremo potere (podere) ch'infatti io
ritengo sbianchi invece la terra sotto ai piedi, tu sei
la mia amante se il cielo s'oscura, e il brivido
è tuo, nell'eterna foresta. Città vuota, città piena, città
che blandisci i dolori per
lo più fantastici dei sensi, ti siedi
accaldata dopo il tuo pasto di me, trastullo al vento spianato
dalle coste non oso più
affrontare, temo la rossa onda
del vero vivere, e le piante che ti dicono addio. Rompi-
collo accavalco i tuoi ponti, e che essi siano
la mia
natura.
Non so più
chi va e chi viene, lascia
il delirio trasformarti in incosciente
tavolo da gioco, e le ginestre (finestre) affacciarsi
spalmando il tuo sole per le riverberate vetra.

From *Bellicose Variations* (1964)

From *Poems* (1959)

Roberto, mum calls out, amusing herself in the white
settee. I don't know
which God wants from me, sober
purposes tearing eternity, or the frank chortle
of the puppet hanging from the
balustrade, balustrade yes, balustrade no, oh
postpone your persuaded oration for
a Babeling deeply felt; *car* the parched and yellow leaves abduct
the wind that beats them. Black vision tree that tends
toward that supreme force (farm) which I in fact
retain bleaches the earth below our feet instead, you are
my lovergirl if the sky darkens, and the shudder
is yours, in the eternal forest. Empty city, full city, city
who blandishes pains for the
mostly fanciful of the senses, you sit
hot after your meal of me, plaything of the wind leveled
by the shores I no longer dare
to face, I fear the red wave
of truly living, and the plants that bid you adieu. Dare-
devil I straddle your bridges, & so they may become
my
nature.
I no longer know
who comes and who goes, leaves
delirium to transform you into an unconscious
game table, and the broomflowers (windows) to peep out
smearing your sun all over the reverberate panes.

*

          del tuo oh nulla è il mondo e nulla
dire è la tua parola, lo mantiene sul suo asse
diagonato il passo degli analfabeti. Ed oltre ogni dire è il vero
libro da scuola. Sorride l'estate in un dolce frugore di molli
verdi foglie, ma l'oscuro della sua trama non racconto.
E la mia collana di ideali (la marina che batteva mentre gli uomini
premevano il fiore solo il terreno sapeva) è un sogno
più reale della tua luce candita pressata nella macchina di oggi.

         *

Non da vicino ti guarderò in faccia, né da
quella lontana piega della collina tu chiami
la tua bruciata esperienza. Colmo di rimpianto tu
continui a vivere, io brucio in un ardore che non
può sorridersi. E le gioconde terrazze dell'invernale
rissa di vento, grandine, e soffio di mista primavera
solcheranno il suolo della loro riga cruente. Io
intanto guarderò te piangere, per i valli
del tuo istante non goduto, la preghiera getta tutto
nelle sozze lavanderie di chi fugge: prega tu: sarcastica
ti livello al suolo raso della rosa città di cui
tu conosci solo il risparmiato ardore che la tua viltà
scambiò.

         *

                    nullo
è il deserto in cui tu mi muovi, e le false facce di
quella cattedrale tu chiami l'ardore
di Dio
s'incoronano di spine mortali. E se il sicuro
ormeggiare della tua candela di notte si
spezza, incolpa il fato, la notte oscura, e le
povere tue
spostate ragioni.

70

*

    of your oh null is the world and null
to tell is your word, the step of the illiterate supports it
on its axis aslant. And beyond every telling is the true
textbook. The summer smiles in a sweet fumbling of damp
green leaves, but I won't recount the tenebrousness of its plot.
And my necklace of ideals (the marine that beat while the men
pressed the flower only the terrain knew) is a dream
more real than your candied light pressed in the machine of today.

*

Not from close up will I look you in the face, nor from
that faraway fold of the hill you call
your scorched experience. Brimming with regret you
go on living, I scorch in an ardor that cannot
favor itself. And the jocund terraces of the wintry
brawl of wind, hail, and whiff of mixed spring
will plow the ground with their bloodying row. Meanwhile
I will watch you weeping, among the rampartance
of your unsavored instant, prayer flings everything
into the filthy laundries of he who flees: pray, you: sarcastic
I level you to the razed ground of the rose city you know only
as the economized ardor your faintheartedness
swapped.

*

                            null
is the desert in which you move me, and the false faces of
that cathedral you call the ardor
of God
crown themselves with mortal thorns. And if the sure
mooring of your candle-of-night
breaks, accuse fate, the dim night, and
your poor
displaced reasons.

Fui, volai, caddi tremante nelle
braccia di Dio, e che quest'ultimo sospiro
sia tutt'il mio essere, e che l'onda premi,
stretti in difficile unione, il mio sangue,
e da quell'inganno supremo mi si renda
la morte divenuta vermiglia, ed io
che dalle commosse risse dei miei compagni staccavo
quell'ansia di morire
godrò, infine,—l'era della ragione;
e che tutti i fiori bianchi della riviera, e
che tutto il peso di Dio
battano sulle mie prigioni.

★

O rondinella che colma di grazia inventi le tue parole e fischi
libera fuori d'ogni piantagione
con te ballerei molto al di là dei nidi precisi saprei la
indulgente cima. Se si ripetono gli
semoventi affanni, se la ribellione deve smorzarsi, se la tua piuma cade
per terra
ch'io almeno sogni! l'indifferenza e che le
bionde tirannie (e che la casa dai matti)
custodiscano il tuo vampo (le tue bionde tirannie).

★

Certe mie scarpe strette, sì vilmente mi causano torture
son paragonabili così come la tua
ascia di perle di amore. E la tua cattiva rubrica
è la meglio allevata dei tori nella palestra non i rubi
li sentimentali cori essi si rubano da sé
fuori dal canestro: scarpe piatte pò i
O! venir rubar
e la tendenza a congiungersi da sé nelle più cruenti
gonfalonerie.

*

        I was, I flew, I fell atremble into the
arms of God, and may this final sigh
be my entire being, and may the wave repay,
bound in difficult union, my blood,
and from that supreme ruse may death
become vermillion be rendered me, and I
who from the heartfelt riots of my comrades detached
that anxiousness to die
will relish, at last,—the age of reason;
and may all the white riviera flowers, and
all the weight of God
strike at my prisons.

*

O little swallow teeming with grace you invent your words and whistle
                      free outside of every plantation
with you I would dance so far beyond the exacting nests I would know the
indulgent summit. If self-propelling
toils repeat themselves, if rebellion must wilt, if your feather falls
                           to earth
may I at least dream! indifference and may the
blonde tyrannies (and may the madhouse)
watch over your blaze (your blonde tyrannies).

*

Certain tight shoes of mine, so contemptibly cause me agony
akin are they to your
hatchet of pearls of love. And your bad rubric
is the best bred of the bulls in the stadium not th' hearts
rubi'd with sentiment who are robbed on their own
out of the basket: flat shoes migh i
O! come rob
& the tendency to couple on their own in the bloodiest
coats of arms.

★

Cos'ha il mio cuore che batte sì soavemente
ed egli fa disperato, ei
più duri sondaggi? tu Quelle
scolanze che vi imprissi pr'ia ch'eo
si turmintussi sì
fieramente, tutti gli sono dispariti! O sei muiei
conigli correnti peri nervu ei per
brimosi canali dei la mia linfa (o vita!)
non stoppano, allora sì, c'io, my
iavvicyno allae mortae! In tutta schiellezze mia anima
tu ponigli rimedio, t'imbraccio, tu,—
trova queia Parola Soave, tu ritorna
alla compresa favella che fa sì che l'amore resta.

★

e se la luna intensa si ripiglia le sue corna
e se il mare è musco e se il sole e brama, cade.

★

o mio fiato che corri lungo le sponde
dove l'infinito mare congiunge braccio di terra
a concava marina, guarda la triste penisola
anelare: guarda il moto del cuore
farsi tufo, e le pietre spuntate
sfinirsi
al flutto.

★

        Questi uccelli che volano,
e questi nidi, di tormento fasciano
le inaudite coste, e l'ombra
che getta l'alabastro violento sui cuori
è l'improbabile vittoria. O sonetto tu suoni con le campane
dei muli,—il passo è muto.

74

★

What ails my heart which beats so suavely
& maketh hee disconsolate, ese
soundings quite steel? lle Those
scomminglings therein 'mprinted fore Ille
be harrowed so
fiercely, alle hath evanished! O shhd mine
hares rampant thru th'nerves &s thru
channels rimed 'f thisse my lymph (o life!)
not stopp, thus yes, th'I, mio
nearyng unto mortae! In alle clandors soul of mine
thou dost propose a cure, thee I imbrace, you,—
find 'at Suave Word, you, return
to the comprehended saying that makes sure love remains.

★

& if the moon intense takes back its horns
& if the sea is moss & if the sun & craving, falls.

★

o breath of mine who races along the shores
where infinite sea joins an arm of land
to marine hollow, watch the sad peninsula
pant: watch the heart's motion
turn to tuff, and the blunted stones
exhaust themselves
in the surge.

★

These birds that take flight,
and these nests, bandage the unheard-of
coasts with anguish, and the shadow
casting violent alabaster unto hearts
is the improbable conquest. O sonnet you sound with the bells
of mules,—the step is mute.

★

le pinze di domani, accendono in gorghi
sordi le linfe del tuo crescere: non
viandare; non trastullare
le tue forze all'inferno di vento e
grandine oggi obbliga tua maestà piegarsi! Se
tu credi alla grammatica dei poveri, ascolta allora
l'invidia nascente dei ricchi,—ti farai presto la mano
a nascere uno di loro.

★

                                    la mia fresca urina spargo
tuoi piedi e il sole danza! danza! danza!—fuori
la finestra mai vorrà
chiudersi per chi non ha il ventre piatto. Sorridente l'analisi
si congiungerà—ma io danzo! danzo!—incolume, perché
'l sole danza, perché vita è muliebre sulle piantagioni
incolte se lo sai. Un ebete ebano si muoveva molto
cupido nella sua
fermezza: giro! giro!—come tre grazie attorno al suo punto
d'oblio!

★

i rapporti più armoniosi e i rapporti più dissonanti, tu povero
che corri armoniosamente tu intelligente che corri con
la dissidenza, voglia io unirvi
in un universo sì cangiante sì terribilmente dissidente
che solo la Gloria di Dio noi crediamo porti gloria
sa riunire. E se veracemente con tutta la fiaccola di dio oh ordine
che cadde consumato, si rinnovò e non fu per sempre e fu solo
una balugine, io perdo! io non resto! riposato sulle erbe
tranquille dei né paradisi né terra né inferno né normale
convenienza con te ho cercato l'immenso e la totale
disarmonia perfetta, ma basse corde risuonano anche se tu non
le premi anche se tu non sistemi le valanghe i gridi e
le piccole sgragnature in quell'unico
sicuro scialle.

★

the forceps of tomorrow, they kindle in deaf
eddies the lymph of your growth: do not
wayfare; do not amuse
your forces in the hell of wind and
hail today oblige your majesty to bend! If
you believe in the grammar of the poor, then listen
to the nascent envy of the rich,—you will soon have a hand in
borning one of them.

★

                                my fresh urine I strew
your feet and the sun dances! dances! dances!—outside
the casement never will want
to shut for those who don't have a flat belly. Smiling the diagnosis
will be conjugated—but I dance! dance!—unscathed, because
th'sun dances, because life's womanly on the fallow
plantations if you know it. A half-wit ebony moved quite
covetously in its
stalwartness: I spin! spin!—like three graces around its point
of oblivion!

★

the most harmonious and the most dissonant relations, poor you
who runs harmoniously, intelligent you who runs with
dissidence, may I unite you
in a universe so changeful so terribly dissident
that only the Glory of God we believe to bring glory
knows how to reunite. And if veraciously with the whole torch of god oh order
which fell consumed, was renewed and was not forever and was only
a glimmer, I lose! I won't stay! resting on the tranquil
grasses of neither paradise nor earth nor hell nor normal
convenience, with you I sought the immense, and total
flawless disharmony, but bass chords resound even if you don't
bear down on them if you don't organize the avalanches the screams and
the little scraplings in that one
secured shawl.

tu rubi da anni l'antico ereditaggio
con cui concubine e ragazze si pegnavano
l'anima—tu rubi i fusti più delicati della
pietà—
e non paghi. Attendi l'ora che suonerà
la tua disfatta immagine, attendi l'oro che suonerà
la tua precipitosa fuga! Ora tu ti abbigli con
gli stalloni della fiertà,—domani ti stirerai
rotta fra gli stracci della pietà.

★

                              o dio che ciangelli
e la tua porta si fracassi—come un'
auto che varca il roso cancello, passa la tua
severa ordinanza, ma io non posso! seguirti!
tu troppo ti nascondi troppo premi il tuo pistone da pericolo.
Tu non hai dolcezza? Tu non distribuisci caldamente le
Felicità?, come un puro flauto dal becco sì sottile è
la tua ostilità—tu attiri
per poi ripulsare le gioie barbare.

*

for years you've robbed the antique hereditage
for which concubines & girls empawned their
souls—you rob the frailest stalks of
pity—
and don't pay. Await the hour that'll sound
your undone image, await the golden ore that'll sound
your headlong flight! Now you bedeck yourself with
intrepidity's stags—tomorrow you'll be stretched out
broken among pity's rags.

*

oh god may you chancel
& your portal be smashed—like an
auto that trespasses the corroded gate, passes your
severe ordinance, but I cannot! follow you!
you hide too much you press too much your perilous piston.
Have you no sweetness? Do you not ardently distribute
Felicities?, your hostility's like a pure flute so thinly
beaked—you attract
only to repel barbàrian joys.

Da *Variazioni* (1960–1961)

Per le cantate che si svolgevano nell'aria io rimavo
ancora pienamente. Per l'avvoltoio che era la tua sinistra
figura io ero decisa a combattere. Per i poveri ed i malati
di mente che avvolgevano le loro sinistre figure di tra
le strade malate io cantavo ancora tarantella la tua camicia
è la più bella canzone della strada. Per le strade odoranti
di benzina cercavamo nell'occhio del vicino la canzone
preferita. Per quel tuo cuore che io largamente preferisco
ad ogni altra burrasca io vado cantando amenamente delle
canzoni che non sono per il tuo orecchio casto da cantante
a divieto. Per il divieto che ci impedisce di continuare
forse io perderò te ancora ed ancora—sinché le maree del
bene e del male e di tutte le fandonie di cui è ricoperto
questo vasto mondo avranno terminato il loro fischiare.

★

Contiamo infiniti morti! la danza è quasi finita! la morte,
lo scoppio, la rondinella che giace ferita al suolo, la malattia,
e il disagio, la povertà e il demonio sono le mie cassette
dinamitarde. Tarda arrivavo alla pietà—tarda giacevo fra
dei conti in tasca disturbati dalla pace che non si offriva.
Vicino alla morte il suolo rendeva ai collezionisti il prezzo
della gloria. Tardi giaceva al suolo che rendeva il suo sangue
imbevuto di lacrime la pace. Cristo seduto al suolo su delle
gambe inclinate giaceva anche nel sangue quando Maria lo
travagliò.

Nata a Parigi travagliata nell'epopea della nostra generazione
fallace. Giaciuta in America fra i ricchi campi dei possidenti
e dello Stato statale. Vissuta in Italia, paese barbaro.
Scappata dall'Inghilterra paese di sofisticati. Speranzosa
nell'Ovest ove niente per ora cresce.

Il caffè-bambù era la notte.

La congenitale tendenza al bene si risvegliava.

From *Variations* (1960–1961)

For the singing that unwound in the air I rhymed
still utterly. For the vulture that was your sinister
figure I was determined to fight. For the poor and the ill
of mind that wound their sinister figures among
the ill streets I sang still tarantella your shirt
is the loveliest song of the street. For the streets odorous
with gasoline we sought in the neighbor's eye a favorite
song. For that heart of yours that I fully prefer
to every other storm I go along amenably singing those
songs that are not for your chaste ear of a singer
prohibited. For the prohibition that prevents us from going on
perhaps I will lose you still and again—until the tides of
good and evil and of all the fables which cover
this vast world will have ceased their whistling.

       *

We count the infinite dead! the dance is almost done for! death,
the blast, the swallow lying wounded on the ground, illness,
and hardship, poverty and the demon are my dynamite
drawers. Late I was arriving at pity—late I was lying amongst
pocketed invoices upset by a peace unoffered.
Close to death the ground rendered collectors the price
of glory. Late it lay on the ground that rendered its tear-
soaked blood peace. Christ seated on the ground upon some
bent legs was lying in blood as well when Mary labored
him.

Born in Paris labored in the epic of our fallacious
generation. Laid in America amid the rich fields of landowners
and of the statal State. Experienced in Italy, barbarous country.
Escaped from England country of sophisticates. Hopeful
in the West where nothing for the moment grows.

The café-bamboo was the night.

The congenitaled tendency toward good was reawakening.

Dopo il dono di Dio vi fu la rinascita. Dopo la pazienza
dei sensi caddero tutte le giornate. Dopo l'inchiostro
di Cina rinacque un elefante: la gioia. Dopo della gioia
scese l'inferno dopo il paradiso il lupo nella tana. Dopo
l'infinito vi fu la giostra. Ma caddero i lumi e si rinfocillarono
le bestie, e la lana venne preparata e il lupo divorato.
Dopo della fame nacque il bambino, dopo della noia scrisse
i suoi versi l'amante. Dopo l'infinito cadde la giostra
dopo la testata crebbe l'inchiostro. Caldamente protetta
scrisse i suoi versi la Vergine: moribondo Cristo le rispose
non mi toccare! Dopo i suoi versi il Cristo divorò la pena
che lo affliggeva. Dopo della notte cadde l'intero sostegno
del mondo. Dopo dell'inferno nacque il figlio bramoso di
distinguersi. Dopo della noia rompeva il silenzio l'acre
bisbiglio della contadina che cercava l'acqua nel pozzo
troppo profondo per le sue braccia. Dopo dell'aria che
scendeva delicata attorno al suo corpo immenso, nacque
la figliola col cuore devastato, nacque la pena degli uccelli,
nacque il desiderio e l'infinito che non si ritrova se
si perde. Speranzosi barcolliamo fin che la fine peschi
un'anima servile.

*

In preda ad uno shock violentissimo, nella miseria
e vicino al tuo cuore mandavo profumi d'incenso nelle
tue occhiaie. Le fosse ardeatine combinavano credenze
e sogni—io ero partita, tu eri tornato—la morte
era una crescenza di violenze che non si sfogavano
nella tua testa d'inganno. Le acque limacciose del
mio disinganno erano limate dalla tua gioia e dal
mio averti in mano, vicino e lontano come il turbine
delle stelle d'estate. Il vento di notte partiva e
sognava cose grandiose: io rimavo entro il mio potere
e partecipavo al vuoto. La colonna vertebrale dei

*

After the gift of God came the rebirth. After the patience
of the senses fell all the days. After the Chinese
ink an elephant was reborn: joy. Afterwards of joy
sank hell after paradise the wolf in its hole. After
the infinite came the merry-go-round. But the lamps fell and the beasts
were refocillated, and wool was prepared and the wolf devoured.
Afterwards of hunger the baby was born, afterwards of struggle the lover
wrote his verses. After the infinite fell the merry-go-round
after the blow to the head the ink rose. Passionately protected
the Virgin wrote her verses: moribund Christ answered her
don't touch me! After his verses Christ devoured the sorrow
afflicting him. Afterwards of night fell the entire brace
of the world. Afterwards of hell the son thirsting to distinguish
himself was born. Afterwards of struggle the acrid
whisper of the peasant seeking water in the well too deep
for her arms broke the quiet. Afterwards of air that
fell delicate around her immense body, the little daughter
with the devastated heart was born, the sorrow of the birds was born,
desire and the infinite that cannot be found again once lost
was born. Hopeful we lurch until the ending fishes out
a servile soul.

*

Prey to a most violent shock, wretched
and near to your heart I sent incense smoke into
your eyesockets. The Ardeatine caves mixed credences
and dreams—I had departed, you had returned—death
was a crescendo of violence that found no succor
in your head of deceit. The murky waters of
my disenchantment were polished by your joy and by
my having you in hand, near and far like the turbine
of summer stars. The night-wind departed and
dreamt grandiose things: I rhymed within my powers
and took part in the void. The spinal column of

tuoi peccati arringava la folla: il treno si fermava
ed era entro il suo dire che sostava il vero.

Nell'incontro con la favola risiedevano i banditi.

*

Ma in me coinvenivano montagne. Nella cella di tutte
le solitudini preparavano bistecche e insalate riccamente
condite. Nella cella delle pulchritudini attendevo
l'ordine di partire, insalata mista, per il tempo
che massacrava: ma nessun ordine attendeva fuori la
porta delle silenziose immagini. Il choc alla nuca
ruppe violento entro la porta—la scalata alla montagna
preparò la discesa precipitosa. Vietate al sole d'entrare,
vietata alla porta d'aprirsi vietata all'ira di soddisfarsi
fuori delle finestre dei poveri. Vietate alla noia
d'allontanarsi vietate. Nelle castelle di tutte le
bellezze moriva un vecchio sagace.

Condizionata ad una presa di potere che non era il
mio entravo in piazza e vedevo il sole bruciare, le
donne stagliare erbe su della piazza che ardeva di
malizia: la milizia.

Il sol fa mi do di tutte le tue battaglie.

*

Nel tappeto di Balzabar era la rinascita. Nell'ombra
dei cipressi che sovrastavano riconoscevo l'alfabeto.
L'assurdo si risolveva con quattro cannonate d'inferno
la mia aspettativa era la vostra! Conducevo una vita
piena di stenti—la castità m'obbligava a frullare
di tra le poetiche vetra delle case di cura, sale
d'ammobigliamento, vetrine di Picasso—insomma l'arte
intiera si rivolgeva ai miei occhi sbarrati per la
stupidità.

your sins harangued the crowd: the train ground to a halt
and it was within its talk that truth paused.

In the encounter with the fairytale resided outlaws.

*

But in me mountains coinvened. In the cell of all
solitudes they prepared steaks and salads richly
seasoned. In the cell of pulchritudes I awaited
the order to depart, mixed salad, for time
which slaughtered: but no order awaited out the
portal of silent images. *Shock* to the nape
broke violent within the portal—the climb to the mountain
prepared the headlong descent. Prohibit the sun to enter,
the portal prohibited to open the ire prohibited to satisfy itself
outside the windows of the poor. Prohibit tedium
to distance itself prohibit. In the castelles of all
beauties an elderly sage was dying.

Conditioned to a power seizure that wasn't my
own I entered the square and saw the sun burning, the
women hacking grasses upon the square that blazed with
malice: the militia.

The sol fa mi do of all of your battles.

*

In the carpet of Balzabar was the rebirth. In the shade
of impending cypresses I recognized the alphabet.
The absurd resolved itself with four cannonshots of hell
my expectation was yours! I conducted a life
full of hardship—chastity obliged me to whirr
amidst the poetical windowing of the cure-homes, parlors
of furnishings, showcases of Picasso—essentially art
entire turned to my eyes wide with
stupidity.

Crescevo a stenti: un giorno perso era la cura delle
mie fanciullaggini. Cercavo l'infinito: trovavo la
pietra di Topazio di tra i graniti del Tibet.

★

Se la colpa è degli uomini allora che Iddio venga
a chiamarmi fuori dalle sue mura di grossolana cinta
verdastra come l'alfabeto che non trovo. Se il muro
è una triste storia di congiunzioni fallite, allora
ch'io insegua le lepri digiune della mia tirannia
e sappia digiunare finché non è venuta la gran gloria.
Se l'inferno è una cosa vorace io temo allora essere
fra di quelli che portano le fiamme in bocca e non
si nutrono d'aria! Ma il vento veloce che spazia
al di là dei confini sa coronare i miei sogni anche
di albe felici.

★

Il Cristo trainava (sotto della sua ombrella) (la sua croce) un
informe materiale; parole trainanti nella polvere del dipinto
del chiostro di vetro. Sotto alla sua chiostra di vetro
il Cristo trainava una sciabola. Dodici pecore sogghignavano
distrattamente alla sua predica. Io montavo in arabeschi
il mio pudore dozzinale, su per le vetrate ricurve della
sua sala da pranzo, margherite colate in piombo su dei prati
e i cieli oscuranti di blu feroce. Io salivo i gradini della
pietà molto ben concentrata in se stessa, con la croce quadriforme
della sua durezza alle spalle. Il Cristo incrociato era una
colomba, che spaziava teneramente, lusingava con la sua coda
i teneri colori del cielo appena accennato. Il Cristo deformava
il mondo in mille maniere, catacombe delle lacrime. I suoi
occhi Bizantini splendenti e crudeli stagliavano rondinelle
nel cavo del cuore. La crudeltà si taceva forse meno maestra
del mondo, o universo con la sottana troppo piccola, se lui
piangeva. Io che cado supina dalla croce m'investo della
sua mantella di fasto originario. Bellezza armonia che scintilli

I grew up with hardship: one day lost was the cure for
my childishness. I sought the infinite: I found the
stone of Topaz amidst the granite of Tibet.

*

If the fault is man's well then shall God come
to call me outside his coarse girdling city walls
greenish as that alphabet I do not find. If the wall
is a sad history of botched conjunctions, well then
shall I chase the fasting hares of my tyranny
and know how to fast until great glory has come.
If hell is ravenous well then I fear being among
those whose mouths bear flames and do
not feed on air! But the swift wind that ranges
beyond borders also knows how to crown my dreams
with happy dawns.

*

Christ hauled (below his parasol) (his cross) a
shapeless material; words being hauled through the dust of the painting
of the glass cloister. Below his glass clauster
Christ hauled a sabre. Twelve sheep smirked
distractedly at his prayer. I mounted my second-rate modesty
in arabesques, up the arched glass windows of
his dining room, daisies cast in iron on lawns
and the heavens dimmed with ferocious blue. I ascended the stairway of
quite self-absorbed piety, with the quadriform cross
of its hardness behind me. Christ upon the cross was a
dove, ranging tenderly, alluring with his tail
the tender colors of a heaven just lit. Christ deformed
the world in a thousand ways, catacombs of tears. His
resplendent and cruel Byzantine eyes hacked little swallows
in the hollow of the heart. Cruelty kept silent, perhaps less mastress
of the world, or universe with too-tight petticoat, if he
cried. I who fall supine from the cross invest myself in
his mantle of originary splendor. Beauty harmony who gleams even

anche per i prati ora secchiti: marmo che non cade, curva
di spalla sepolta e rinata, con la spala che intacca i geroglifici
del mondo. Forma cunea, alfabeto—triangolo,—punta al cielo
le tue dita sporcate di terriccio.

★

I quattro contadini spostavano la rete, depositavano nella
cassaforte i loro averi. Ho scritto:—il falegname nella
sua artiglieria piangeva. Il colloquio con la natura era
di natura eterodossa. Per una civile scempiaggine non
era possibile partire. La maniera di asciugarsi la fronte
era di non badare alle forme. Se nel paradiso dei cantastorie
vigeva un'altra alta personalità era perché la mia mentalità
divergeva troppo dalle bassezze.

★

Nell'elefantiasi della giornata si conduceva un rapido
sbaraglio di cause ed effetti. Affetti si concludevano
dentro e fuori del ruscello. La somministrazione
di ogni bene avveniva dentro e fuori la cella. La
cellula di tutte le freschezze si appartava desolata
nel suo vecchiume. Conducevo una gara magniloquace
e la pulchritudine delle giornate era una barriera
alla comunione. Per perdonare la gara reinventavo
sillabe astruse, magniloquaci come il vento che germoglia
in fioritura secca. Condizionata a condonare la folla
ed i poveri rialzare la gara terminava fasulla per
le camminate colpevoli dentro la gara e fuori la gara
degli ricchi ed idioti fuori dal passatempo del sole.

★

Cercatemi e fuoriuscite.

upon now-arid lawns: marble that does not fall, curve
of shoulder buried and reborn, with the shovel that eats into the world's
hieroglyphs. Cuneiform, alphabet—triangle,—point to the heavens
your digits polluted with soil.

★

The four farmers were shifting the net, depositing their
belongings in the safe. I wrote:—the carpenter in
his artillery wept. Colloquy with nature was
of heterodox nature. A civil foolishness made it
impossible to leave. The way to dry one's forehead
was not to abide by forms. If in the storytellers' paradise
another high personality was in force it was because my turn of mind
swerved too much from lowliness.

★

In the elephantiasis of the day one conducted a rapid
wrout of causes and effects. Affects concluded
inside and outside of the brook. The administration
of every good took place inside and outside the cell. The
cell of all freshnesses would retire desolate
in its old rubbish. I conducted a magniloquacious race
and the pulchritude of the days was a barrier
to communion. To excuse the race I reinvented
abstruse syllables, magniloquacious as the wind that sprouts
in dry flower. Conditioned to condone the crowd
and the poor to raise the race was terminating false for
the guilty walks inside the race and outside the race
of the rich and idiotic outside the pastime of the sun.

★

Seek me & banish.

★

Il fratello della signora digiunava a poco prezzo.
Io m'ero messa in testa che dovevo accompagnarlo. Salvati
mi gridò morendo. La tua giacca è tesa di fil di panno
lavato alla riviera. L'ideale se ne va con voci infantili
ed incoscienti a lavarsi i panni alla riviera. L'ideale
se ne va infantile e risoluto a cercar voci nell'aldilà.
L'ideale è un prodotto borghese dell'agiatezza femminile.

★

Il tuo sorriso ambiguo curvava ogni mia speranza.
Sottoposta ad un esame di coscienza stiravo le membra
in un giocondo gioire del nulla. Il bene era rimasto
allontanato.

Per i riflessi casalinghi il mio corpo si circondava
di nuove cose: luci e fallimenti, sparimenti e castelli
dipinti a difficoltà di rosa.

Luce di mattina calcolava la rosa e spariva la bruma
in un incontro di fiabe, il gigante si mordeva le
mani.

★

Con tutta la candida presunzione della mia
giovane età stabilivo inventarii. Rose coronavano
le mie pezze e la luce brillava attraverso un
occhio quasi crudele.

La regola d'onore era l'inesperienza! Regolatevi
secondo il momento giusto esclamò l'analfabeta.

*

The lady's brother was fasting at low cost.
I'd gotten it into my head that I had to join him. Save yourself
he screamed at me dying. Your jacket is taut with the thread of linen
cleansed at the shore. The ideal takes off with infantile and
unconscious voices to cleanse its linens at the shore. The ideal
takes off infantile and resolute to seek voices in the beyond.
The ideal is a bourgeois product of feminine comfort.

*

Your equivocal smile curved every hope of mine.
Subjected to a test of conscience I stretched limbs
in a jocund rejoicing of the void. The good had been
distanced.

For housewifeish reflections my body encircled itself
with new things: lights and bankruptcies, vanishments and castles
painted with rose difficulty.

Morning light would calculate the rose and the mist would vanish
in a collision of fables, the giant chewing his
hands.

*

With all the candid arrogance of my
young age I established inventories. Roses crowned
my patches and light gleamed across an
eye nearly cruel.

Inexperience was the rule of honor! Regulate yourselves
according to the right moment exclaimed the illiterate female.

La farfalla che nei tuoi occhi si schiuse
per un istante era la mia gioia nell'essere
così addolorata dal tuo rifiuto. Un istante,
un essere—e il muro apre verso i campi la
sua tetra missione. Coinvolgendo il tuo specchio
felice nelle mie mani adoranti ritrassi la
figura di un eroe, e tu apristi il cielo
e il muro alla mia finestra. Nell'interno
della tua figura vi erano gli specchi, eterno
paradiso, mia fantasia subacquea, che soggiace
ai tuoi mordenti distinti dalla fraseologia
comune, abbronzatura d'inverno e fallace segno
della tua invidia.

   Il corso del mio cammino era una delicata fiamma
d'argento, o fanciullezza che si risveglia quando
tutte le navi hanno levato àncora! Corso della
mia fanciulezza fu il fiume che trapanò un monte
silenzioso contro un cielo scarlatto. Così si
svolse la danza della morte: ore di preghiere
e di fasto, le ore intere che ora si spezzano
sul cammino irto e la spiaggia umida, il ghiaccio
che muove.

   Tutto il mondo è vedovo se è vero che tu cammini ancora
tutto il mondo è vedovo se è vero! Tutto il mondo
è vero se è vero che tu cammini ancora, tutto il
mondo è vedovo se tu non muori! Tutto il mondo
è mio se è vero che tu non sei vivo ma solo
una lanterna per i miei occhi obliqui. Cieca rimasi
dalla tua nascita e l'importanza del nuovo giorno
non è che notte per la tua distanza. Cieca sono
chè tu cammini ancora! cieca sono che tu cammini
e il mondo è vedovo e il mondo è cieco se tu cammini
ancora aggrappato ai miei occhi celestiali.

*

The butterfly disclosed in your eyes
for an instant was my joy in being
so sorrowed by your refusal. An instant,
a being—and the wall opens its tetric mission
to the fields. Involving your happy
mirror in my adoring hands I with-
drew the figure of a hero, and you opened the sky
and the wall to my window. Inside
your figure were mirrors, eternal
paradise, my underwater reverie, subjected
to biting of yours distinct from common
phraseology, winter suntan and illusory sign
of your envy.

*

The course of my journey was a delicate flame
of silver, o girlhood that reawakens when
all the ships have lifted anchor! Course of
my girlhood was the river that drilled a silent
mount against a scarlet sky. Thus did the
dance of death unwind: hours of prayer
and of pomp, the hours entire that break now
upon the bristling journey and damp beach, ice
that moves.

*

All the world's a widower if it's true that you walk still
all the world's a widower if it's true! All the world
is true if it is true that you walk still, all the
world's a widower if you do not die! All the world
is mine if it is true that you are not alive but solely
a lantern to my oblique eyes. Blind was I left
by your birth and the consequence of the new day
is naught but night for your distance. Blind I am
because you walk still! blind I am that you should walk
& the world's a widower & the world is blind if you walk
still seizing my celestial eyes.

Da *Serie ospedaliera* (1963–1965)

settanta pezzenti e una camicia che si rompeva
nel nulla, per un capriccio io mi stendevo nel
nulla e tutto era alloro e beneficenza, benefatto
il re dei poveri, cammello che strisci. Una pioggia
dura, sottile, penetrava, per un bisogno d'assistenza
io penetravo in camere arredate ad una vera vita
che con le maiuscole si scostava dalla mia, gentilmente
servizievoli erano i condannati a morte. Inviti
strisciavano per i cardini piovosi d'una città
permeabile: nessuna bestia nascosta spolverava
le capre che marciavano estasiate per i monti della
Trinità: un cammello, due indiani e la gente maestra
di tutte le arti, musica e matematica, il furore
di sogni realizzabili. Perduta nella vasca d'ombre
le ragnatele bianche e la polvere per le ciglie,
granelli e piccole perle sotto una pioggia miserissima
decidevano per il meglio una vita chiusa.

★

Due scimmie solcarono l'anima di tracce invisibili,
ne soffrì il cuore, vecchia sentinella baffuta, corrotta,
ubriaca, tenace, senza speranza eppure aspettandosi l'intero
curvo cielo in mano. Il cuore ha una mano? chiedi tu e
l'ironia anch'essa con la sua mano (crivellata di biscotti)
disegna o gratta un arabesco tremulo sulle colline opache
del cervello: l'ironia è un ago, le tempeste bagnano di
opache tristezze il sangue lascivo, oh come corre il fiato

From *Hospital Series* (1963–1965)

seventy destitutes and a shirt that ripped itself up
in the null, by some caprice I lay back in the
null and all was laurel and beneficence, benefacted
the king of the poor, camel that would crawl. A rain
hard, thin, penetrated, in need of assistance
I penetrated rooms furnished to a real life
that with capital letters drew itself away from mine, courteously
obliging were the condemned to death. Invitations
crept along the rainy cornerstones of a city
permeable: not one hidden beast dusted
the goats that marched ecstatic upon the mounts of the
Trinity: a camel, two Indians and the people master
of all the arts, music and mathematics, the fury
of realizable dreams. Lost in the basin of shadows,
the white spiderwebs and the dust on lashes—
specks and small pearls beneath a rain most wretched
settled for the best a life closed.

*

Two monkeys ploughed the soul of invisible traces,
the heart suffered it, old guard whiskered, corrupt,
drunk, tenacious, without hope and yet expecting the entire
curved sky in hand. The heart has a hand? you ask and
irony too with its hand (riddled with cookies)
draws or scratches an arabesque tremulous on the opaque hills
of the mind: irony is a needle, the tempests bathe lascivious
blood with opaque sorrows, oh how the breath rushes

a smozzare le sentinelle! (qua follia arrangiasti tu una
specie di festa, mi liberasti).

⋆

Severe le condanne a tre. In rotta con l'arcipelago fummo
travolti dal fiume, inorganica vicenda, terra e mare sputavano
sangue invece. Mentre tu partisti, io mi rimirai nel vasto
arcipelago che era la mia mente molto severa, logica,
disperata di tanto vuoto: una battaglia, due, tre battaglie

perdute. Ma il furore dei nostri sguardi, tu lanterna
che credevi guidare, io manovella rotta, ma il furore
di questi nostri due sguardi c'inceppò: la vittoria scontata
la battaglia vinta i banditi più forti di noi, l'unione
di due anime una tarantella.

⋆

L'infelice luna si chinò piangente.

Rivoli innocenti, barche semivuote, larghi laghi delle montagne
premettono ch'io sia tua, e obbediente.

⋆

Le tue acquerelle scomponevano la mia mente
loquace per l'invernizio. Con lo scompiglio della
primavera, nave in tormenta, io scalinavo ancòra
per le giostre colorate con astuzia: il tuo il mio
tesoro affogato. Il pennello dolcemente vibrava
nella modestia di un tugurio scomposto per l'inverno
che fu una crudeltà continua, un tuo dormire nascosto
dalle mie preghiere, uno scostarsi dalla ferrovia
che spesso invece s'accostava al mio capo, reclino
quando v'era luce.

to lop off the guards! (here folly you managed a
sort of feast, released me).

*

Severe the threefold sentences. En route with the archipelago we were
swept up by the current, inorganic event, land and sea spit
blood instead. As you split, I stared at myself in the vast
archipelago that was my mind, very severe, logical,
desperate before so much void: a battle, two, three battles

lost. But the furor of our looks, you lantern
who thought to guide, I routed crank, but the furor
of these two looks of ours blocked: the victory taken for
granted the battle conquered the bandits stronger than us, the union
of two souls a tarantella.

*

The unhappy moon bowed down in its lament.

Innocent rivulets, halfempty boats, the mountains' lakes agape
premise that I should be yours, and obedient.

*

   Your aquarelles discomposed my
mind loquacious for the winterice. With the mess of
spring, storm-tossed ship, I cut footholds still
among the merry-go-rounds colored with cunning: your my
drowned treasure. The paintbrush sweetly shook
in the modesty of a hovel discomposed for the winter
that was a continual cruelty, a sleep of yours hidden
from my prayers, a straying from the railway
that often rather veered toward my head, reclining
when there was light.

E la luce scomponendosi in parti eguali evolse
economiche colorazioni sulla carta del ferroviere.

Pallido, estenuato, iracondo, stornavi rondinelle
mentre io dipingevo egualmente innamorata della
natura e del mio bisogno.

⋆

un sole celeste, una irrorazione di grumi di cristallo
mattino presto, la luce non s'è spenta: quartieri traboccanti

di senilità, la lavandaia con il cesto ma le sue spalle
tremano. Dedicata tranquillità a piccole dosi! rosso il

malore, se la tua testa sonnecchia.

⋆

Il sesso violento come un oggetto (cava di marmo imbiancata)
(anfora di creta ricurva) e nascostissimo in forma
d'uovo assaltava il solitario, come se fosse la grandine
a tempestare, nel salotto. Non gaudente, non sapiente
serpentinamente influenzato da esempi illustri o illustrazioni
di candore, per la pace e per l'anima purulava. Non sapiente
non gaudente, ma sapiente e mercantile speronato come
il vascello contro rocce pipistrelle, cadeva di colpo
dall'alto del rigore e della danza, dal sol fa mi do di
un'altra giornata; non sapiente e non gaudente travestito
da soldato annaspando e arrischiando tra capanne di maiale
rovistando, come forma e come oggetto, il sesso si serviva
di lui.

⋆

Facce appese, bronzi al muro, facce di bronzo, santi appesi
al muro in una camera solitaria in affitto, per quattro

And the light discomposing itself in equal parts evolved
economical colorations on the map of the railroadman.

Pallid, enervated, irascible, you warded off swallows
while I painted on, equally enamored of
nature and of my need.

         *

a celeste sun, a sprinkling of crystal clots
early morning, the light hasn't spent itself: quarters teeming

with senility, the washerwoman with the basket yet her shoulders
tremble. Devoted tranquility in small doses! red the

seizure, if your head drowses.

         *

Sex violent like an object (quarry of marble blanched)
(amphora of crooked clay) and most clandestine in the form
of an egg would assault the solitary one, as if it were hail
to storm, in the sitting-room. Not voluptuary, not wise
serpentinely influenced by illustrious exempla or illustrations
of candor, for peace and for the soul it purulated. Not wise
not voluptuary, but wise and mercantile rammed like
the vessel against rock bats, it fell of a sudden
from the heights of rigor and of dance, from the sol fa mi do of
another day; not wise and not voluptuary crossdressed
as a soldier groping and risking among huts of swine
rummaging, as form and as object, sex helped itself
to him.

         *

Faces hung, bronze to the wall, brazen faces, saints hung
to the wall in a lone rented room, for four

giorni aspetto. Una camera povera, sovraccarica di fiori
di plastica, e leoni alla porta. Un mare trombante, e un
paese grossolano, verdi porte all'aperto dietro la strada
nuova, i monti inosservabili, la luce è un diadema. Le
colline poi sono verdi cavalli, il galoppo un imbroglio,
uno stratagemma per perdersi. Fa caldo ancora, e il cielo
è macchiato di tombe oscure.

5 poesie per una poetica

I

Permettimi catene d'indulgenza, salvami dalla barca che cola
a picco, levatura del pensiero scaccia gli argonauti da questa
mia dimora di dimensioni ignote; redivivi le mie labbra supplicanti
all'elemosina, porta alla cenere il resto dei miei giorni
non tanto squadrati da non poter giudicare la giustezza, trasparente
se la verifichi, ma tutt'altro che una serena esplorazione.
Dov'è il chi viene, il chi parte, incomprensibile rimango
e salgo e scendo per i ritrovi notturni d'un contadino: mani
grosse fiato corto cristallemi della noncuranza, me ne frego!
e precipito nel tuo bersaglio. Premendo i bottegai disonorati
frangendo peripezie, no—volevo dire, ma m'è scappata, la
urina e la luna e il commercio si sono cristallizzati innocentemente
per farmi fuori—premi dunque, sofisticato ambascio delle
lune—fammi dunque capire! Prassi della notte (una notte spiritosa
era la notte) prassi del mio non trovare non capire non perdonare
l'inezia che è il mio refrigeratore, manganellate alla bestia
che si concentrò così fermamente in se stessa da starnutire.
Collisione delle bestie e delle frane, i miei sogni non mi
lasciano tranquilla, premi dunque il rapporto di piacere,
te solo cerco.

2

Praticamente imbestialita mi stendevo rinoceronte forte sulla
collina del tuo capitale: cioè: non so: non voglio: non sei:
non vedo: non rimango: non, non, non, non, capitale delle
mie destrezze perché t'ho perso contadino urlatore semantica
all'infinito, non so se sono stata chiara, ma non ti vedo
apparire più tra le mie braccia desolanti per la partitura

days I wait. A poor room, overtaxed with plastic
flowers, and lions at the door. A sea trumpeting, and a
coarse country, green doors to the open behind the new
street, the inobservable mountains, the light is a diadem. The
hills then are green horses, the gallop a scam,
a stratagem for getting lost. It's hot still, and the sky
is stained with obscure tombs.

5 Poems for a Poetic

I

Permit me chains of indulgence, save me from the boat that
sinks, calibre of thought oust the argonauts from this
my abode of dimensions unknown; revivify my lips begging
for alms, reduce to ash the rest of my days
not so squared as to be unable to judge justice, transparent
if you verify it, but by no means a serene exploration.
Where is the he who comes, who leaves, incomprehensible I remain
and bound and descend through a farmer's nocturnal haunts: fat
hands short breath crystallemes of noncaring, I don't give a shit!
and fall headlong into your target. Pressuring the disgraced shopkeepers
breaking vicissitudes, no—I wanted to say, but it escaped me, the
urine and moon and commerce crystallized innocently
to do away with me—press on therefore, sophisticated anguish of the
moons—make me therefore understand! Praxis of the night (a witty night
was the night) praxis of my not finding not understanding not pardoning
the trifle that is my refrigeratore, bludgeoning the beast
that concentrated on itself so steadfastly as to sneeze.
Collision of beasts and landslides, my dreams won't leave
me alone, press therefore the rapport of pleasure,
it's you alone I seek.

2

Practically embeasted I stretched out rhinocerous strong on the
hill of your capital: that is: I do not know: I do not want: you are not:
I do not see: I do not stay: not, not, not, not, capital of
my dexterities because I've lost you farmer howler semantics
to the infinite, I don't know if I have been clear, but I don't see you
appear anymore in my arms desolant for the score

che si fece attendere. Quel che desideravo dire se n'è andato
per la finestra e le mollezze del tuo sguardo non corrodono
il tuo dono di freschezza: il pensiero non c'entra! non ti
vedo, non c'entro: il pensiero coalizzato non è per me che
una coagulazione collisione di infarti su della testa parrocchiale
dei segreti. Segreto della notte e della tomba pericoloso
avversario dei senza luna, il tuo miracoloso scolpire parrocchiale
principia la mia fine e ne comincia un'altra. Chiarezza deserto
dell'intelletto corridore in vena di sandwich, presso alla
fontana si siede la putta, crematorio della linguistica è la
farsa delle nostre credenze delle nostre credenziali.

   3
Perché cercavo essere chiara. Perchè ti morivo, insonne nottambulo
le mie emozioni. Per le notti che presero la lungaggine di
un infarto rimai lussureggiante lussuria permanente. Per le
notti birichine nell'incastro delle notti veramente non ho
fine. Per le membra insaziabili per la bestia insensibile
per le notti per lo sguardo, per l'occhio che nel frangente
s'appese al vocabolario, corta ricetta di ricotta tu mi guardi
e non mi vedi tu mi senti e mi disperi. Per la protagonista
che si bilanciava settimanalmente ti rispondo: non ho, non
vedo, non chiarisco il settimanale rispondere che sono brava.

   4
perchè non ti posso dire che sono brava. Credi a me, v'è,
per esempio, per critica delle cose, un segno, nelle mie labbra
che tu sei fermo.

Prendi la penna e impara a guardare, rischia la tosse nel
vestibolario, quasi, piccolo cerchio anche, dozzine
ma che dico, centinaia di sguardi puliti alle mie spalle,
la notte invece un rimare senza spalle.

   5
Una pulita notte. Permanente la luce nella stanza ovale. Gridi
sommessi, il tuo pensare. Patatrac, non v'è più luce. Gridare
sommessamente e gesticolare ma non trovare risposta alcuna
è necessario è naturale ai miei piedi rosa. Particolareggiate
sensibilità non ho ambizione di soccorrere né di essere io
ventilata dalle primizie: cioè: dedicata alla verità. Che

that made one wait. What I wanted to say fled
through the window and the softness of your gaze does not corrode
your gift of freshness: thought has nothing to do with it! I don't see
you, I don't have anything to do with it: coalited thought is nothing to me but
a coagulation collision of infarctions up from the parochial head
of secrets. Secret of the night and of the tomb perilous
adversary of those without a moon, your miraculous parochial sculpting
initiates my end and begins another. Clarity desert
of the intellect runner in the mood for a *sandwich,* against the
fountain the strumpet sits, a crematory of linguistics is the
farce of our credences of our credentials.

3

Because I sought to be clear. Because I died of you, tireless sleepwalker
my emotions. For the nights that took the prolixities
of a heartattack I rhymed lush permanent lust. For the
nights impish in the recesses of the nights I truly have no
end. For the insatiable members for the insensitive beast
for the nights for the look, for the eye that at this juncture
hung itself from the vocabulary, curt recipe for ricotta you watch
and don't see me you hear and despair of me. For the protagonist
who balanced herself weekly I respond to you: I do not have, I do not
see, I do not clarify the weekly responding that I am good.

4

because I cannot tell you that I am good. Believe me, there prevails,
for example, for the critique of things, a sign, in my lips
that you are firm.

Take the pen and learn to watch, risk the cough in the
vestibulary, almost, small circle also, dozens
but what am I saying, hundreds of sterile glances behind my spine,
the night instead a spineless rhyming.

5

A sterile night. The light in the oval room permanent. Subdued
screams, your thinking. Crash!, there is light no more. To scream
subdued and gesticulate but not to find any response
is natural is necessary to my rose feet. I have no
ambition to succor itemized sensibilities nor to be I
aired by the latest news: that is: dedicated to truth. What

mondo crudele è questo esclami ma non vedi ch'io penso cerca
quel che puoi, un incastro qualsiasi, puttana dalle lunghe
orecchie sornione, credimi la battaglia non è che una semantica
revoluzione.

Primeggiava nel suo sguardo prontamente riflesso nel mio cervellotico
corpo la primizia. Cioè: guarda bene: sono tre i punti: larga
la spalla stretto il collo e le labbra sono molli.

Versatile odorare insieme di certe piccole ambizioni non dico
nascoste ma evidenti tutti lo sanno. Credimi le barche nei
fiumi impasticciati sono rotonde: non ho altro da dire, il
fiato è una strategia per confondersi nel linguaggio, che
se tu vuoi, e puoi, e ricordi, e chiara è la tua mente sofferente
dalle meningiti chiare, predomina l'assemblea in piccole discussioni
ritornate al vocabolario, spezzami l'osso pretendi ch'io
sia come voi, che nella lingua catatonica travestite l'ingaggio
di vostra madre.

★

Sollevamento di peso e particolarità della sorte
sbirciavano colombelle le mie forze sono
prese dal tuo volare via come una
caramella, liquefatta la vocazione ad
una semantica revisione delle beghe
ed uccelli nostri. Nessuno dei soldati che veramente
intendeva risposarsi seppe dirmi
chi è che veramente marcia.

. . . solitaria alle regioni didascaliche
sorreggevo brigantella delusa di
una così miserabile sorte, oh
vedi io scoppio e tu non correre, la
mitra del pianoforte rimuove
sensazioni, metrò, canfora, rosse
e curve labbra mattoni della cassaforte.

a cruel world this is you cry but don't see that I think seek
what you can, any recess, whore with long
sly ears, believe me the battle is nothing but a semantic
rivolution.

The latest news prevailed in its gaze readily reflected in my queer
body. That is: look: there are three points: the
shoulder broad the neck narrow and the lips are soft.

Versatile smelling ensemble of certain small ambitions I won't say
hidden but evident everyone knows it. Believe me the boats in the
muddled rivers are round: I have nothing more to say,
breath is a strategy for confusing oneself in language, that
if you want, and can, and recollect, and clear is your mind afflicted with
clear meningitis, the assembly prevails in small discussions
sent back to the vocabulary, break my bone pretend that I am like
all of you, who in catatonic language disguise *l'engagement*
of your mother.

                    ★

Weight heaving and oddities of fate
stockdoves were eyeing my forces are
seized by your flying away like a
sweet, liquefied that vocation to a
semantic revision of our quarrels
and fowls. Not one soldier who truly
intended to remarry could tell me
who it is that truly marches.

. . . brigandelle disillusioned by
so miserable a fate I surged
solitary toward the didascalic zones, oh
you see I explode & you, don't go, the
piano's miter submachinic removes
sensations, metro, camphor, scarlet
and curved lips bricks of the coffer.

★

Il cielo caprino che curvava le suole
quasi vigorosamente prometteva: ignoranza
e terracotta.

Credere momentaneamente, rivedersi, pubblicare
pentatonica delusione il ridere è sempre
amaro; presto rivedrai rivivere le lustre
piantagioni e la raccolta, un provvisorio
accecamento della sorte.

   Premi il tuo disingaggio nella notte
rivedi i programmi, *amour je t'ai tué:* notte
di nuovo le caramelle una lavagna io
ti scorro nelle tue dita misogene. Presto
rivedrai il cantare della sorte, coniglio tu
ed io insieme nelle sere della morte
confinata ad un industriale amare.

          ★

la vita è un largo esperimento per alcuni, troppo
vuota la terra il buco nelle sue ginocchia,
trafiggere lance e persuasi aneddoti, ti semino
mondo che cingi le braccia per l'alloro. Sebbene
troppo largo il mistero dei tuoi occhi lugubri
sebbene troppo falso il chiedere in ginocchio
vorrei con un'ansia più viva ridirti: semina
le piante nella mia anima (un tranello), che
non posso più muovere le ginocchia pieghe. Troppo
nel sole la vita che si spegne, troppo nell'ombra
il gomitolo che portava alla capanna, un mare
gonfio delle tue palpebre.

The goatlike sky that curved the soles
quasivigorously promised: ignorance
and fired clay.

To believe fleetingly, to meet again, to publish
pentatonic delusion to laugh is always
tart; soon you will revisit to relive the lustrous
plantations and the harvest, a provisional
blinding of fate.

　　You push your disengagement in the night
you revise programs, *amour je t'ai tué:* night
again the candies a blackboard I
course through your misogynous fingers. Soon
you will revisit the singing of fate, rabbithearted you
and I together in the evenings of a death
confined to an industrial loving.

　　　　　　★

life's an experiment agape for some, too
empty the earth the hole in its knees,
to transfix lances and persuaded anecdotes, I sow you
world who girds the arms for laurel. Although
too agape the mystery of your lugubrious eyes
although too false the asking on one's knees
I would like with more live anxiety to tell you again: sow
the plants in my soul (a snare), since
I can't move these folded knees anymore. Too much
in sun the life that extinguishes itself, too much in shadow
the ball of wool that led to the cottage, a swollen
sea of your eyelids.

"Lentement, et tres tendrement, quoy que mesuré"
(Couperin: 14ème ordre, livre III)

I

Tirannia dei rapporti; assoluto
del focolaio spento monotonamente e
grigio il tuo disfare della mia notte
a piena notte la lunaria cresima il
veramente essere, volere parimenti alle
lotte sconcertare. Prima di volere il
rapportare dei tuoi sogni bigi, spensi
la lucerna che nell'angolo criticava
questo male incandescente nelle tue
braccia bianche murarie e se la sonda
infallibile dei miei scarsi pensieri
indivisibile difesa del filtro credi
a me: incompleta
la descrizione del tuo malore, il resto
è sangue blu e vivace: nella notte della
mia deposizione quando a piccoli grappoli
l'uva si disingaggiava dalle mie dita
credenti caritatevoli sembra un sogno
opportuna vendi l'anima e la bilancia
cede.

2

Quando le fitte al cuore ti appagano
sembri un disastro e se lo sei vendi
pure le duecento dita che ti fecero
credere io volevo, nella notte disturbata
da piccoli sogni senza sonno, senso
ha questa rivolta perfetta. Ma sembra
che crack il boom cede, ovale nelle renitenti
catacombe e il cuore, una lavagna cancellata
tanto ha fatto il toro. Confidati
presto perché sembri, tutt'ora un accecamento
periglioso nel tuo, disfacendo la melagrana,
armonico prospetto: unghia uguale alla
carne se non ti spari, quando la gioventù
col suo violino attaccava un paesaggio
simile all'era nuova subdivisa

"Lentement, et tres tendrement, quoy que mesuré"
(Couperin: 14ème ordre, livre III)

1

Tyranny of rapports; absolute
of the hotbed quenched monotonously and
grey your undoing of my night
in full night the lunary confirms
true being, wanting likewise
at battle to disconcert. Before wanting the
rapporting of your grey dreams, I quenched
the oil-lamp that from the corner criticized
this incandescent evil in your
white masonry embrace and if the drill
infallible of my scant thoughts
indivisible defense of the filter believe
me: incomplete
the description of your illness, the rest
is blood blue and vivacious: in the night of
my deposition when in small clusters
the grapes disengaged themselves from my believing
charitable fingers it seems a dream;
opportune you sell the soul and the scale
gives in.

2

When the pangs at the heart gratify
you seem a disaster and if you are sell
by all means the two hundred fingers that made you
believe I wanted, in the night disturbed
by little dreams without sleep, this perfect
revolt makes sense. Yet it seems
that *crack* the boom gives in, oval in the recalcitrant
catacombs and the heart, a blackboard erased
so much has the bull accomplished. Confide
quick because you seem, even now a perilous
blinding in your, pomegranate-undoing,
harmonic prospect: fingernail equal to
flesh if you don't shoot yourself, when youth
with its violin attacked a landscape
like the new subdivided era

nel grattacielo della tua anima sento
l'odore d'un fiammifero, spento appena
arso e il cielo, costante nella sua
nuvolosità a braccia aperte ha soddisfatto
l'esigenza della carne
(anni) sembrò anch'essa un fiore quando
si macellavano le bestie nel retro della
bottega impestata, per il caso che
nella mano cede, quando la carne presto
si sfascia girotondo.

Risposta

contrasto tra le ferite e l'ingranaggio una colomba spaziava
ma mi persi a cercare colombelle. Seduta stante convocai
anzi cominciai per bere, e il limone questa volta spartito
in parti eguali cresceva nel vaso da notte riempito di tè.
Ruvido il guanciale mentre non dormi, una rosetta sul porta
calza, tiracalze; strettoie delle difficoltà. Per essere
nelle mani di Dio giunsi le mani, le punte alleggerite da
una pressione civica interna.

O un Dio o un'ombra: era lo stesso per chi cerca il sonno.
Rivoltàme nelle giungle dei sampietrini oppure chiare acque
e fresche ombre, il mangiame dei nostri polli è abituale,
tu non ridi se ti sparano. Volli tentare il pieno ne ricavai
strette misure.

★

Le sentinelle al di là dei ponti, i sacro santi
doveri impongono triplici considerazioni: se
tu sei davvero un cielo cristallo quasi verde
oppure la tenacia confonde le anguille, la tenacia
che lotta contro il contraddirsi, un ennesimo volo
per me nelle periferie delle illusioni ch'io possa
congiungere a me le coste azzurre, la tenacia
appena, ecco cos'è, il non volerti e lo averti

in the skyscraper of your soul I sense
the odor of a match, quenched scarcely
lit and the sky, constant in its
cloudiness with open arms has sated
the exigency of flesh
(years) it too seemed a flower when
the beasts were slaughtered in the back of the
plague-afflicted shop, for chance that
in the hand gives in, when flesh quickly
collapses ring a round of roses.

Response

contrast between the wounds and the machine a dove ranged
but I lost myself in seeking stockdoves. Without delay I convoked
no I commenced by drinking, and the lemon divided this time
in equal parts bloated in the night vase full of tea. The pillow
coarse as you do not sleep, rosette on the stocking
holder, stockingpull; bottlenecks of difficulties. To be
in the hands of God I joined hands, the points eased by
a pressure civic, interior.

Either a God or a shade: it was all the same for her who seeks sleep.
Revoltment in the jungles of saintpeterstones or clear waters
and fresh shades, the feed of our chickens is habitual,
you do not laugh if they shoot at you. I resolved to try the full & extracted
strict measures.

★

The sentinels beyond the bridges, the sacro sanct
duties enforce triple considerations: if
you are truly a crystal sky almost green
or tenacity confounds the eels, tenacity
that battles selfcontradiction, an nth flight
for me in the suburbs of illusions that I might
tether the blue coasts to me, tenacity
barely, that's what it is, that not wanting you and having you

invano, tenebrosamente sconsigliando sorveglianze
io ti ricevo oh notte nelle cristalline mani che
mi giunsero separate. Separazione e il distillarsi,
delle erbe dal fondo del boccale un barlume
di voci, e l'eterno al di là una canzone imbastita
con orgoglio.

Non vidi nella serata nessuno degli angioli chiedermi
perdono, le braccia più pesanti dell'aria, l'ira
un coordinare impossibilmente le battaglie
quando la foce del fiume ci travolse.

*

Carta da bollo per gli incendiati un papavero
rosso accende come se fosse le tue speranze
grottesche direi se non fosse che così facendo
io cerco un illuminarsi dei progetti malgrado
le difficoltà inerenti alla tua rozzezza. Nel
sasso della strada un verificarsi di oggetti
casti se li misconosci e nella grossezza
della strada anche un tandem. Nella
verecondia di soggetti illuministici governavano
pozze di piccolo sangue sparsa la terra di
ondeggianti calamai rinascita quando
sei rotto.

*

L'ironia un ginocchio ancora più duro.

Pensi pensi pensi e è la fine. Di tutti i tuoi incartamenti
incantamenti. Mentre menti io me la filo, sulla linea del
sonetto montagnaro. Associa associa i tuoi guanti non toccheranno
mai cosa viva.

Il sonetto una cosa barbara. La lapide un fiammifero
che nell'inscenare la grand'istanza si dischiuse instantaneamente
una linea dell'avvenire la tua mano e nella faccia, la

in vain, tenebrously dissuading surveillance
I receive you oh night in crystalline hands that
reached me separate. Separation and being distilled,
in herbs from the depth of the jug a glimmer
of voices, and the eternal beyond a song drafted
with pride.

I did not see in the evening any of the seraphim begging my
pardon, arms heavier than air, the ire
an impossible coordinating of battles
when the mouth of the river swept us up.

★

Legal paper for the victims of fire a red
poppy ignites as if it were your hopes
I would call grotesque except that thus
I seek an enlightening of projects despite
the difficulties inherent in your coarseness. In the
stone of the street a coming-true of objects
chaste if you deny them and in the street's
corpulence a tandem even. In the
pudor of enlightened subjects governed
puddles of petty blood the earth strewn with
undulating inkwells rebirth when
you are broken.

★

Irony an even more rigid knee.

Think think think and it's the end. Of all your files
enchantments. As you lie I take off, along the line of the
mountain sonnet. Associate associate your gloves will never touch
a living thing.

The sonnet a barbarous thing. The tombstone a match
disclosed instantaneously in the staging of grand instance
your hand a line of becoming and in your face, the

scontenta mob degli arrivisti, l'innocenza che è rimasta in te
un perdono.

La mob un perdono.

La moto una querela. L'allucinazione un trasporto

al cimitero. Ne è senz'altro il più degno
rappresentante.

(L'unica cosa che m'importa
è di non sfigurare
con le sue apparenze.)

★

Di sollievo in sollievo, le strisce bianche le carte bianche
un sollievo, di passaggio in passaggio una bicicletta nuova
con la candeggina che spruzza il cimitero.

Di sollievo in sollievo con la giacca bianca che sporge marroncino
sull'abisso, credenza tatuaggi e telefoni in fila, mentre
aspettando l'onorevole Rivulini mi sbottonavo. Di casa in casa

telegrafo, una bicicletta in più per favore se potete in qualche
modo spingere. Di sollievo in sollievo spingete la mia bicicletta
gialla, il mio fumare transitivi. Di sollievo in sollievo tutte

le carte sparse per terra o sul tavolo, lisce per credere
che il futuro m'aspetta.

Che m'aspetti il futuro! che m'aspetti che m'aspetti il futuro
biblico nella sua grandezza, una sorte contorta non l'ho trovata
facendo il giro delle macellerie.

malcontented *mob* of the arrivistes, the innocence that lasts in you
a pardon.

The *mob* a pardon.

The motorcycle a plaint. The hallucination a haul

to the graveyard. It is certainly its most worthy
representative.

(The one thing that matters to me
is not to disfigure
with its appearances.)

        ★

From relief to relief, the white stripes the carte blanche
a relief, from passage to passage a bicycle new
with bleach that sprays the graveyard.

From relief to relief with white jacket that juts out umber
over the abyss, belief as tattoos and telephones in line, as
awaiting Congressman Rivulini I unbuttoned myself. From house to house

I telegraph, one bicycle more please if you can in some
way push. From relief to relief push my yellow
bicycle, my smoking of transitives. From relief to relief all

the cards sparse on the ground or the table, sleek with belief
that the future awaits me.

That the future awaits me! that it awaits that it awaits me the future
biblical in its grandeur, a contorted fate I have not found
doing the rounds of the slaughterhouses.

Dolce caos, un addolcimento visionario
mi porta stanca nel tuo quadro giardino
perfettamente atto alla libertà,
alla libidine e a ogni cosa che insieme
procura distensione, dal tuo viso
così cangiante.

Nell'interiore di questo pacifico
piccolo parco vedo te partire, a
passi ancora lenti, per altro giardino
e so che piovana attenderò che completamente
risorta sia la tua figura dal cimitero
delle mie penombre, i miei pensieri.

Tu sordo sembri rimanere incerto
all'entrata, fili di ferro ben raddrizzati
ad una tua possibile partenza, e
tutt'intorno il vuoto gentile sembra
pensare ad altra cosa che il tuo
ritorno—sembra, scacciandoti, infestarti
d'una punizione—io non cado ma sempre
sono che pezzo per pezzo muoio. Ed
in questa liquefazione delle attitudini
si rovescia il piano del parco, si
silenzia l'odore del bosco, e tutt'intorno
ancora travasa la gioia piccola d'esser
quasi salvi.

★

Questo giardino che nella mia figurata
mente sembra voler aprire nuovi piccoli
orizzonti alla mia gioia dopo la tempesta
di ieri notte, questo giardino è bianco
un poco e forse verde se lo voglio colorare
ed attende che vi si metta piede, senza
fascino la sua pacifità. Un angolo morto

*

Sweet chaos, a visionary sweetening
brings me tired into your square garden
perfectly apt for liberty,
for the libidinal and for each thing that in
ensemble draws distension, from your so
changeful face.

In the interior of this pacific
little park I see you depart, with
pace still slow, for another garden
and know that rainfall I will await
your figure's total resurgence from the cemetery
of my penumbras, my thoughts.

Deaf you seem uncertain still
at the entrance, iron wires well rectified
toward a possible departure of yours, and
all around the courteous void seems
occupied with something other than your
return—it seems, driving you off, to infest you
with a punishment—I do not fall but always
am that piece by piece dies. And
in this liquefaction of aptitudes
the plane of the park capsizes, the scent
of the forest silenced, and all around
still pours off the little joy of being
nearly saved.

*

This garden that in my figurate
mind seems to want to open small new
horizons to my joy after last night's
tempest, this garden is somewhat
white and perhaps green if I wish to color it
and waits for one to set foot inside, its
pacificity without allure. A dead corner

una vita che scende senza volere il bene
in cantinati pieni di significato ora
che la morte stessa ha annunciato con
i suoi travasi la sua importanza. E nel
travaso un piccolo sogno insiste d'esser
ricordato—io son la pace quasi grida
e tu non ricordi le mie solenni spiagge!
Ma è quieto il giardino—paradiso per scherzo
di fato, non è nulla quello che tu cerchi
fuori di me che sono la rinuncia, m'annuncia
da prima doloroso e poi cauto nel suo

crearsi quel firmamento che cercavo.

★

E accomodandosi tutto lei piangeva, disperatina
nella sua cella, biochimica la sua reazione. Son
un tantino rincretinita, rispose al padrone di
casa—ma che fai con la pistola?

La spingo nel suo buco.

E ne partì un colpo che traversalmente prese la
rete retinica, poi si lasciò cadere morbido sul
divano, ma era per terra i mattoni quadri rossi
e grigi.

★

Attenta alla medusa: un bianco un po' livido, la Giulietta
Alfa Romeo che ti passa in testa, arguisce il silenzio
d'oro e s'accende nella tua fede una speranza di
delusioni. Senza paradiso fummo, castrati, nell'ignota
fede di un domani che non vuol apparire vano ma spara
boccioli sulla tua testa abituata ai sonniferi.

Una cacca sul parabrezza s'adagia mollemente
nell'interruzione del tuo sogno. Liquefatta torni
ai tuoi doveri, un'intenzione in meno.

a life that sinks without wanting the good
in cellarings full of meaning now
that death itself has announced its importance
through its effusions. And in
effusion a small dream insists on being
remembered—I am peace it nearly screams
and you don't recall my solemn shores!
But the garden is quiet—paradise as a joke
of fate, null is what you seek outside
of I who am renouncement, at first
dolorous and then cautious in its self-creation

that firmament I sought announces me.

★

And with all made at home she wept, little wretch
in her cell, her reaction biochemical. I have been
driven a wee bit mad, she responded to the master of
the house—but what are you doing with the pistol?

I'm pushing it into its hole.

And from that a crosswise shot took the
retinal net, then let himself fall limp on the
couch, but was on the ground the square bricks red
and grey.

★

Look out for the medusa: a white a bit livid, the Juliette
Alfa Romeo that passes through your head, shimmers
silence of gold and ignites a hope for disillusions
in your faith. We were lacking paradise, castrati, in the anonymous
faith of a tomorrow that doesn't want to seem empty but shoots
buds on your narcotized head.

Shit on the windshield a slack adagio
in the interruption of your dream. Liquefied you return
to your duties, one intention less.

Che belli papaveri che sono. Spiritualizzano
l'erba, che ne sgratta i formaggi.

Rio Claro: centro meccanizzato: fiori (non
hanno nome) stendono la mano amica, pioviggina
e triste (se lo sei) stendi il braccio al
vento e la rara pioggia.

Poi ti senti soprassedere: le hanno levate tutte
le mammelle alle gigantesse! Stendi di nuovo
mano amica all'ombrello, e stendi il piede
frugale alla terra, piccola polvere mostruosa
che starnutisce. Senza l'ombrello non puoi
stare: piove da dannati ora che tu hai sentito
tutto l'odore dei fiori (se vi erano).

★

Archi di connivenza al mare, Pasqua
del bello, archi del freddo nella tua
personale arca di Noè: un frigido guantarsi
anima e corpo: per un puledro, polpastrello
indicibile affermazione della noia,
distensione del guanto nella mano e
anche una biro che aiuta ad aggiustarsi
le vere cose.

Le quali preferiscono starsene là sedute
incuranti bagnanti, che stirano stemmi
dal tuo linguaggio, lo pianificano e
poi lo mostrano al pubblico.

Cosa mostrano? Le tue incongruenze,
poi uno smacco al sedere, poi un'altra
piccola cosa: il suo cuore, che s'identifica
col vino. Smacco lesbico, o fannulone
poi un'altra piccola tristezza, le tue

★

What pretty poppies they are. They spiritualize
the grass, which grates cheeses of them.

Rio Claro: mechanized center: flowers (they
have no name) extend a friendly hand, drizzly
and sad (if you are) you extend an arm to the
wind and the rare rain.

Then you sense yourself superseded: they've snatched all
those breasts off the gigantesses! Again you extend
a friendly hand to the umbrella, and frugal
foot to the earth, little monstrous dust
that sneezes. Without an umbrella you cannot
stay: it's raining like hell now that you have taken in
the whole scent of the flowers (if they were there).

★

Arches of connivance by the sea, Easter
of the beautiful, arches of the cold in your
personal Noah's ark: a frigid gloving of oneself
soul and body: for a foal, fingertip
unspeakable affirmation of boredom,
relaxing of the glove in the hand and
a ballpoint pen that helps the true things
adjust themselves.

Which prefer to sit there,
indifferent bathers, who pull coats of arms
out of your language, strategize and
then show it off to the public.

What do they show? Your incongruities,
& a shame to the bum, & another
little thing: that heart, which identifies
with wine. Lesbian, or do-nothing, shame
& another small sadness, your

forbici, che recidono, ogni attitudine
al dovere.

(trasparente insonne il tuo bagnare
la testa al gatto, la sua coda, quando
col suo calore smaniava).

★

Ti vendo i miei fornelli, poi li sgraffi
e ti siedi impreparato sulla scrivania
se ti vendo il leggiero giogo della
mia inferma mente, meno roba ho, più
contenta sono. Disfatta dalla pioggia
e dai dolori incommensurabile mestruazione
senilità che s'avvicina, petrolifera
immaginazione.

Dialogo con i Poeti

Da poeta a poeta: in linguaggio sterile, che
s'appropria della benedizione e ne fa un piccolo
gioco o gesto, rallentando nel passo sul fiume
per lasciar dire ogni onestà. Da poeta in poeta:
simili ad uccellacci, che rapiscono il vento
che li porta e contribuiscono a migliorare la
fame. Di passo in passo un futile motivo che
li rallegra, vedendosi crescere in stima, i letterati
con le camicie aperte che s'abbronzano, al sole
di tutte le tranquillità: un piccolo gesto sfortunato
li riconduce all'aldilà con la morte che sembra
scendere e stringerli.

Ironicamente fasulla, o v'è una verità? ch'io
possa dire anche tua?

Ma nel fiume delle possibilità sorgeva anche
un piccolo astro notturno: la mia vanità, d'esser

scissors, which crop, each aptitude
for duty.

(transparent tireless your bathing
the head of the cat, its tail, when
in its heat it was craving.)

                    ★

I sell you my hotplates, then you grate at them
and sit yourself unprepared on the desk
if I sell you the light yoke of my
infirm mind, the less stuff I have, the
happier I am. Undone by the rain
and by pains incommensurable menstruation
senility that nears, petroliferous
imagination.

Dialogue with Poets

From poet to poet: in sterile language, which
embezzles benediction and makes a small
game or gesture of it, slowing its pace on the river
to let every honesty be told. From poet to poet:
like hawks, who abduct the wind
that carries them and support the bettering of
hunger. From pace to pace a futile motive that
cheers them, seeing themselves grow in stature, the literati
with open shirts who tan themselves beneath the sun
of all tranquilities: a small unfortunate gesture
reroutes them to the hereafter with death that seems
to lunge down and clench them.

Ironic sham, or does a truth prevail in it? that I
might say is yours as well?

But in the stream of possibilities there surged
a small evening star: my vanity, to be

fra i primi gigante della passione, un Cristoemblema
delle rinunziazioni. Annunciando castità, problemi
risolvibili e no, sapendo stornare l'emblema
dalle bocche virili, seppi che t'eri sparato
con un colpo secco alla nuca: dominio di sé se
nella notte tuona l'uragano. Uragano particella
di così vasto dominio da rigare anche la tua fronte
di pudori inesistenziali.

E al tocco ti rividi, morto sul pavimento, sbandierare
nonsensi, stirarti la camicia ai quattro angoli
e alla terra sputando pedate conformiste.

★

Cercando una risposta ad una voce inconscia
o tramite lei credere di trovarla—vidi le muse
affascinarsi, stendendo veli vuoti sulle mani
non correggendosi al portale. Cercando una riposta
che rivelasse, il senso orgiastico degli eventi
l'ottenebramento particolare d'una sorte che
per brevi strappi di luce si oppone—unico senso
l'azione prestigiosa: che non dimentica, lascia
i muri radere la pelle, non subisce straniamenti
e non rivolta, contro questo male stritolante
e singhiozzante, che è la mia luna sulla faccia
l'odore di angeli sulle braccia, il passo certo
e non nascosto: la rovina lenta ma adempiuta:
un non staccarsi dalle cose basse, scrivendone
supina.

★

Poter riposare nel tuo cuore, nel tuo fuoco
a bracie spente, liberamente rinnegando
la mia libertà. O commuoverti in perdono
perdendo l'ora, che trionfante vuole
un cuore duro, selciato, minaccioso
finché ne perdi la causa, l'origine
dell'ardore.

among the first, giant of passion, a Christ-emblem
of renunciation. Announcing chastity, problems
resolvable and non, knowing how to ward off the emblem
from the virile mouths, I knew that you had shot yourself
with a single blow to the nape: dominion of the self if
the hurricane thunders in the night. Hurricane particle
of such vast dominion as to furrow even your brow
of inexistential reserve.

And at the stroke I saw you again, dead on the floor, to brandish
nonsense, to stretch your shirt to the four corners
and to the earth spitting conformist footprints.

★

Seeking a response to an unconscious voice
or through her thinking to find it—I saw the muses
bewitch themselves, spreading void veils on their hands
not correcting themselves at the door. Seeking one replaced
that would reveal, the orgiastic sense of events
the particular darkening of a fate opposed
through quick rips of light—sole sense
the illustrious act: that does not forget, allows
the walls to graze the skin, suffers no estrangement
and does not revolt, against this grinding and
sobbing ill, which is my moon on the face
the smell of angels on my arms, the step certain
and unconcealed: the ruin slow yet accomplished:
a nondetachment from the low things, writing about them
lying down.

★

To be able to rest in your heart, in your fire
of spent embers, liberally denying
my liberty. O to move you in pardon
losing the triumphant hour that wills
a heart hard, paved, menacing
so that you lose its motive, the origin
of ardor.

Poter danzare con le ore, gaiamente
intravedendo scienze, e non stampare
la tua faccia sul sasso. Poter rinsaldare
con te le mille pietre, che congiunte
in anello, sono edera leggiera
avvinta ai nostri occhi. Poter castrare
i desideri, slacciarli puri nel fiume
dove orgiastiche passano le ballerine
suicide di notte. Poter annunciare
che i desii non sono assurdi, ma
canto vero, una pulce nell'orecchio
atto d'amore, oppure vero verbo
che sale nel tuo cuore.

★

Inesplicabile o esemplare
generosa e trita ti concedi qualche piccolo
ritorno alle abitudini.

La lingua scuote nella bocca, uno sbatter d'ale
che è linguaggio.

Sentì bisogno allora di inalzare, piramidi alla
verità (o il suo mettersi in moto).

★

tuo motivo non urlare, dinnanzi alla
cattedrale; esilio o *chance* non ti perdonano
la locomotrice.

Io sono molto improdiga di baci, tu scegli
in me una rosa scarnificata. Senza spine
ma i petali, urgono al chiudersi. Mio
motivo non sognare, dinnanzi alla realtà
ignara. Mio motivo non chiudersi, dinnanzi

alla resa dei conti.

To be able to dance with the hours, gaily
glimpsing sciences, and not to stamp
your face on the stone. To be able to fortify
with you the thousand rocks, which linked
in a ring, are slight ivy
bound to our eyes. To be able to castrate
desires, unlace them pure in the river
where orgiastic the suicidal dancers
of night pass. To be able to announce
that amors are not absurd, but
true song, a buzzing in one's ear
an act of love, or veracious verb
that rises in your heart.

*

Inexplicable or exemplary
generous and trite you allow yourself some small
return to habit.

The tongue tosses in its mouth, a beating of winglets
that is language.

And so it sensed the need to raise, pyramids to
truth (or its setting itself in motion).

*

your motive not to scream, facing the
cathedral; exile or *chance* don't pardon you
the locomotrix.

I am quite improdigal of kisses, you choose
in me a rose stripped of flesh. Missing thorns
but the petals—those urge to close. My
motive not to dream, facing reality
unacquainted. My motive not to be closed, facing

the settling of accounts.

Tu scegli in me un motivo non dischiuso
dinnanzi alla rosa impara.

★

Primavera, primavera in abbondanza
i tuoi canali storti, le tue pinete
sognano d'altre avventure, tu non hai
mica la paura che io tengo, dell'inverno
quando abbrividisce il vento.

Strappi rami agli orticoltori, semini
disagi nella mia anima (la quale bella
se ne sta in ginocchio), provi a me
stessa che tutto ciò che ha un fine
non ha fine.

Oppure credi di dileguarti, sorniona
nascosta da una nuvola di piogge
carica sino all'inverosimile.

Ma il mio pianto, o piuttosto una stanchezza
che non può riportarsi nel rifugio
strapazza le foglie, che ieri
mi sembravano voglie, tenerezze anche
ed ora sperdono la mia brama.

Di vivere avrei bisogno, di decantare
anche queste spiagge, o monti, o rivoletti
ma non so come: hai ucciso il tuo grano
nella mia gola.

Assomigli a me: che tra una morte
e l'altra, tiro un sospiro di sollievo
ma non mi turbo; o mi turbo? del tuo
sembrare agonizzante mentre ridi.

E bestemmia la gente: è più fiera
di te che dello spazio che ti strugge

You choose in me a motive nondisclosed
facing the unpaired rose.

*

Spring, spring in abundance
your crooked canals, your pine-woods
dream of other flings, you don't at all
share this fear I harbor, of winter
when the wind enshivers.

You snatch branches from horticulturists, sow
unease into my soul (who stays put
pretty on her knees), prove to my
self that all that has an end
has no end.

Or you think to dispel yourself, sly girl
clandestine in a cloud of rain
implausibly laden.

But my plaint, or better, a fatigue
that can't take you back to shelter
abuses the boughs, which yesterday
seemed like vows, even tendernesses
and disperse my longing now.

I would need to live, to decant
these beaches, or mountains, or rivulets
as well but don't know how: you've killed your grain
in my throat.

You resemble me: between one death
and the next, drawing a sigh of relief
yet unbothered; or am I? by your
seeming to be in death's throes as you laugh.

And the people curse: they're prouder
of you than of the space that consumes you

portandoti fra le mie braccia. E io
stringo una pallida mummia che non
odora affatto: escono semi dai suoi
occhi, pianti, virgole, medicinali
e tu non porti il monte nella casa
e tu non puoi fruttificare, queste
sorelle che ti vegliano.

Sembri infatti un morto nella cassa
e non ho altro da fare che di battere
i chiodi nella faccia.

*

Di sera il cielo spazia, povera
cosa è dalla finestra il suo bigio
(ma era verde) ondulare. Oppure

colori che mai speravo riconquistare
abbaiavano tetri al davanzale. Se
questa tetra verginità non può

rimuovere dal cuore i suoi salmi
allora non v'è nessuna pace per
chi scuce, notte e dì, trite cose
dai suoi labbri.

Non è la casa (cucita con le mattonelle)
a farti da guida; è il mistero
disintegro delle facciate aeree

che ti promette gaudio sottilmente.

*

Tu con tutto il cuore ti spaventi
di aria che ti scuote e ti perde;
giù per le facciate analfabete
sprigionano i sogni, il sangue

as it takes you into my arms. And I
clench a pallid mummy that doesn't
smell at all: seeds exit its
eyes, tears, commas, medicinals,
and you don't take the mountain into the house
and you cannot fructify, these
sisters who keep vigil over you.

You seem in fact a corpse in the strongbox
and I have naught to do but to beat
the spikes into its face.

★

At evening the sky ranges, poor
thing from the window is its grey
(but it was green) undulating. Or

colours I never hoped to reconquer
bayed tetric at the windowsill. If
this tetric virginity cannot

remove its psalms from the heart
then there prevails no peace at all for
she who unstitches, night and day, trite things
from the lips.

It isn't the house (stitched with tiles)
to act as your guide; it is the disintegral
mystery of the airy facades

that promises you gaudfulness subtly.

★

With all your heart you're scared
of air that rouses and loses you;
down through the illiterate facades
the dreams, the blood discharge

in grosse gocce che tu conti
cadere a precipizio sulle mani
ritirate dall'angoscia di sapere
dov'è l'aria cosa muove perché
parla, di mali così annaffiati
da sembrare, tante cose insieme
ma non una che si scordi quel tuo
trascinare per immense giornate
notte e sangue.

*

C'è vento ancora e tutti gli sforzi
non servono a tenere la radura
ferma nel suo proposito.

Sento tintinnire l'erba, essa non
può, amarsi. Salvo che immettendo
nell'aria fragranze, disobbediendo
alla natura.

Rocce covano serpi che correggono
quest'idillio nascente.

*

Diana la cacciatrice soleva avvicinarsi
a questi boschi, irrimediabilmente
perduti per lei che nella caccia
giocava con le parole.

Se mi muovo c'è chi mette piede
innanzi a me e mi crea la trappola
delle elementari immagini. Se mi
sposto anche la linea del cielo
subisce mutazione. Le parole scendono
in basso nella vallata si ricordano
dei miei tre archi. Non si scosta
il parallelo della mia costanza

in fat drops that you count
falling headlong onto hands
withdrawn from the anguish of knowing
where the air is what it moves why
it speaks, of ills so showered
as to seem, so many things amassed
but not one that would disrecord that
dragging of yours for days immense
the night and blood.

★

There is wind still and all efforts
fail to keep the clearing
steadfast in its design.

I hear the grass tinkling, it cannot,
love itself. Save in releasing
scents into air, disobeying
nature.

Boulders brood over snakes that correct
this nascent idyll.

★

Diana the huntress was apt to approach
these woods, irrecoverably
lost to her who in the hunt
played with words.

If I move someone sets foot
ahead of me to craft the trap
of elementary images. If I
shift the line of sky also
suffers change. The words plunge
low in the valley recalling
my three arches. The parallel
of my constancy does not stray

se urlo nel passo le rocce scavano
orbite. Diana cacciava: un cuore

scavò tre orbite, l'una nell'occhio
le altre intristiscono sulle mie
labbra. Animali perplessi sono le

parole, esse guastano il mercato
non feci in tempo a firmare l'assegno
che già mi volarono. Diana spinse

la freccia: caddero le parole, nella
vallata volano. Io mi muovo, le
riacchiappo, solendo metterle all'occhiello
dopo la caccia.

*

I bambini sono i padroni del paese
ladrocinii non vi sono solo incanti trasformati
in urgenti compere e vendite, un po'
di lana per i piedi odorosi, e un gonfio
materasso per la china. Vi sono solo
donne in gramaglie, vecchie ninne-nanne
e il voler esser concittadini, come
gli altri.

Non vi sono affatto gramaglie in paese
solo donne col turbante o altre scimmiotterie
i bimbi giocano con l'arpa, tenendo
in mano un ramo.

*

Attorno a questo mio corpo
stretto in mille schegge, io
corro vendemmiando, sibilando
come il vento d'estate, che
si nasconde; attorno a questo

if I howl in the passage the rocks dig
orbits. Diana would hunt: a heart

dug three orbits, one in the eye
others that languish on my
lips. Perplexed animals are

words, they break the market
I did not sign the check in time
as they had already flown from me. Diana shot

the arrow: the words fell, in the
valley they fly. I move, recapture
them, apt to eyelet them
after the hunt.

★

The children are the masters of the town
thieveries do not exist only charms transformed
into urgent purchases and sales, a bit
of wool for fragrant feet, and a swollen
mattress for the slope. There are only
women in palls, old lullabies
and the will to be fellow-citizens, like
the others.

There are no palls at all in town
only women in turbans or other mimicries
the kids play with the harp, keeping
a branch in hand.

★

Around this my body
narrowed in a thousand splits, I
run grape-harvesting, sibilating
like the summer wind, which
hides; around this

vecchio corpo che si nasconde
stendo un velo di paludi sulle
coste dirupate, per scendere
poi, a patti.

Attorno a questo corpo dalle
mille paludi, attorno a questa
miniera irrequieta, attorno
a questo vaso di tenerezze
mal esaudite, mai vidi altro
che pesci ingrandire, divenire
altro che se stessi, altro
che una incontrollabile angoscia
di divenire, altro che se
stessi nell'arcadia di un
mondo letterario che si forniva
formaggi da sé; sentendosi
combattere, nelle vacue cene
da incontrollabili istinti
di predominio: logori fanciulli
che stiravano altre membra
pulite come il sonno, in vacue
miniere.

*

Cercare nel rompersi della sera un nascondiglio
meno adatto di questo che stimola i miei
riflessi in lunghe nappe obbligatorie. O
ritrovare tra le erbe frammiste di tenerezza
un'obbligatoria crudeltà il giorno che
tu fermasti gli occhi al solco della primavera
incantando un mondo di bestie con vetrali
lacrime che non scendevano ma s'imbrogliavano
nel tuo sonno tutto rose.

Cercare nel sonno che concede qualche mal
posto ristoro un'ombra gracile che fu quella
giovinezza persa fra stenti, quando doravi
il libro d'ore.

old body which hides
I spread a veil of fens upon the
abrupt coasts, so as to come
down, to terms.

Around this body of a
thousand fens, around this
fretful mine, around
this vase of tendernesses
ill fulfilled, I never saw other
than fish enlarging, becoming
other than themselves, other
than an uncontrollable anguish
of becoming, other than
oneself in the arcadia of a
literary world that catered itself
to its own cheeses; sensing itself
embattled, in the vacuous suppers
of uncontrollable instincts
of dominance: worn-out youths
who stretched other members
sanitary as sleep, in vacuous
mines.

*

To seek in the breaking of the evening a hiding place
less fit than this that rouses my
reflections in long obligatory naps. O
to recover among the grasses intermingled with tenderness
an obligatory cruelty the day that
you halted eyes at the furrow of the Spring
enchanting a world of beasts with glassy
tears that did not fall but were embroiled
in your sleep all roses.

To seek in sleep that concedes some ill
place of relief a frail shadow that was that
youth lost among starts, when you would gild
the book of hours.

Da *Diario ottuso: Nota* (1967–1968)

1/1/67

Intenta a descrivere il paesaggio mi intromisi; ne sgorgava irrequieta la scena primaria: trottole, caverne, demistificatorie scene. È una scena questa che mi impedisce di ragionare mentre con un mitra elegantemente vi spiàno.

Che corvée di matti! Che elegante ritrovo! Che scamiciata eleganza! Orari fuori turno e benedetti calamai.

Una struttura per ingigantirmi. "Storia di Ada": determinismo della forma e stesura dell'incanto. Quante mattonelle per disegnarti un approccio!

Basilari differenze: innanzi a te la stesura d'un compito che abbracciando la totalità non neghi la formosa individualità.

La quale essendo fatta di materiale sparso armeggiò per distinguere il vero dal falso, il falso dal crudo, il crudo dal bello, il desiderio dalla bontà! Era delirante quel giorno che l'impiegai a torcere il desiderio.

Io essendo un paradiso non posso avvicinarmi all'eterno, bruciare della pelle che non ha confini distinguibili.

Perché batti il petto? Esso ha bruciore che tu non immagini nella scura notte che trascinandosi dietro una pelle d'asino, fece quel che non poteva nascondersi: si bruciò.

Urla delle belle armi, alloro che si merita, io non nego di meritarmi ma: cerco qualche bicicletta più nuova al desiderio. Non vedo d'altronde quale intavolata discussione possa sembrare meno difficile. E vedendovi vi convinsi a non lasciarmi indietro.

Quale nero velo: quale bianca rima: quale grigio pudore.

138

From *Obtuse Diary: Note* (1967–1968)

Intent on describing the landscape I butted in; the primary scene gushed out disquieted: spinning tops, caverns, demystifying scenes. This is a scene that bars me from reasoning while they spy on you all elegantly with a submachine gun.

What a corvée of lunatics! What an elegant haunt! What shirtsleeves elegance! Timetables out of turn and blessed inkwells.

A structure for colossifying myself. "Ada's Story": determinism of form and draft of enchantment. How many tiles to plot yourself an approach!

Fundamental differences: before you the draft of an exercise which embracing totality would not negate buxom individuality.

Which being wrought of material scattered hustled to distinguish the true from the false, the false from the crude, the crude from the beautiful, desire from goodness! It was delirious that day I employed it to wring desire.

I being a paradise cannot come close to the eternal, burn skin that lacks distinguishable borders.

Why do you beat your chest? It has burning you don't imagine in the shady night which dragging a jackass's skin behind, did what couldn't be concealed: it burned itself.

Shrieks of stunning weapons, laurel that is deserved, I do not deny deserving but: I seek some bicycle newer to desire. Besides I do not see which dispute brought to the table could seem less difficult. And seeing you all I convinced you not to leave me behind.

Which black veil: which white rhyme: which grey pudor.

Da *Documento* (1966–1973)

Ossigeno nelle mie tende, sei tu, a
graffiare la mia porta d'entrata, a
guarire il mio misterioso non andare
non potere andare in alcun modo con
gli altri. Come fai? Mi sorvegli e
nel passo che ci congiunge v'è soprattutto
quintessenza di Dio; il suo farneticare
se non proprio amore qualcosa di più
grande: il tuo corpo la tua mente e
i tuoi muscoli tutti affaticati: da
un messaggio che restò lì nel vuoto
come se ad ombra non portasse messaggio
augurale l'inquilino che sono io: tua
figlia, in una foresta pietrificata.

*

Pietre tese nel bosco; hanno piccoli
amici, le formiche ed altri animali
che non so riconoscere. Il vento non
spazza via il sasso, quelle fosse, quei
resti d'ombra, quel vivere di sogni
pesanti.

Resti nell'ombra: ho un cuore che scotta
e poi si sfalda per ingenuamente ricordarsi
di non morire.

Ho un cuore come quella foresta: tutta
sarcastica a volte, i suoi rami lordi
discendono sulla testa a pesarti.

From *Document* (1966–1973)

Oxygen in my tents, it's you, to
scratch my entryway, to
heal my mysterious not going
not being able to go along with the others
in any way. How do you do it? You surveil me &
the step that joins us is full of
God's quintessence, above all; his raving
if not quite love something
greater: your body your mind and
muscles all fatigued: by
a message that stayed there in the void
as if I couldn't bring an augural message
to shade, tenant that I am: your
daughter, in a petrified forest.

*

Stones tense in the wood; they have little
friends, the ants and other animals
I cannot identify. The wind doesn't
sweep away the rock, those holes, those
remains of shadow, that living of heavy
dreams.

Remains in shadow: I've a heart that scorches
and peels away to remind itself ingenuously
not to die.

I've a heart like that forest: all
sarcastic at times, its filthy boughs
descend upon your head to weigh you down.

Con la malattia in bocca
spavento
per gli spaventapasseri
rose stinte e vi sono macchie sul muro
piccolissime nel granaio dei tuoi pensieri:
e con quale colore smetti di
dipingere?

Avevo trovato il mio proprio opposto.
Come lo divorai! Poi lo mangiai. E ne
fui divorata, in belle lettere.
E correre poi
al riparo mentre corrono anche certe
vecchie, all'orinatoio.

Poi smettono di correre.

★

Uno strepitare svelto di ali smorzate
questo incesto non
si ha da fare.

Nel cavo della mano rimane
solo un fluorescente pensarsi?

Le scienze
naturali e colte
il mio grido di fanciulla senza colomba.

a Shubert

Una melodia colore arancione aveva suonato
nelle mie orecchie così attente al solfeggio
d'un violino abbastanza netto da toccarmi

With illness in my mouth
I scare
among the scarecrows
faded roses and there are stains most small
on the wall in the silo of your thoughts:
and with which color do you give up
painting?

I'd found my own opposite.
How I devoured it! Then I ate it. And I
was devoured by it, in belles lettres.
Then to run
for cover while certain old
ladies run, too, for the urinals.

Then they give up running.

A swift uproar of muffled wings
this incest one
must not commit.

Is a fluorescent self-contemplation
all that's left in the hollow of the hand?

The natural
and cultivated sciences
my scream of a maiden lacking a dove.

to Shubert

A melody colored orange had sounded
in my ears so attentive to the sol fa mi do
of a violin keen enough to touch

perfino quelle mie fibre nervose (il
gran cuore) che mi tiravano per i capelli
mentre danzavo con la melanconia quella
sera che non ci fu posta.

Melodia eterna e inesplosa, melodia
di sentimenti che non possono violarsi
nel segreto tombale dell'apostolo: apostolo
di cosa?—d'una quasi disperata a volte
allegra, esposizione dei vostri quadri
mentali, sentimentali e ordinari: l'amore
in una scatola ben chiusa non ebbe tempo
di chiedere scusa.

⋆

Innesto nel vivere
la tua colpa (un
pedinaggio)
non mi feci avanti coi miei fiori, perché
tu eri ancora meditabondo
il cuore
curvo per eccellenza nella sua dimora
guardando se qualche verità inedita
ancora potesse provocarmi.

La piazza come una vecchia tristezza
alle due di notte deserta era e distante
parasentimenti
cerchi contusi (l'inutile
ronda)
nel senso guardigno della parola ti
credesti libera per un istante.

⋆

Solo i fatti, reprimere i sentimenti
poi ritrovi una "persona" che s'aggancia
fortemente al pavimento, i bricconi

even those nerve fibers of mine (the
great heart) that pulled me by the hair
as I danced with Melancholy that
evening when there were no stakes.

Eternal and undetonated melody, melody
of sentiments that cannot be violated
in the depths of the apostle's grave: apostle
of what?—of an almost hopeless at times
allegro, exhibition of your mental, sentimental
and ordinary paintings: love
in a box shut tight had no time
to apologize.

★

Graft in living
your fault (a
tailing)
I did not come forward with my flowers, because
you were still meditative
the heart
curved par excellence in its abode
watching to see if some unpublished truth
could still provoke me.

Like an old sadness the piazza
at two a.m. was deserted and distant
parasentiments
bruised circles (the useless
rounds)
in the guarded sense of the word you
believed yourself free for an instant.

★

Just the facts, repress the sentiments
then recover a "person" that's yoked
steadfastly to the floor, the rogues

le piccole vie pannellate, le testate
anche i grandi riverberi della tua immaginazione.

Piccoli neri su corona di fil di ferro
fatti concordano, espongono, giustificando
ed altri (che poi divennero te) quel
obliterare ogni passo della tua vita
sentimentale.

Furono una corona? La portasti espellendo
fiori mescolati all'avena? Rimanendo
un logico bastonarsi quel correre dei
tempi fu come una grafia utile, desiderabile
necessaria.

Rivale al cuore alle passioni (molto
usate e celebrate) desti filo da torcere
a quel nesso giuridico che operava nella
tua testa che forzutamente rubando al
ventre (ombra delle tue pupille) un

rafforzarsi della ragione, salvò quel
che poté, nell'ombra ragionando d'amore
mentre in via di trapasso celebravi
la quinta edizione del tuo errore.

         ★

Quanti rami hanno gli oliveti che tu
vedi solo come carta vetrata! Il palcoscenico
preme per sostituire la tua bellezza
al volo obliquo, distrutto, del tuo
amore e della tua scoraggiata rinuncia

a quel che offriva il dono della solitudine
terrorizzata, terrorizzante, che premeva
rompendo gli scaffali, e quell'intruglio

che ti querelava. Questi campi ottusi
nel tuo fieno!

the little billboarded routes, the blows to the head,
even the great ricochets of your imagination.

Little, black, on a crown of iron wire
facts concur, expose, justify
and others (which later turned into you)
obliterating each passage of your
sentimental life.

Were they a crown? Did you wear it shedding
flowers mixed up with wheat? Lasting as
a logical self-thrashing that rush of
times was like a useful, desirable, necessary
signature.

Rival of the heart of (quite used and
celebrated) passions you gave wire to twist
to that juridical nexus at work in
your head which robbing a
fortification of reason brawnily from the

belly (shadow of your pupils), salvaged what
it could, reasoning in the shadow about amore
while in the passageway you were celebrating
the fifth edition of your error.

                       ★

How many boughs fill the olive groves that you
see as nothing but sandpaper! The stage
presses to substitute your beauty
with the oblique, devastated, flight of your
love and your dispirited renunciation

of what offered the gift of terrorized,
terrorizing, solitude that pressed,
busting the shelves, and that concoction

which prosecuted you. These fields obtuse
in your hay!

Hai avvelenato la tua esistenza cercando
il conforto della prosa mentre poesia
ricercava la tua gloria.

*

E veleno forzarsi per nervi occulti
fino a rimaneggiare le vie occulte
mentre l'affanno consideravo indubbio
gli affetti sospiravano senilmente
nell'impianto d'una civiltà costruita
sul rimpianto.

Il balbettare
grandi frasi
la luna come un pezzo di carta straccia
fertili visite alle donne
mentre con le mammelle incrostate
verdi stanze analfabete coprivano invariabili
finestre.

*

La severa vita dei giustiziati rinnoverava
la scoperta d'un abisso che era e non
era il loro disinteresse ma una cosa
ben più sicura: la loro costanza, la
loro incostanza, il loro regime feudale
e le cagnotte tenute al laccio. La costanza
di questa loro interessata fedeltà che
era fedeltà tout court, quella loro
fedeltà a speranze perché venissero
deluse, quel loro sperare! così tragici
nell'immedesimarsi nella tragica farsa.

Un gioco o un altro, una carestia o
un'altra, un gioco di circostanze o
un altro, una fama mondiale o un dovere

You've poisoned your existence searching for
the comfort of prose while poetry
researched your glory.

*

And venom to force its way through occult nerves
until it rearranged the occult routes
while the affects pined dodderingly
for the toil I took to be undoubted
in the framework of a civilization erected
on regret.

The babbling
great phrases
the moon like a piece of wastepaper
fertile visits to the women
while with encrusted udders
green illiterate stanzas covered invariable
windows.

*

The severe life of the condemned renewed
the discovery of an abyss that was and was
not their disinterestedness but something
far more secure: their constancy, their
inconstancy, their feudal regime
and lackeys kept ensnared. The constancy
of their interested fidelity that
was fidelity tout court, that fidelity
of theirs in hopes that they'd be
disillusioned, that hoping of theirs! so tragic
in identifying themselves with the tragic farce.

One game or another, one famine or
another, one game of circumstances or
another, a global fame or a duty

obbedito—il resto è da cancellarsi
sì che il resto non appaia più fra le
liste degli annegati, i perseguitati
i rimpianti e le loro doleanze.

Cara vita che mi sei andata perduta
con te avrei fatto faville se solo tu
non fosti andata perduta.

★

Mentre mi avvicinai alle pareti odoravano
anche di sangue queste pareti che invece
sudavano.

Notti fà ho visto sperdersi ardori che
punendosi e pulendosi si dimostrarono
incapaci di anelare verso l'infinito.

Ma mare e giostra hanno ugual ardore
vi fu un caldo precipuo amore—precipitoso
nel garantirsi agli altri.

A se stessi finsero bombe aperte e a
mano dire: notte tempo ho rivaleggiato
con l'ardore!

A se stessi finsero bombe a mano dire
notte tempo ho rivaleggiato con l'ardore
e non mi sommuove rissa alcuna.

A se stessi finsero di dire amore ardore
a se stessi dissero perso l'amore che
tanta battaglia dette a l'odore di questa

condiscendente rivalità.

obeyed—the rest are to be erased
so that the rest don't show up any longer in the
lists of the drowned, the persecuted
the mourned and their dolors.

Dear life who has gone astray from me
with you I would have made sparks fly if only
you hadn't gone astray.

★

As I came closer to the walls these walls were odorous
of blood as well but they were
sweating.

Nights ago I saw ardors disperse that
self-castigating & cleansing proved themselves
incapable of hankering after the infinite.

But sea and merry-go-round possess equal ardor
there was a hot principal amour—precipitate
in guaranteeing itself to others.

They faked themselves open & hand grenades
to say: night and time I have rivaled
ardor!

They faked themselves hand grenades to say
night and time I have rivaled ardor
and no riot agitates me.

They faked saying amour ardor to themselves
they said to themselves lost the amour that
so much battle gave to the odor of this

obliging rivalry.

★

Un orrore di bombe che cadono tremanti
voracemente impegnate a sostituirti
il pane, oh sommossa contadina che vai
cercando invece il brodo, il buono brodo.

Vittoria armata sino ai denti e una
sinistra causa appariscono povere al
contrasto che si fece tra due banditi
e le loro circostanze.

Tubi rosa, rosi dalla pioggia che indaffarata
scuote le vigorie del mondo.

★

Nelle cene distillate
l'ombra si grattava la pancia
astratta.

L'idea
di un libro mi venne in mente per sbaglio
scegliendo per amministrare questi miei
beni una scena vuota.

Vi fu invece una
iterazione,
interurbana coraggiosa:
nelle ore inferme del mattino.

Dialogo con i Morti

scendete voi, abbracciate questa vostra
figlia che annaspa tra tomboloni e
mussulmani che giocano con le sue braccia
che invece, bianche, vorrebbero abbracciare

A horror of bombs that fall trembling
insatiably devoted to substituting for your
bread, oh peasant uprising in search
of broth instead, good broth.

Victory armed up to the teeth and a
sinister cause appear poor to the
contrast once made between two bandits
and their circumstances.

Rose tubes, rosed from the rain which, busied,
rouses the vigors of the world.

*

In the distilled suppers
shadow scratched its abstract
stomach.

The idea
for a book came to my mind by mistake
choosing for administration of my
goods an empty vista.

Instead there was an
iteration,
courageous intercity train:
in the infirm hours of early morning.

Dialogue with the Dead

come down, all of you, embrace this daughter
of yours who gropes amid crashes and
muslims who play with her arms
that, white, would like to embrace

o strozzare ma mai fallire questi colpi
che diurnamente ricevono, pieni
di lividi e lividamente promuovete una
sete di dolcezza e aspra giustizia
oppure non lasciate più ch'io tormenti
(ed essi mi tormentano) questa mente
che muore ad ogni istante piena di
stretti nodi che ingombrano la sua
piana marcia ad un paese più bello introvabile
mentre muore lividamente anche la voglia
di essere più belli di quello che si
è.

Scendete, e scendete ancòra—e infilate
nella vostra banale gioia il significare
d'una vita che ballonzola rattristata
dalla piena potenza del male degli
altri e del mio—il non sapere difendermi
da ottusa voglia.

Vivere un istante o mezz'ora e poi

ritrovarsi per una svista del pensiero
ancora più ingombra di inessenziali
rabbie!
Voce in capitolo non ebbero le sagge
mani: vi incontrai per poi farmi ostinatamente
massacrare da voi.

E il massacro volge in lussuria: e
la lussuria in estasi contemplata nel
grano sifilitico che s'attorciglia al
mio collo, stremato dai troppi abbandoni.

Abbandonarsi al vuoto sesso e poi ritenersi
anche insudiciati dalla nera pece del
fare così angusto dei poveri.

Sesso e violenza s'abbandonarono e
si ritrovarono infradiciati quel mattino
glorioso ove tutto cadde a pezzi, e

or throttle but never to miss these marks
they daily receive, full
of bruises and bruisingly advance a
thirst for sweetness and harsh justice
or else don't let me torment
(and they torment me) this mind any longer
which dies with each instant full of
taut knots that encumber its
slow march to a more beautiful illocatable country
as bruisingly there dies even the wish
to be more beautiful than one
is.

Come down, and keep coming—and slip
into your banal joy the meaning
of a life that stumbles along saddened
by the total power of the evil of
others, and my own—not knowing how to defend myself
from obtuse wishes.

To live an instant or half an hour and then

find oneself through an oversight
even more encumbered by trifling
rage!
Sage hands had no say in the
matter: I met you all so as stubbornly to make you
massacre me.

And the massacre turns into lust: and
lust into ecstasy contemplated in the
syphilitic wheat that coils around
my neck, worn out by too much abandonment.

To abandon oneself to empty sex & then think to be
unsoiled by the black pitch of
such petty doings of the poor.

Sex and violence were abandoned and
rediscovered sodden that glorious early
morning when all fell to pieces, and

se saggezza con le sue microscopiche
usanze non ritira truppe dal votarsi
all'angoscia, e se una piccola fierezza
o svista può provocare angosce ritardate
allora cade a pezzi la giornata triste
per la tua feconda grettezza.

Ed è inerme che io battaglio per una
chiarezza che non ha permesso d'esistere
sinché tu giochi con questa providenza
che ci stampò in faccia quell'ansia
di esistere fuori d'un commerciale

attenersi alle più basse voglie; ma
vidi anche nella tua faccia il sigillo
della noncuranza e del vuoto armarsi
alla morte senza pensare alla vita!

*

Vento d'Oriente e libeccio di malavita
costipazione d'origine flemmatica; orizzonte
di perle e vita senza forza.

Condividono la mia pena d'essere disarmata
in una strada tutta gas.

Vento d'inverno rabbrividisce d'estate
l'onda della vita ha le sue imprese
venti orrendi tastano la tua fronte
e hai imparato a disamare, finalmente
quando con grandi forbici tastavi un
incontro.

Armata ribelle e voce dall'interno
la libertà soffocata in un sofà
guanti forzati a dimostrarsi maneggevoli
ma avrei voluto prenderlo a pugni
quando lo slacciasti seduto sul sofà
fredda accoglienza a chi ti vuole
verde orario che sempre imbandisce.

if wisdom with its microscopic
habits doesn't withdraw troops from its devotion
to anguish, and if a small pride
or oversight can provoke agonies postponed
then the sad day falls to pieces
for your fecund miserliness.

And I battle unarmed for a
clarity that has no permit to exist
so long as you play with this providence
which stamped our faces with that anxiety
of existing outside of commercial

clinging to the basest wishes; but
I saw in your face the seal
of heedlessness as well and of the void arming itself
for death without a thought to life!

★

Orient wind and southwesterly wind of a life of crime
constipation of phlegmatic origins; horizon
of pearls and life without force.

They share my punishment of being disarmed
in a street full of gas.

Winter wind shivers in summer
the wave of life has its ventures
horrible winds feel your forehead
and you learned disamour, at last
once you felt out an encounter with great
scissors.

Rebel army and voice of the interior
freedom suffocated in a sofa
gloves forced to prove themselves tractable
but I would have wanted to take it to fisticuffs
when you unlaced it sitting on the sofa
cold welcome to the one who wants you
green timetable that always lays out the feast.

Ho sognato libidini che invece hanno
finte remore pasticciando con il vicino,
la pietà che non ha altro angolo visuale
che quello di ingigantire le promesse,
un avvenire che è uguale a quel passato
spossato.

E te cerco sul binario spossato, e te cerco
nella campagna svuotata.

Dame svuotate . . . Che pianto!
(fra le tue braccia allargate)
piccola giostra nella spossatezza
che ti riguardava . . .

Ho nelle braccia formicolanti tutta la forza
di un avvenire coinvolto nel tuo che è assenza
di peso e di noia,
e nell'immenso calderone dei nuvoloni una
peste di canti svogliati.

Essa è deliberatamente impegnata
(nell'immenso sorriso del cielo)
vele rimaneggiate

buona partita di calcio.

Nelle tue braccia abbandonate alla polvere
il torto ch'io subii tastandoti.

★

Rimai, verso una proda
e mi ritiravo sull'orlo
invece tutto si faceva passato lugubre
una impreparata decisione
di afferrare con ambo le mani la decisione

★

I have dreamt of libidos that have
phony qualms messing with the neighbor,
pity having no visible angle but
that of magnifying promises,
a future equal to that enervated
past.

And I look for you on the enervated platform, and I look for you
in the emptied countryside.

Emptied ladies of rank . . . Such plaint!
(between your outstretched arms)
small joust within the enervation
that regarded you . . .

My thronging arms hold all the force
of a future involved in yours which is absence
of weight and of boredom,
and in the immense cauldron of clouds a
plague of listless songs.

It is deliberately occupied
(in the immense smile of the sky)
sails rearranged

good game of soccer.

In your arms abandoned to dust
the wrong that I suffered feeling you.

★

I rhymed, versus a shore
and withdrew to the rim
instead everything being rendered lugubrious past
an unprepared decision
to seize the decision in my hands bloodied

nelle mie mani sanguinose
per le pratiche quotidiane.

Un rosso ardore
svuotata ogni forma dal suo perfetto
senso,
e sui velodromi correvano le piste
per il futuro furto di anime umane.

Riparare
più vicino al mare
placida esistenza non riparata
dalle bombe a mano,
placido shock che risorge
dalla sua abituale placidità
veneree discussioni di principio
i contendenti una rivolta che partecipa
a tutta la tragicità della comicità
tra gli alberi del mare.

Quale vuoto
hai voluto portare in questo vuoto
con desiderio di fuga e di vuoto
a capire il perché del furto.

*

Ed hanno soffici manti quei ragazzi
imprigionati nelle loro sostanze: verniciate
folte chiome. Versano acqua nell'emporio
buono a tutto: la libidine. Essa ha
cangianti colori foschi e gialli convenientemente
ridotti ad un livello immaginario a
sua soddisfazione privata.

Hanno sondato tutte le possibili sonde
e hanno forti del loro avere scelto
odori minaccianti colorati di dispetti
e anche spesso di valutazioni errate.

for daily practices
with both hands.

A red ardor
each form of its perfect
sense
emptied, and on the velodromes the tracks were racing
for the future robbery of human souls.

To repair
closer to the sea
placid existence unrepaired
by hand grenades,
placid *shock* that resurges
from its habitual placidity
venereal discussions of principle
the adversaries a revolt that takes part
in all the tragedy of comedy
between the trees of the sea.

What emptiness
you have wished to bring to this emptiness
with a desire for flight and for emptiness
to understand the reason for robbery.

★

And they have soft mantles, those kids
imprisoned in their substances: dyed
thick tresses. They pour water into that emporium
good for everything: the libido. It has
changeful dusky colors and yellows profitably
reduced to an imaginary level of
its private satisfaction.

They've sounded all possible sounding lines
& have fortresses of their having chosen
menacing odors colored with spite
and often erroneously appraised.

Nella Pearl Harbor che sono io esprimersi
mai ebbe a miglior sorte altro che
vanagloriosa espulsione dei resti, il
lavoratore non per questo distratto
dalla sua missione: che era oligarchica,
e sentenziosa, mentre dietro alle finestre
stringeva il mazzo di rose. Oltraggiò
pubblicamente la bestia, promosse una
crocifissione di così minor conto da
drasticamente contaminarne l'ambiente.

Mossa dal vento in piccoli grappoli
redivivi dalla parte sbagliata sopperire
ma con placide finestrelle tu hai invece
decolorato il cielo, stesso e steso
nella lavanderia delle nostre buon anime.

Chiusi in un sacco gli impiegati cominciarono
a rendere ragione delle loro azioni
e non erano poche quelle che turbavano.

        ★

Condurre con sé gli impiegati
fronteggiare l'impreveduto
impossibili attitudini
scoperte di avanguardie scoperte
confinate nella notte d'una vecchia
conoscenza; nell'alberazione
d'una quotidiana coscienza.

Quale fracasso assembri
nelle montagne vivaci
pur tacendo. Hai manomesso frontiere

mai ebbi da voi altro che prigioni.

In the Pearl Harbor that I am self-expression
never had a better fate than a
vainglorious expulsion of remains, not
for this was the worker distracted
from his mission—which was oligarchical,
and sententious, as he clutched the bouquet of roses
behind the windows. He publicly
desecrated the beast, promoted a
crucifixion of such minor account as to
drastically pollute its environment.

Moved by the wind in small clusters
resurrected by the wrong side to provide
yet with placid little windows you have
bleached heaven itself instead, spread out
in the laundromat of our good souls.

Shut up in a sack the employees began
to rationalize their actions
and those agitating were not scarce.

                    *

To lead the employees with oneself
to confront the unforeseen
impossible attitudes
discoveries of discovered avant-gardes
confined within the night of an aged
knowledge; within the treeing
of a quotidian conscience.

What sort of hubbub you assemble
in the mountains vivacious
yet hushed. You have tampered with frontiers

never did I get anything from you all but jails.

*

l'inaccettabile realtà
manipola così bene la realtà
ogni
cosa attorno o dentro mentre con cose

terra che fra le tue
ginocchia non poteva crescere nello
spazio

un fine gioco che è d'un altro giro
compatrioti
stanchi la pallida
èra dei nostri trasporti
visibile a vista un continuo getto di
grattacieli

*

Hanno fuso l'ordigno di guerra con le
mie dita troppo occupate a servirsi
di cibi cannibaleschi e tutto il mondo
è corso a vedere.

Pene infranto e rotta condotta sono
lì a farvi da guida: l'esperienza è
maestra degli svogliati, i poveri d'immaginazione
che rotolandosi nell'aldilà hanno voluto

imprigionarvi. Voglia di fare temprata
da consuetudini che hanno invece tremebonde
pratiche: quelle di non sapere dove
le hanno lasciate.

Ed è il dovere a farti strada come fosse
una sbiadita lanterna e spaccata che
nulla illumina salvo che il tuo piede
che sbaglia.

*

unacceptable reality
manipulates reality so well
each
thing around or within while with things

earth that between your
knees could not grow in
space

a game's end from another round
compatriots
tired the pale
era of our transport
visible to sight a continual casting of
skyscrapers

*

They have fused the war device with
my fingers overly occupied in helping themselves to
cannibalistic foods and all the world
has run to see.

Shattered penis and cracked conduit are
there to be your guides: experience is
governess of the listless, those impoverished of imagination
who wallowing in the beyond have wished

to jail you all. Wish to do something tempered
by habits that take on rather tremulous
practices—of not knowing where
they have left them.

And it is obligation that shows you the way as if it were
a faded shattered lantern which
illuminates nothing but your foot
that errs.

Gli aeroplani hanno cominciato a sparare
sulla folla poi hanno tradito così come
è normale nella pioggia di ogni giorno
e anche la sera.

Ogni giorno tentano un tranello e ogni
giorno torna la purezza e ogni notte
mettono in dubbio quello che hanno fatto
di giorno.

Di giorno sognano; di notte vegliano;
il pomeriggio dormono; la mattina pregano.

Pregano che non se n'andrà così presto
la vita che ha nascosto la morte per
tanto tempo finché un giorno ritrovarono
la notte stesa come un morto.

                        ★

Viene
soffiata giù per le scale,
similitudine ch'io faccio di ogni cosa
che passa per la mente
come se fosse sempre pronto lì il perdono.

Barattare le sigarette altrui
per una mansarda piena di buoni libri . . .

Ho visto nella curia e nelle percentuali
stendersi il processo tra le righe
e io ho assolto il comandante
perché tu eri il solito massacratore

di donne nel labirinto
spaventate dal grido
tra montagne di roccia
nell'orrore di una bomba
non scoppiata

The airplanes have begun to fire
upon the crowd then have betrayed as
is standard in the rain of every day
and evening as well.

Every day they attempt a snare and every
day purity returns and every night
they call into question what they have done
by day.

By day they dream; by night they keep watch;
afternoons they sleep; mornings they pray.

They pray that life which has concealed
death for so long will not take leave so soon
until one day they recovered
the night laid out like a corpse.

                ★

It comes
blown down the stairs,
likeness that I make of each thing
that passes through my mind
as if forgiveness were always at the ready there.

To barter the cigarettes of others
for a dormer full of good books . . .

In the court and the percentages I saw
the trial extended between the lines
and I acquitted the commanding officer
because you were the usual slaughterer

of women in the labyrinth
frightened by the scream
between mountains of stone
in the horror of a bomb
undetonated

come tutte le nostre cose migliori:
politica nella sua dozzinale vendita
largisci i tuoi poteri assembrati
tra gli analfabeti del quartiere

e tra la polvere che tu portavi intatta
nel grigio bagaglio.

★

questo è il mare oggi
in ondate più serene che squarciano
quel tuo grido e quel tuo affanno deliberatamente

fondendosi la
visione di uno strazio con uno strazio
tutto si rifà,

e da capo e di nuovo

★

i canali linfatici odorosi
di zanzare
nella baracca vuota
ormai nessuno può più metter mano
nodose storie
scambiandole per una metafora.

★

C'è come un dolore nella stanza, ed
è superato in parte: ma vince il peso
degli oggetti, il loro significare
peso e perdita.

C'è come un rosso nell'albero, ma è
l'arancione della base della lampada

like all of our best things:
politics in its chintzy sale
you bestow your assembled powers liberally
amongst the illiterate of the neighborhood

and amongst the dust you were carrying intact
in grey luggage.

★

this is the sea today
in waves more serene that slash
that scream & that toil of yours deliberately

fusing the
vision of a gash with a gash
everything remakes itself,

& from the top & again

★

the fragrant lymphatic canals
of mosquitoes
in the empty shack
no one can any longer lay hands on
knotty histories
trading them for a metaphor.

★

There's something like pain in this chamber, and
it is partly overcome: but the weight
of objects wins, their signifying
weight and loss.

There's something like red in the tree, but it is
the orange of the lamp base

comprata in luoghi che non voglio ricordare
perché anch'essi pesano.

Come nulla posso sapere della tua fame
precise nel volere
sono le stilizzate fontane
può ben situarsi un rovescio d'un destino
di uomini separati per obliquo rumore.

Sciopero generale 1969

lampade accesissime e nell'urlo
d'una quieta folla rocambolesca
trovarsi lì a far sul serio: cioè
rischiare! che nell'infantilismo
apparente schianti anche il mio
potere d'infischiarmene.

Un Dio molto interno poteva bastare
non bastò a me il mio egoismo

non bastò a queste genti il sapore
d'una ricchezza nella rivincita

del resto strozzata. Dovevamo
esprimere il meglio: regalarsi

ad una retorica che era urlo
di protesta ad una distruzione

impavida nelle nostre impaurite
case. (Persi da me quell'amore
al verticale, a solitario dio
rivoluzionandomi nella gente
asportandomi dal cielo.)

purchased in places I don't wish to remember
because they also weigh.

Like nothing I can know of your hunger
the stylized fountains are
precise in wanting
a reversal can be settled of the destiny
of men divided by oblique noise.

General Strike 1969

lamps wholly alight and in the howl
of a calm audacious crowd
to find yourself there, acting with seriousness:
taking risks! May this apparent
childishness shatter even my own
power not to care.

A deep inner God could have sufficed
my egotism did not suffice for me

the taste of riches in a revenge
nonetheless smothered did not suffice

for these people. We had to
express something better: allow ourselves

this rhetoric that was a howl
of protest against undaunted

destruction in our frightened
houses. (I lost on my own that vertical
love of solitary god
revolutionizing myself in the people
removing myself from heaven.)

★

Tento un mercato—poi ne tento un altro
sorvolo sulle difficoltà e poi vi rimango
impantanata: è come dire, sì, se mi volete
sarò come voi: la stessa pasta ai vostri
affetti da ventriloqui!

Poeticamente si scansa, tenta il massimo
ancòra più ambigua: non ha fine la ricerca
di chi sta bene.

Dieci scellini all'anno assicurano la
sopravvivenza, se bene accalappiata,
destreggiata servirvi come se lavorassi.

Soldi situati nel minimo organizzabile
per commentare poi la situazione da voi
spalancata, su questi abissi che sono
l'urlare in punto di morte per non morire
di inedia o di scoraggiamento: nessuno

vuole i tuoi sporchi versi: mentre fai
il verso a Fidel, o a qualche altra scelta
d'eroizzare la tua esistenza appena tracciata.
Tenti altri eroi, altri sacrifici finché
t'accorgi che non ti vogliono e la rivoluzione
poi non esiste, è tutta da farsi, non

certo da noi. Allora anzi decidi di separarti
fra due assurdi è preesistente il primo
fra due stranezze scegliere la meno bella

e spiegarti così, come se te lo chiedessero
(e infatti oggi tutto è mercato). Ma
se tutto è stato e sarà sempre mercato?
Se volendo il mercato ti ritrovi rivoluzionario
e volendoti rivoluzionario-capo ti ritrovi

★

I try one market—then I try another
I soar over difficulties yet remain
bogged in them: it's like saying, sure, if you want me
I'll be like you: the same pap to your
ventriloquist affects!

Poetically one dodges, tries one's best
even more ambiguous: the research of those who are well
has no end.

Ten shillings a year ensure
survival, if well ensnared,
manipulated to serve you all as if I worked.

Money situated within the minimum manageable
to comment on the situation you've
thrown open, on these abysses that are
a howling at the verge of death so as not to die
of starvation or discouragement: no one

wants your dirty verse: as you write
the line to Fidel, or to some other choice
to heroize your faintly traced existence.
You try other heroes, other sacrifices until
you realize they don't want you and the revolution
doesn't even exist, it's all to be done, not

certainly by us. So you decide instead to separate yourself
between two that are ludicrous the first is preexistent
between two oddities to choose the less attractive one

and explain yourself thus, as if they asked you to
(and indeed these days everything's a market). But
if everything has been and will always be a market?
If wanting the market you find yourself revolutionary
and wanting to be head revolutionary you find yourself

mercato? Nulla volle la volontà ma si
spostò da un canale all'altro, misteriosamente
la Sua volontà si fece, a cambiar l'altro
(il mondo intero fa come te, se può) perché
certamente ciò che aveva deciso era ciò
(come se per caso). Esitante ti riscrivi o riiscrivi
all'aristocrazia-élite dei
cervelli artistici: nessun conto in banca
ma quel minimo assicurato ti predestina
al forgiarsi rivoluzioni dei contenuti
e tentativi di rivoluzioni *nei* contenuti.

★

colle di limone: solitudine
impeccabile! pregno di luce

sono io stasera: non buia
la verde estate o estatica

la marcia violetta
alla vendetta . . .

★

Continenza europea, semmai venne
con un carico di bestiame
come la terapia della scienza
che fu questo nostro pensare ogni
dì, la libertà di pensare.

Si travagliavano in vano corto
e spento quel che mai fu scritto
su di creta neutra
egiziana inaspettata
o semplicemente ambizione di propria
voce?

a market? Will willed nothing but
shifted from one channel to another, mysteriously
your honor's will was done, to change the other
(the whole world does as you do, if it can) because
certainly what it had decided was that
(as if by chance). Hesitant you rewrite or reinscribe yourself
into the aristocracy-élite of
artistic minds: no account in the bank
but that minimum ensured predestines you
to the forging of revolutions of content
and attempts at revolution *within* content.

★

lemon hill: impeccable
loneliness! impregnate with light

am I this evening: undark
the green summer or ecstatic

the violet march
toward vendetta . . .

★

European continence, if ever it came
with a load of livestock
like the therapy of science
that was this our thinking each
day, the freedom to think.

They worried in short and stifled
vain what was never written
upon neutral sudden
Egyptian clay
or simply the ambition of one's own
voice?

Quattro stanze indivisibili
quattro angoli nascostissimi
polvere o grigiore e smemoratezza
v'hanno composto questa ballata
(angoli delle mie quattro stanze)
non disturba il vostro io trafelato

non volge in canto forte.

★

nel nordico
palmeto di chiese sconsacrate,
forzate risate
la città in palmo,
vita da carbonizzare

Neve 1973

Neve, a bricconi sulla pianta della testa
rivoluzione pesante delle maniere, manierismo
anche quello se tu non puoi più andare

avanti col soliloquio (arancione naturalmente)
così come avevi condotto a sperare. Non

puoi più mentire a te stessa!—s'è scippata
la burrasca, e t'hanno chiuso dentro per
farti meglio ragionare.

Io non sono quello che apparo—e nel bestiame
d'una bestiale giornata a freddo chiamo
voi a recitare.

Four indivisible stanzas
four most hidden corners
dust or greyness and forgetfulness
have composed you all this ballad
(corners of my four stanzas)
does not disturb your gasping I

does not turn into forceful song.

★

in the nordic
palm grove of deconsecrated churches,
forced laughs
the city in the palm,
life to carbonize

Snow 1973

Snow, in rogues upon the plan of the head
a heavy revolution of manners, mannerism
even that if you can no longer go

ahead with the soliloquy (orange naturally)
such as you had driven to hope. You can't

lie to yourself any longer!—the tempest
has been snatched, and they've shut you inside to
improve your reasoning.

I am not what I appear to be—and in the cattle
of a cattlish day chilled I call
on you all to recite.

★

E nell'acquedotto
si rintanano le rane, hanno spulciato
anche loro le acque
in attesa
d'una divorazione semplice
sanno che tu sgarri
come prima, come
se fosse
nel tuo vivere naturalissimo
scambiare rane per acqua.

Veloci foglie
sentitemi arrancare
non ho la vostra pazienza—
rimugino sino in fondo
le salde attese.

★

Corruzione nel giornale di ieri
centoventimila tiratori scelti.

Senza lezione
scemava nella tenerezza costrittiva
l'inconscia palla del nemico divertito.

Sovente nell'arte illustrata
consiglio donò
scempio tutt'intero—

*

And in the aqueduct
the frogs take refuge, they too have plucked
fleas from the waters
in expectation
of simple devourment
they know that you go wrong
as before, as
if there were
in your living most natural
exchange of frogs for water.

Swift leaves,
hear me trudge along
I lack your patience—
I ruminate utterly
the staunch expectations.

*

Corruption in yesterday's paper
one hundred twenty thousand shooters chosen.

Without lessons
the unconscious bullet of the enemy diverted
abated in constrictive tenderness.

Oftentimes in illustrated art
counsel donated
ruin entirely whole—

Da *Appunti sparsi e persi: Poesie* (1966–1977)

Improbabile sonetto
una vita errabonda
condotta sul filo del rasoio.

Macchiandosi le punta delle dita
l'infarto premeditato
una carovana del tutto obliqua.

*

Cambiare la prosa del mondo,
il suo orologio intatto,
quel nostro incorniciare le giostre
faticose di baci.

Hai inventato di nuovo la luna,
è una povera isola
ti chiama con contingenza disperata
imbastardita dalle lunghe cene.

*

Esso ha radici molto profonde infatti
nel tuo cuore che sanguina ininterrottamente

                              il tuo romanticismo
(io parlo ai muri, che sono io) il tuo
romanticismo ti svena ai polsi. Vivendo (ma
non è vivere questo), vivendo t'accorgi

From *Notes Scattered and Lost: Poems* (1966 – 1977)

Improbable sonnet
an errant life
conducted along the razor's edge.

Staining the fingertips
the strategized heartattack
a caravan wholly oblique.

$\star$

To change the prose of the world,
its intact clock,
our framing of merry-go-rounds
fatigued with kisses.

You have invented the moon again,
it is a poor island
it calls you with desperate contingency
bastardized by lasting suppers.

$\star$

It has very deep roots in fact
in your heart which bleeds uninterruptedly

                               your romanticism
(I speak to the walls, which are me) your
romanticism slits your wrists. Living (but
this is not living), living you realize

d'aver travisato il rospo, di non averlo
mai ingoiato!

L'uscita dai boschi cavernosi era verde
di misurata larghezza e impegno; ma
le sue scabre rocce non puzzavano della
gioia che m'aveva invasa.

. . . invece

un aratro scavava paziente la sua
storia nel folto del mondo.

★

Figlia del sereno giorno
nera pece degli industriali
culto della vergine Maria, picchiando
donne e donne.

Vuoto attorno alle donne
trascendere quel vuoto
armarsi di una punta vuota di sarcasmo
mai vi si immaginava condottieri esperti
e neppure si contava molto su di voi.

L'impermeabile rosso
muove con catene un prodotto bellico
che ha infantilmente tradito
con intatte virtù lavoratrici,
ribelli finti dietro le porte
nel buio delle loro simboliche notti

stanchi di servire il pane
col suo lustro sorriso fatto di ponti.
statistiche pedonate da serene
macchine calcolatrici
che incanto guardarle suonare il bordone.

Furenti appelli ad una pace con guerra
sogni di un aldilà divenuto insopportabile

you have misinterpreted the toad, never
having swallowed it!

The egress from the cavernous forests was green
in measured width and commitment; but
its rugged rocks did not reek of the
joy that had invaded me.

                          . . . instead
a plough, patient, dug its
history in the thick of the world.

★

Daughter of the serene day
black pitch of the industrials
cult of the virgin Mary, beating
women and women.

Hollow around the women
to transcend that hollow
to arm oneself with a hollow point of sarcasm
never did one imagine expert soldiers of fortune there
& neither did one count much upon you all.

The red raincoat
moves with chains a bellic product
that has childishly betrayed
with work ethics intact,
rebels faked behind the doors
in the dark of their symbolic nights

tired of serving bread
with its bright smile made of bridges.
statistical races by serene
calculating machines
such enchantment to watch them sound the drone.

Furious appeals for a peace with war
dreams of a hereafter become intolerable

si trafigge un popolo
stanco.

Questi versi
che sono la prova della mia durata,
ritardi giornalieri degli autobus
col vuoto che hanno loro nei loro cuori
mentre in piazza si scende a parlare
con le mani.

O è in piazza che si scende a patti
per le scale del disastro pensando di
pensare agli altri,
libertà di badare al coltello
ponti a crollare
mentre ammazziamo solo donne e bambini.

★

Luna verde di rabbia
folta foresta grigia
volontaristica senza finalità
mente con sensitiva espressione.

In me mistero d'esplosione
io luna esploitata
pallida la fronte si riempie
di diagrammi.

★

Follie fantascientifiche
valorose malattie

impedimenti a scrivere
totalità da descrivere

volontà di scrivere
volontà di sopravvivere

a tired people is
impaled.

These verses
that are the proof of my duration,
daily delays of buses
with the hollow they have in their hearts
while in the square one stoops to talking
with one's hands.

Or it's in the square that one stoops to terms
along the stairs of disaster thinking to
think of others,
freedom to mind the knife
bridges to crumble
while we murder only women and children.

⋆

Moon green with rage
thick forest grey
voluntaristic without aim
mind with sensory expression.

In me explosion's mystery
I exploited moon
pallid my forehead fills
with diagrams.

⋆

Science fiction follies
valorous illnesses

impediments to write
totality to describe

will to write
will to survive

volontà d'impedire
la tirannide.

(a Pier Paolo Pasolini)

E posso trasfigurarti,
passarti ad un altro
sino a quell'altare
della Patria che tu chiamasti
puro . . .

E v'è danza e gioia e vino
stasera:—per chi non pranza
nelle stanze abbuiate
del Vaticano.

Faticavo: ancora impegnata
ad imparare a vivere, senonché
tu tutto tremolante, t'avvicinavi
ad indicarmi altra via.

Le tende sono tirate, il viola
dell'occhio è tondo, non è
triste, ma siccome pregavi
io chiusi la porta.

Non è entrata la cameriera;
è svenuta: rinvenendoti morto
s'assopì pallida.

S'assopì pazza, e sconvolta
nelle membra, raduna a sé
gli estremi.

Preferii dirlo ad altra infanzia
che non questo dondolarsi
su arsenali di parole!

will to impede
tyranny.

(for Pier Paolo Pasolini)

And I can transfigure you,
hand you over to another
as far as that altar
of the Fatherland that you called
pure . . .

And there is dance and joy and wine
this evening:—for those who do not dine
in the dimmed rooms
of the Vatican.

I toiled: still engaged
in learning to live, except that
trembling all over, you came close
to show me another way.

The curtains are pulled, the violet
of the eye is round, it is not
sad, but since you were praying
I closed the door.

The maid did not come in;
she fainted; discovering you dead
she dropped off pallid.

She dropped off mad, and shocked
in the limbs, gathers
the extremes to herself.

I wished to tell this to another childhood
and not to this rocking
upon word-arsenals!

Ma il resto tace: non odo suono
alcuno che non sia pace
mentre sul foglio trema la matita

E arrossisco anch'io, di tanta esposizione
d'un nudo cadavere tramortito.

★

Benediva la casa il tepore finto
e starnutiva nel
silenzio una cicala
l'abitudine facente a meno dei suoi
complessi dionisiaci.

Paraffinato, l'olioso acquedotto
intenso.

★

Situazionista tra un campo e l'altro
il paesaggio magnifico nella sua esuberanza
la stanca parola bacia
i piedi nudi sul tavolo di marmo.

Poi si spande per la chiassata
delle strade
come le stelle
continuamente baciando
il
globo torturando.

★

Il colore che torna dal nero
al verde d'un prato affamato

But the rest is silent: I hear no
sound that is not peace
as the pencil trembles on the page

And I blush as well, at such display
of a nude cadaver stunned.

★

Fake lukewarmth blessed the home
and a balm-cricket
sneezed in the silence
habit doing without its
dionysian complexes.

Waxed, the oily intense
aqueduct.

★

Situationist between one field and the other
the magnificent landscape in its exuberance
the tired word kisses
the naked feet on the marble slab.

Then it spreads amidst the ruckus
of the streets
like the stars
continually kissing
the
globe torturing.

★

The color that returns from black
to the green of a famished lawn

fiori scesi giù tranquilli
posano per gli artisti

guardandomi girare tranquillamente
per le strade a volte bianche.

*

E se posando nuda per vecchi *cameramen*
la governante intenta
al suo nazismo
alla buona
mentre miagolando
perfino il gatto si dava un'esistenza
e dappertutto un odore di chiuso
di mobili fuori uso.

Verifichi l'incidente
e poi crederesti di saperne di più
mostrandoti arrogante.

Perle pendono sul collo fresco
d'una Madonna dipinta di fresco.

E poi arrotoli la sigaretta e fai
un gesto non di diniego ma di
arrendevolezza.

*

Pel cielo che
nelle sue gondole passava
per porte
lontane dalla sorgente
le parole scappavano, esterefatte
senza rumori d'amore.

Bullo per strada sostituisce amicizia.

flowers gone down mellow
pose for artists

watching me ramble mellowly
amidst the streets to white vaults.

★

And if posing nude for old *cameramen*
the governess intent
in her workaday
Nazism
while meowing
even the cat took on an existence
and everywhere an odor of closure
of furniture out of use.

You verify the incident
then presume to know more about it
displaying your arrogance.

Pearls hang on the fresh
neck of a Madonna depicted in fresco.

And you roll the cigarette and make
a gesture not of denial but of
pliability.

★

Across the sky that
in its gondolas passed
across doorways
far from the spring
words escaped, aghast
without amorous noise.

Punk on the street stands in for amity.

★

Eri come si deve essere
nel verde nulla della passione spenta
calando verso il suolo leggermente chino
come quel monte di cui la pagina non ha spazio

*

You were as one has to be
in the green null of passion spent
dropping toward the ground barely bowed
like that mountain for whom the page has no room

Da *Impromptu* (1981)

I.

Il borghese non sono io
che tralappio d'un giorno all'
altro coprendomi d'un sudore
tutto concimato, deciso, coinciso
da me, non altri—o se soltanto

d'altri sono il clown faunesco
allora ingiungo l'alt, quella
terribile sera che non vi
fu epidemia ma soltanto un
resto delle mie ossa che
si rifiutavano di seccarsi
al sole.

Non v'è sole che non sia
lumière (e il francese è
un *par terre*) quando cangiando
viste, cangiasti forme, anche
nel tuo nostalgico procedere
verso un'impenetrabile morte.

Nel verso impenetravi la
tua notte, di soli e luci
per nulla naturali, quando

l'elettrico ballo non più
compaesano distingueva tra
chi era fermo, e chi non
lo era. Difendo i lavoratori

From *Impromptu* (1981)

I.

I am not the bourgeois
as I trallop from one day to the
next covering myself with a sweat
fertilized, settled, coincided, all
by myself, not others—or if I am only

the others' fawnish *clown*
then I issue the command to halt, that
terrible evening there was
no epidemic, only some
relic of my bones which
refused to be dried
in the sun.

No sun exists that isn't
lumière (and the French is a
par terre) when altering
sights, you altered forms, even
in your nostalgic advance
toward an impenetrable death.

In verse you impenetrated your
night, of suns and lights
that weren't natural at all, when

the electric dance no longer
paisanic distinguished between
those who were unmoved, and those who
were not. I defend the workers

difendo il loro pane a denti
stretti caccio il cane da

questa mia mansarda piena
d'impenetrabili libri buoni

per una vendemmia che sarà
tutta l'ultima opera vostra

se non mi salvate da queste
strette, stretta la misura
combatte il soldo e non v'è

sole ch'appartenga al popolo!

2.

Quando su un tank m'avvicino
a quel che era un *tango,* se

la misericordia era con me
quando vincevo, o invero

se la tarda notte non fosse
ora ora di mattino, io non

scriverei più codeste belle
note!—Davvero mi torturi?
e davvero m'insegni a non
torturare la mente in agonia

d'altri senz'agonia, ma mancanti
al sole di tutti i splendidi
soldi che hai riconosciuto
nella Capitale del vizio

che era Roma? E tu frassine
oh lungo fratello d'una volta
chiamato Pierpaolo, un ricordo

soltanto ho delle tue vanaglorie
come se in fondo fosse l'ambizione

I defend their bread with clenched
teeth I drive the dog from

this loft of mine full
of good impenetrable books

for a harvest of grapes which will be
the entirety of your final work

if you don't all rescue me from these
trenches, clenched the measure
battles the coin & no sun exists

that belongs to the people!

    2.

When on a *tank* I approach
what used to be a *tango,* if

mercy was with me
when I was winning, or indeed

if the late night were not
this instant early morning I would

no longer compose yon beautiful
notes!—Are you really torturing me?
and are you really teaching me not to
torture the mind in agony

of others without agony, but missing
from the sun of all the splendid
money that you've recognized
in the Capital of vice

that was Rome? and you Fraxinus
oh long brother of once upon a time
named Pierpaolo, only one memory

do I have of your vainglory
as if in the end it were ambition

a gettar l'ultimo sguardo
dall'ultimo ponte.

3.

questa notte con spavaldo desiderio
scesi per le praterie d'un lungo fiume
impermeato d'antiche abitudini
ch'al dunque ad un segnale indicavano

melma, e fiato. Solo sporcizia
sì, vidi dall'ultimo ponte, dubitando
d'una mia vita ancora rimasta al
sole, non per l'arrosto ma per

il fuoco è buona: se a tutti divenne
già prima ch'io nascessi indifferente

la mia buona o cattiva sorte, dall'altr'angolo
che da questa visione crematorizzata

dalla mia e vostra vita terrorizzata
se resistere dipende dal cuore

piuttosto dalle sottane s'arrota
la *Mistinguette,* la vita sberciata
per un attimo ancora, se sesso
è così rotativo da apparire poi

vano a questo recitativo che mi
faceva passare per pazza quando
arroteandomi dietro ad ogni scrivania

sorvegliavo i vostri desideri d'essere
lontani dalla mia, rotativa nella
notte specchiata nel lucido del

vetro che copre le vostre indifferenze
alla mia stralunante morte.

that cast the final look
from the final bridge.

3.

this night with brazen desire
I went down among the grasslands of a long river
impermeated by ancient habits
which at a signal ultimately marked

mire, and breath. I saw only filth,
yes, from the final bridge, doubting
in a life of mine remaining to the
sun, good not for the roast but for

the fire: if my good or bad fortune became—
even before I was born—a matter of indifference

to everyone, from any outlook
other than this carbonized vision

of my and your terrorized life
if resistance depends on the heart

Mistinguette is ground instead on the axis
of her skirts, life mocked
for an instant more, if sex
is so rotative as then to appear

vain to this recitative that made
me pass for crazy when
reeling behind each desk

I oversaw your desires to be
far from mine, rotative in the
night mirrored in the luster of the

glass that covers your indifference
to my moonstriking death.

6.

Se risentimento ha per causa
questa lunga campagna militare
per forza v'aggiungo ch'era
nel mio sogno una intera
visione del vostro dipinto
non di difficoltà di rosa
ma come se fosse, nell'esistenza
di qui, l'alloro che morale
m'aveva ingiunto a dirmi

ch'io sono tra i grandi e
nascondo perfino il piccolo

di tra i miei sospetti ora
stretti ora larghi, sulle

vostre mancerie d'una volta
per scherzo ci sputavate sopra
qual'è la guerra a cui m'ingaggiaste?
se nel vedervi tutti stesi
in un grano di turco, là
nel campo di fieno non secchito
dalle pioggia io vi mangio

era per meglio appropriarmi
delle vostre giuste lezioni

che lesinavano il tocco alla
bocca che ora non sente il

vostro odore di santità politica
nel campo, dove riposo ingiunta
dal massacro a massacrarmi
come voi, nei desideri intensi
curvati nel blé, the *grass*
che vi fa invidia perché
è soltanto il grano che
non si piega mentre mi circonda
di felici visioni d'un cielo
non più tanto tetro, anzi

6.

If resentment has as cause
this long military campaign
I add perforce that it was
a total vision of your
painting in my dream
not of rose difficulty
but as if it were, in this existence
here, the laurel that moral
had commanded me to tell myself

that I am among the great and
I hide even the minor

of my sometimes narrow
sometimes broad suspicions, upon

your come-ons of once upon a time
you spit on us as a joke
in which war did you enlist me?
if in seeing you all lying down
in wheat of turkey, out there
in the field of hay unarid
from the rain, I eat you,

it was so I could better conform
to your just lessons

that eased their blow to my
mouth which doesn't sense now

your smell of political sanctity
in the field, where I rest commanded
by the massacre to massacre myself
like all of you, in the intense desires
curved in the navy blue, *the grass*
that is the envy of you because
it is only the wheat that
doesn't bend as it surrounds me
with cheerful visions of a sky
no longer so tetric, in fact

è primavera o fa quasi caldo
mentre contemplo il mio unico

prigioniero mentre voi fate
alla guerra io mi beo nel
sole, difesa da rami distanti
all'orlo del campo, un infinito

di secche penzolanti, schiaccio
col mio corpo la venustà
lo stile, di questi ultimi
arrampicatori d'una futura
celebrità, sognando sempre
ad occhi aperti quel sogno
che già c'è, è il cielo nel

suo azzurro benefico che m'ammicca
mentre finalmente circondata
dai steli d'una pulita polizia
che era il grano prima che
lo schiacciassi, io mi difendo

dal vostro aldilà che non
è su codesta terra che l'ha

già mangiato mentre io mi
stendevo sui steli piatti
nelle lunghezze appariscenti
dei loro confratelli ben
più saccenti nell'oscurare
quel volto, quel corpo, ora

il mio, di cui posso a tratti
obbedire, in vece che al
vostro.

    8.
Si farà quel suo pane quando
l'avrà travasato d'una setola

it's spring or nearly hot outside
as I contemplate my one and only

prisoner while you make
war I bask in the
sun, defended by distant boughs
at the edge of the field, an infinity

of dangling buckets, with my body
I crush the beauteousness,
the style, of these last
climbers toward a future
celebrity, dreaming ever
with eyes open that dream
that already exists, it's the sky in

its beneficent azure that winks at me
while finally surrounded
by the stalks of an unsoiled police force
that was the wheat before
I crushed it, I defend myself

from your hereafter that is not
upon yon earth which has

already eaten it while I
stretched out on the flat stalks
in the gaudy lengths
of their confraternity brothers far
more presumptuous in their obscuring
of that face, that body, now

mine, of which I'm able at intervals
to obey, in stead of
yours.

8.
That bread will be made when
it has been decanted from one bristle

all'altra—sull'altopiano v'era
il ripiano su di cui giaceva.

Tarda tornavo alle parole che
mi sfuggivano; bloccata la promessa
d'un semplice linguaggio, il

languire era per esteso una fiaba
d'innocenza nella solitaria trovata

d'un riposo in piena aria, fingendo
di non essere massacrata da voi;
ognuno ha il suo obbligo e il

mio era, o non è di non morire
per quelle mire con mitra che
avete spianato tutte contro questo

mio muro d'un più alto silenzio
di cui mai immaginavate la portata
scherzosa ora che spiombano finte
bombe sul naso della gente, finto

rumore non è per un bel niente,
quando v'è la guerra si aspetta
e si spera, se sperare si può
in questa giardiniera d'un agente

non in borghese ma con solenne
gesto, rimpalmava il sospetto

d'una più orrida fine che infinitamente
si sposta, nella lontananza ora

vedo un futuro, è fatto di questa
gente che proprio non ne sa niente.

    10.
Se permisi al mio ginocchio di
toccare la terra, fu con il permesso

to the next—on the plateau
was the shelf it lay upon.

Late was I in returning to words that
fled from me: the promise of a simple
language blocked, to

languish was far and wide a fable
of innocence in the solitary discovery

of repose in the open air, pretending
not to be massacred by all of you;
everyone has an obligation and mine

was, or isn't to fail to die
for those submachinic targets
you've razed one by one against

my wall of a higher silence
whose range you never imagined
jocose now that they hurl fake
bombs in the people's faces, fake

noise is for naught at all,
when war is on one waits
and hopes, if one can hope
in this jardinière of a cop

not in leisure clothes but who with solemn
gesture, was resmearing suspicion full

of an end more horrid that infinitely
shifts, in the distance now

I see a future, it's wrought of these
people who know naught about any of it.

10.

If I permitted my knee to
touch the earth, it was with the permission

del granoturco che s'inchinò
al mio passaggio non obbligatorio

d'una solare necessità d'infischiarmene
di tanto in tanto di tutto ciò
che non è terra e sole e grano
e pittoresca viltà, o riposo con
le gambe non all'aria ma stese

nel ventre di quel pittorico
campo fatto d'altri, il loro

suicidio con la terra ben cotta
contro o sopra o sotto quegli
steli, tappeto garantito se te
lo immagini, coprente la terra

che non più coinvolgi. Pistola
non hai né puoi bucarti la testa

come se fosse possibile in questi
grandi tempi, quando violenza
fa male perché è benevola e perciò

s'irrida di permessi al ridere
tanto fa la morte quando ti squadra

non da lontano ma anche da vicino.
Paesano non langue nell'ombra
d'uno stelo, non sono migliaia risposi
inchinandomi a terra, quasi fosse
possibile col dorso permissibile

duramente sottratto all'aria
alla posizione retta, risi
quando quel poco sole s'infilò

sotto altra nuvola che non quella

che era curva.

of the corn that bowed
to my nonobligatory passage

of a solar necessity not to give a damn
from time to time about all that
is not earth and sun and wheat
and picturesque cowardice, or rest with
legs not in air but stretched out

in the belly of that pictorial
field made of others, their

suicide with the earth well fired
against or above or below those
stalks, carpet guaranteed if you
imagine it, covering the earth

that you involve no longer. You have
no pistol nor can you bore holes in your head

as if it were possible in these
great times, when violence
does harm because it's benevolent and thus

one is mocked with permissions to laugh
death does as much when it squares you

not from a distance but also from close up.
No paisan languishes in the shade
of a stalk, they are not thousands I answered
bowing to the earth, should it almost be
possible with my permissible back

arduously withdrawn from uprightness
in the air, I laughed
when that modicum of sun sneaked in

below a cloud other than the one

that was curved.

11.

Che è e rimane curva nel salotto
borghese del campo squadrato
dal pittore in borghese. Si diradano
le nuvole ora femminili, ora
se svolazzano mi credo un mostro.
Ma nel sacro terrore d'una notte

insonne, permisi alla sofferenza
d'allontanarsi per un poco: quando
giacque partorì un bimbo, si salvò

cercando un altro gioco che non
era già di partenza vinto. Ma

che campo è questo esclamando
rintronai, sempre con alla bocca
penzolante uno stelo, fina erba
indurita da pioggia e sale della
terra, che congiunta in adorazione
mi faceva da benedizione.

12.

Lo spirito della terra mi muove
per un poco; stesa o seduta guardo

non l'orologio; lo tasto e lo
ripongo al lato della testa, che

non sonnecchiando ma nemmeno
pensando, si rivolse al suo dio

come fosse lui nelle nuvole! Rinfiacchita
l'infanzia muraria di questi versi
non sono altro che pittorica immaginazione
se nel campo di grano rimango

a lungo stesa a pensarci sopra.

11.

Which is and remains curved in the bourgeois
sitting-room of the field squared
by the painter in leisure clothes. The clouds,
feminine now, dispel themselves, & now
if they fly about I believe myself a fiend.
But in the sacred terror of an insomniac

night, I permitted suffering
to distance itself for a while: when
it lay down it gave birth to a child, saved itself

in search of another game that wasn't
already decided in starting out. But

what field is this I roared
in exclamation, with ever a stalk dangling
from my mouth, thin grass
hardened by the rain and salt of the
earth, which commanded into adoration
served as my benediction.

12.

The spirit of the earth moves me
for a while; lying back or sitting I look

not at the watch; I feel it and place
it aside my head, which

neither dozing nor even
thinking, turned to its god

as if it were him in the clouds! Rewearied
the childhood's masonry of these verses,
I'm nothing but pictorial imagination
if I remain in the wheatfield

laid out for a long while to think it over.

13.

Soffiati nuvola, come se nello
stelo arricciato in mia bocca
fosse quell'esaltazione d'una
primavera in pioggia, che è il
grigio che ora è era appeso nell'aria . . .

Quando vinti ci si esercita in
una passione, d'ingaggiarsi per
altri versi che non questa miopìa
non si sente l'uomo che è donna
coi pantaloni piuttosto sul grigio
che se non fossero al dunque lavati

per quel forzato amore che è
la detronizzazione: quando vinta
rispècchiati nella vittoria, che

è l'indifferenza per tutto ciò
che riguarda la Storia, di quell'ebete
femmina ingaggiata per una storia

d'amore di cui mi racconterai
pur ancora un'altra volta, quando
l'avrai vista storta. E se paesani
zoppicanti sono questi versi è

perché siamo pronti per un'altra
storia di cui sappiamo benissimo

faremo al dunque a meno, perso
l'istinto per l'istantanea rima

perchè il ritmo t'aveva al dunque

già occhieggiata da prima.

13.

Cloud, blow yourself up, as if the
twisted stalk in my mouth
were that exaltation of a
spring in rain, which is the
grey that now is was hung in the air . . .

When defeated one drills oneself in
a passion, to be enlisted versus
something other than this myopia
one doesn't sense the man that is woman
with the pants more greyish
than if they were ultimately laundered

for that forced romance that is
dethronement: when defeated
mirror yourself again in victory, which

is indifference toward everything that
has to do with History, of that idiot
female enlisted in a history

of romance you'll tell me all about
yet one more time, once
you have seen it aslant. And if hobbling
paisans are these verses it is

because we're ready for another
history we know perfectly well

we'll ultimately do without, the instinct
for instantaneous rhyme lost

because rhythm had ultimately

been eyeing you from the start.

Uncollected

Perché non mai morii, seppia e sé
con altri fu gioconda spaccata in
pezzi uguali.

Scrivo oscuro, beata nebbia e senza
sole il cielo, infarinato di stanchezze
le monotonie del vivere a sbalzi
acuti e bassi.

11.3.'95

Uncollected

    Because I never did die, sepia and self
with others was jocund smashed in
equal pieces.

I write obscure, blissful fog and without
sun the sky, floured with wearinesses
the monotonies of living by jolts
acute and low.

11 March 1995

Between Languages

From *October Elizabethans*
(October 1956): *On Fatherish Men*

Great Pompous Ague, and Vapid Arguments
do they use, to Use you. The Branch is Loaded
with Ripe Oats, smothered into the Air. With Tinkling fingers
I do Shake it down. So you would have me 'pon your Knees
quite Freely? Pay then First! Then will I Join you
at the Feverish tree, and sing a song of
Exstasie (short-cut, 'tis the Youths we Turn to).
Or would Ye be my Grande-Father? No, too Dulle this proves:
an Olde Man, well ripe in Lust,
or None. Thine Fine Rumbunctious Talk
but Whiffs at Me; 'tis the Bed I want, and
Respect of my Maidenhood, too: till you Die
of Excess. Would you Return (after Judiciously
Leaving me) and take up Habits again? Then come Crawling
'pon your two blind Knees. Have thee not recognized I bee
a Devilish Maiden, pulling at thy flucid Beard? Yet
I do Love thee, and beg thee be
a True Father. Mine is Gone
into the Grave, waving a Banner
of Idiocee: be thou more Intelligent; Keep
from Policee, and Take Mee. Humbly shall I
Spit at thee, Crawling my Hand at your Hind-
Pocket, as you Kisse Me. But no Lucrous
Intents had I, see; twas but to wipe the Loaden sea
of my Love-tears, with Thine Hankerchiee. Come, come,
be though Brave, and Come to Mee,
a-Loaden with rich Jewelree. All Night long
shall we Curry the Milke 'f Innocenciee.

Da *Diario in tre lingue* (1955–1956) /
From *Diary in Three Tongues* (1955–1956)

IX.

Speranza, non abbandonarmi. E pure la speranza di ritrovarti
m'abbandonava.

forse il tuo male è di prefiggerti degli scopi.
o no?

we have come home

l'avarizia presuppone che vi sia un uomo forte

paralogismo
paramagnetico

atteggiamento di coscienza senza meta né intenzioni: Mandala.

see Gibbeon (architt.)
see Aut-Aut

. . . He takes a shallow decision, and dominates Chaos

yes?

la poesia è fatto di liberazione, non di riflessione

Jesù, Jesù, va!
Joseph cherche la Marie de ses entrailles victorieuses (les
                    anges qui rient avec leur dents cassés,
                    leur chemises abricot)

cosa vogliono da me le forme quando premono ecc.

Ecco, il paesaggio degl'uomini è davvero infinito

— o o o —' o o —' o o —' o o —' o

glauco

      di colore tra il celeste e verde (Gk. ceruleo); color
      cielo-glauque, glaucous

glaucome

      en eye-disease

———

l'accordo

      è timbro spaziale. Terza dimensione

intensità,   cioè forza, applicata dall'esterno

              durata

           volume

      è quarta dimensione

   cubo —architettura:

        timbro spazio -accordo

        tempo ritmo

      altezza

        forza-intensità esterna (messa in moto,
        dinamica psicologica)

timbro in rapporto a volume è qualità dinamica (vedere spettri
del mutamento linea-timbro coll'aumento volume. confrontare

varii timbri ai quali sia stato applicato lo stesso aumento
di volume. legge che ne deriva?)
timbro-spazio accordo è cubo statico
timbro-volume, o timbro-accordo-volume è cubo dinamico

Courant & Robins
                    what is mathematics

La geometria analitica

see music, see Mathm. see Aut Aut, see Gibbeon

                    (Tao not satisfact. stati Yoga? – rinuncia
                    realizzazione salvo per D.)

                    creative end? or return comuni.

                    dreams

                    sincerità vs. bocca chiusa

                    sfondare o segreto

                    rapporto creativo con Dio

                    il voler «spiccare il volo» –
                                        il «salto»

                    psycological tar under problem? or to be
                    experimented?

                    Sogno Silvana-Jacobi matrim. «petit-père»
                            assassinio Abramo
                            etica sospesa sorpassata la morale
                            posso uccidere il matrimonio?

                            vita normale negata da Celia (matrim.)
                            Silv. ammazzata con brutale sincerità.

libertà scelta
l'essere conseguente
determinismo:

       see dream
       1, 2, 3, ———

Jung:

      la vita dell'uomo è un continuo titubare tra spirituale e
      concreto
      ogni soluzione dell'uomo è sempre la penultima
certo che vi può essere anche arte non-religiosa!
                    (Proust, Penna?)

il sonno provoca la musica
il sonno provoca il ritmo

      gli accenti sono le travi costruttorie del
      cubo: -lo provocano. piazzamento accenti
      provoca variazioni dinamiche (volume, ritmo,
      piazzamento verso) nell'interno del cubo.

      veux-<u>tú</u>

aller chez le prince?

il tempo nella poesia diventa volume del cubo; cioè
profondità tramite le attesa-spazio tra verso e verso.

   XI.
Cosa si deve fare pur che Esca?

($\overset{o}{—}$ o o o o ȯ o o o $\overset{,}{—}$)

(You're stuck with your own Scheme of Beauty)

dovresti badare a rimanere coscienzioso e conseguente

(le fruit n'a parlé: <u>donc</u> o o o $\overset{,}{—}$ o)

seule isolée à la maison (s'il t'arrive de parler au moins tu peux
le faire entre 4 murs sans danger)

<u>Batter my Heart, Three-Person'd God</u>, at the round point of earth
where angels stand

and watch me Curiously

(twom<u>e</u>nfriends and twow<u>o</u>menfriends)

Let Go your hold on Contents (or the Loss of them)

T'is a Formal Solution you Seek?
the ineluctable modalities of

rage
humiliation
despair
calm

Batter my heart, Three-Person'd God, at all points meeting
for joy.

he Himself has set the hill
   R a i s i n g
            against you

do not be afraid my Honeycombed child, he will lead you
quiet at the steepest hill

.   Yea, when one depends from external moods, and *hits* (hints)
(hilts) upon them, the World Crumbles

FIND

formalsolution

(the hard heart concentrated upon itSelf)

(Others Mock when you Tempest the ground with your
Hoof

of rage, holiness, despair.)

(Dear John:
      i'd come within 2 weeks. Would that suit you? Will
      bring writings, for you to look at)

Is it only when you are beaten you can have Him? the Angels
Hack, Play, and Torture me (o tortoise with the broken shell)

Senti gli strilli degli angioli che vogliono la mia salvezza
ma il sangue è debole e la saliva corre a peccare . . .

(try not to smoke)

Caro Albanese
      ecc.
            la mia vita è una lieta infermità. l'autunno si è
            abbattuto su di noi come una condanna.

time after time have I searched in, the tombs of my fathers the
secret hebraic inscription. I must pronounce myself faithless.
Dead is the mirror upon the hill.

      O come heart of Sorrow
      be thou tomorrow
      ever-present

            . . . sharp
      . . . l'art de classifier les complications

non è dall'esterno che tu puoi risolvere il tuo mal de Dieu
(ritrovare Dio . . . – chiamiamolo pure tale)

Tao not satisfactory
      (is a mechanism of <u>living</u>)

i King mécanique ondulatoire
      meccanica ondulatoria

you want the Cube

      it is not necessary to live

(diretto e unico rapporto con Dio).

Attenta alla voglia di accaparrare

fait no calculs (ambi.)

io non sono dio?

poesia di umile
poesia di culturalone

at the 4 points of the turning wheel

———

Surrealism is (si sa) rebellion to the Gods

                    they think <u>they</u> can construct the universe
                                destruct

miss point of perfect harmony

we do not make the universe

it was there

↑   are infinite directions, cannot be wholly followed

↑   followed holily

do not <u>play</u>

do not play with words
see what you mean
do not care what is given or taken

lv. with holiness

si bada alla forma secondariamente (details of)

non è il contenuto che deve <u>fit in</u> lo spazio

    ma <u>tu</u> che devi plasmare lo spazio

    cioè il tuo contenuto deve provocare lo spazio

ie: 1ᵃ il timbro vocali ecc. (o ritmo ecc.) determinava
inconsciamente il contenuto

    ti accostavi allo schema   ex-temp. dal fuori in
dentro

    «instrument» determined you
          (form -descrip 1ᵉ fantas. la lune tombée dans
          son béon lit how ends: solution) (poulêt rôti,
          et puis?)
                 quel soleil au ciel pourpre?

sapere interpretare proprie visioni tematica surrealiste
                         (psicol. Jung)

Il punto di visione –

    il punto di sintesi tra mondo estrov. e
    mondo introv. sono io, il fluire.

    lo scarafaggio non è per me! punte
    basta.

        · · · · ·

vision lune qui tombe, femme de chambre: soleil

rêve-vision Trocadérò
vision des cercles
    surréalisme
        fleurs

rêve-poussière
    papier
  Hindu-Chinois?

———

MT
Marionravie?

. . .

surréalisme
rouge-vert

rouge-vert-bleu
(pas d'intuition pour s'en aller)
oeuf
presque noir
rails du train
fleurs

Ulisse non è soluzione

brings to train-raies?
(Finnegan)

Montale? . . .

———

(je suis un génie, <u>tous</u> sont des génies, s'ils <u>veu</u>lent)

———

Rimbaud oggi?

la sua era una soluzione di praticità (inserirsi nella storia)

<u>giusta</u>

non poteva fare altrimenti, benché scelse.
la sua fu una soluzione di continuità

(ce n'est pas en fermant les yeux que tu trouveras
quelque chose.)

(la 1ª donna

     (souvent je me hais)

la lune est dans son peigne noir souvent elle se haìt

         (Tahiti)

Gauguin-Tahiti

    <u>pas</u> une solution . . .

  . . . breaks out and breaks the silver gong of ———

Esthétique des Fendue

Eliot

    autumn is a season of gold
    autumn is a season of age and decision
        is a land of gold
        is a land of cold decision

          . . .

is the humble ever ironic?
is the humble ever clever?

          . . .

music is not feeling
music is religion
all arts are religion
the four points meet

<u>II Mite</u>

Obey with Holiness

humility and gentleness toward your Self, and God

cleverness lack of simplicity

see how the flower rises devoid of expectation

(spostato il rapporto
 aiuto-uomo, a
 aiuto-dio)

nemmeno il freddo distacco o il disincantato disinteresse

Si è <u>vinti</u>

       non v'è né sù
          né giù

ma solo il <u>mezzo</u>

(né ascesi né disintegrazione)

non è ancora illuminato

(una stretta gola in una stretta valle)

                . . .

non badare ai suoni colori ritmi ecc. il contenuto propone
le sue forme.

    e il contenuto è sempre <u>Uno</u>

    dunque la forma <u>Una</u>

. . . verrà.

tutto si compensa:
    if you're gay in the night you're foolish in the
    morning, & vice-versa

    o the pain of the turning stars!

    o o — o — from Iacobo

    yes, but mildness, <u>not</u> Biblical

228

a holy text done with technique, not technicism . . .

. . . you're tired, sleep. Everything will be resolved . . .

Tao

potersi tenersi in tal modo sul piano orizzontale della
vita (impegnati)
we live on the superficie of the earth, not in its
substance, not in the air

(no crude harsh, extreme vocabulary)

simplicity

each thing has its name, simple, not to be substituted by
secondary subjects (word-mirroring)

find perfect grammar

no subtle confusion

(adverbs are adverbs, verbs are verbs)

limpid

offuscato

dark

black

white

. . . . .

bright

illuminated

limpid

quality of style as you wish it

les terribles guerres:

>   not clear, determined by form, not substance
>   avoid colourfull prose

simplicity (or control) of expression, complexity of means
consciousness of meaning

I sit, and wait, for death's fine door.
Open the door, open the door
>   (farsi una bella camomilla) . . .

>   But God doesn't always work, or does he? Or is it I who
cannot follow him?

>   la volontà
>   (mine
>   in opposition. The
War with God.
>   (prose a little too flamboyesque)

they say Tao is nature
>   (you must fill your stomach with juice)

(House-arbor)
>   (you must scratch the moss on the arbour)

hoary-hoe

you usually have a rhytm-pattern in your head (or style
– imitation) into which you inser words (when fit rhytm and
mood of style)

now

>   upsa ipsa
>   upsa versa

l' ascensione

c'est un livre secret.

———

    ce n'est pas la pensée qui te sauvera (where 4 points
meet), c'est à dire

(tes technicismes) (Padova, la ditta del Santo)

the sense of the holy
                        (belonging or devoted to Gd.)

what comes is given. il <u>serio</u>

(culture-technique)
<u>Thought</u> is vanity

<u>Work</u> is vanity

Creativeness is?

feeling is pap

sensitiveness complacency
intuition? unconscious

collop = slice of meat (E)

collywobbles = rumbling in the intestine
                               (collq.) (imit.)

col = dépression in mountain chains . . .

the snow-leopard . . .

———

gentleness toward men
humility towards Gd.

il telegrafo (il termometro)

the humble

the sensorial and the spiritual

soul

loins

both have their centers, at <u>all</u> points of the turning world

at all points of the world

at all 4 points of the world

Lets see if we can sleep now . . .

(Tu fai troppe cose con la tua Volontà, ci vuol Pazienza)

now we'll see it its worth it.

From *Sleep: Poems in English* (1953–1966)

What woke those tender heavy fat hands
said the executioner as the hatchet fell
down upon their bodily stripped souls
fermenting in the dust. You are a stranger here
and have no place among us. We would have you off our list
of potent able men
were it not that you've never belonged to it. Smell
the cool sweet fragrance of the incense burnt, in honour
of some secret soul gone off to enjoy an hour's agony
with our saintly Maker. Pray be away
sang the hatchet as it cut slittingly
purpled with blood. The earth is made nearly
round, and fuel is burnt every day of our lives.

*

Well, so, patience to our souls
the seas run cold, 'pon our bare necks
shivered. We shall eat out of our bare hand
smiling vainly. The silver pot is snapped;
we be snapped out of boredom, in a jiffy-
run. Tentacles of passion run rose-wise
like flaming strands of opaque red lava. Our soul
tears with passion, its chimney. The wind cries oof!
and goes off. We were left alone with our sister
navel. Good, so we'll learn to
ravish it. Alone. Words in their forge.

Webern Opus 4

military melancholy reverberates softly
on slender walls, as the sipid music rapidly
counterbounces against walls thicker than
can permit the rapid brain. Cultivation
of flowers is a soft pose in a bent garden
the gallant fingers reaching into crooked
petals are as if placing against an even
beat slow triolets.

★

radioactive confusion bit into my
brain radiant with multitudes. Unexpectedly
the lights warm in a heart went out
for the pleasure of separation. Encountering
the bell flashing in the eyes of
the partisan of a good cause, I
collapsed into fits of apology:
bragging into the tear-rid apostrophes
of saints.

Belonging to a race of saints the
upshot of this long separation which
we ourselves must set to our pleasures
the wind entered the broken boned
part of the heart freezing in a winter
grip.

Assertion of individuality broke
up the cupid love he held for senseless
mates of joy. Regardless of impossibility
the fire turned over the spittled
chicken, as it twisted plumed. Against
triviality the spit hung a banner
pierced through your heart encountered
flames of lust. Through the key hole
of an old woman's bed room door appeared
to the distraught eye the weight
of all disaster.

Sleep

slightly nauseated with all cry I fell
into bemused sleep, oh the tender dangerous
virgins on the mountain top watch a sleep
which is not mine since the radiant bed
of earth covered me moss like. I am a
broken fellow cried the fish monger, and
belayed his true nature. I am the bemused
man on the tree top cried the arch duke
pleased he had slept with divinity. I am
the cry in the night explained the author
as his book fell. The sun slept into a
douche of cloud like sun drop, the earth
rounded the point. All cry is a massacre
when sleep is the virgin; the reason is
lost when all impatience is neglected.

The banality of all superiors is a danger
for the host. The intricacies of court
life is the danger. I am the danger of
a court massacre, exclaimed the virgin
on the tree top as the tree fell, swarmed
down to putritude. Sleep fell on, the reason
went, and the host remembered he had forgotten
the power and the glory.

 ★

   Straight as a shaft of light she fled from
the cunning race, fled into the hangar, black
almost since its grey was clear. And in the straights
of these definite standings she understood perhaps
to have beloved all the world with too much
intensity, and herself, the queen of it, as it
ran ramshackle into the hangar, a plane on its
way to triumph or its own perdition.

The hangar closed down: bent on practicability.
She returned head lowered and a bordered belt
on the sides, a trifle blowsy, but perhaps moderate

enough in her judgment, to an old apprehension
or acceptance of the causes: lower your nets
when the fish drag, and clear the decks from
all damaging surf! A plane, then a ship, all
moderate means, and her belted waist in accordance
with these laws of speed.

*

Do come see my poetry
demand it sit for a portrait
in silence recalling
all past experiences
with no boredom enslaving
its cheeks which wait.

Do come see my poetry
be forceful and desperate
(if ever desperation were ever
a nest in the mind). In kind
it is suave almost, but rather
uncertain as to its premises
and as to its finalities
it avoids gaps, principles,
rests on unconscious decision
while you paint.

With a stroke of the brush you
empower it, with a bliss which
was not there, before we talked.
With a slip of the pen you
endow it, with thoughts which
were never there at all, save
that you lurked in the shadows
finding out its message.

And now the sitting is at end
your new principle stares
you in the eyes, and with dread
it surmises, you were never

born before you wrote
of tender surmises.

*

you sweet, sweet, sweet, child, onwards, you
delicate overhauled train turning into pale
crimson detail; you belligerent waste, you
penetrating delicacy, you saliva watching
into the mystery of death which is a penetration
overhauling its entries, the way out is paved
with bad intentions, I summarize, that you
could not know he that made you. He is gentile
in his fashion and descending tent-wise to
the general hospitals; he is a tender fright
and a refrigerator; he is myself even, though
obtenebrated by joy.

You self-taught heart who has understood
its weak point, obduring through winters
too great for harmony. You tent of oxygen
you pale brown orange-leaved overhauling
though with your pen you may think, and analyse
encounters or things into being, they escape
you not without poverty, they take your hand
and beg: express me!

*

they scrabble: hiss and fear and belittle
every twitch of your nerves: serving higher
ideals as if it were a soup: to be fried
in, or held astance with light grip. They
swallow the meat in the jargon as if it
were a pauper's den, this hell (the naked
word) (or world).

They multiply your reflexes, enjoy your
causing them trouble and their firm (not
so very firm) grasp is a hold on your imagination

which crouching, affirms: you're not my
sorry king; it's gone, that king, he's gone
that shaft of marmalade lightning, the hiss
in the prayer.

And bent to ground your hips devout verify
there is no lightning, but only more soup
more meat, more fast—the choice of which
is almost left to chance.

Faro

be kind be kind be kind I hear this phrase
screaming in my ear each day, be sweet
be sweet be sweet be sweet this is all
I can say (or seem to say). Alas the phrase the
flare the open door the glare the blare the fan
the flight the high tower reaching up towards glaze
are all I am fit to say, to see to hear to feel
to sway. And the open door fitted into a present
day, most say most say most say most die
on this cross.

The watch-tower, the barrel-hill, the lights go
out, upon the swaying of the hill. It's a plague!
and all bemoan the day the clay the meat
on your fingers.

So that's what they're for, the lighthouse watching
anxiously.

★

Oh, you sweet heart, oh you condescending
minstrel of my tuberculous heart oh the
belly-ache testifying to my withdrawal in
the field of war. Oh the horrors which can not
bring other filth into my nestled heart not
melting in its couch, but the plastic cover

supervising all sing-song. Oh death of
war: oh heart of steel oh the elements withdrawing
from racket.

Oh since you left you wept and felt this
strong tie terminating in exercise of pen
needless to say it was with a hen that he
identified the self—the pen rusting in its
rustic balloon, oval-shaped.

You shaped my heart: it took on a tinge of bartering
softnesses and the tenderness never really died
down. It never really did pry on as it had
previously to the marriage in the kitchen.

*

A mind quite narrow yet
exalted: a mind transmitting
its morse code brutally
on chairs painted white.
A mind tapping out the
message you'll not want
to read, pleasing yourself
with my confusion. Yet
it's a telegram! to make
you sigh, or verify me
or explode into rapture.

A mind that does not know
its code, yet in shallow
waters so cold braces up
against the mortified soul.
You may hear its squinting
its tearing the map with
large fat hands, or withdrawing
to diversified code. Its
code! Its tail: its mush
grey matter, and the needle
thrust, fattening the air.

Has it a balance? Has it
a balanced view? Has it
bands and feet, watering
the air? No, its raptures
are too short for comment
and withdraw into caverns
larger than your mouths
when you start speak.

I am no mind—I am a brain
made fast to cajolery, its
breath interlocked with
separate time. No brain
no time—no stinging smile;
a grey lump, an electric
swerve—then all is gone.
Mind sever me from matter
do not lose time, lose it
if you must on despair's
hills, but mock me not!

Quite quiet the breath
takes time: its cajolery
is fast hung to your silent
mind of the matter.

Poetics

Introduction to "Metrical Spaces"

Having read all sorts of poetry from the time that I was very young, at times in English (classics and non), at times in French or in Italian, and having read a lot of prose (Faulkner, for example, or the poetic prose of Eliot), I asked myself how to escape from the banality of the usual free verse, which at the time seemed unhinged, lacking in historical justification, and above all, exhausted. Though I was reading and writing a lot, in reality I was studying musical composition, and intensely; already at the age of seventeen, finding myself in London, I became acquainted with the problems of modern music, and studied its various new theorizations (Bartók for the Hungarian school, and research into different notations for popular folk song, to be found in music that wasn't "educated" in the tempered system of the seventeenth and eighteenth centuries, by the usual intonations defined by Leibniz and above all by Bach). (This system seemed so rich that it is presumed to be the only one even today. In reality, systems called "dodecaphonic" were already being formulated from the years of the Second World War forward, in Austria—systems which aimed to amplify the field of musical writing outside of the tonal or modal.)

In the writing of poetry many intuited this need, and made gestures toward long, elastic lines, alluding to a classical form that was still unknown; they did this not wishing to return to sterile neoclassical forms, nor, in fact, to the so-called free verse that had already been so exploited at the beginning of the century by the surrealists and by fashion. It was possible for all to express themselves in this vague scansion, and few knew how to use free verse as a form inherent to their discourse (Neruda; Breton; Hopkins; Whitman), and with prosaic and primarily musical elegance. The gesture toward forms of the past, this intuiting of fixed but new forms, was common to many important poets, but the poet rarely theorizes his or her form even if it is innovative; the poet instead "feels" it, and doesn't want to analyze it, and renews free verse aiming at intuited forms and dreamt metrics, which would nevertheless break out of every neoclassical scheme. In García Lorca's poetry, in that of Dylan Thomas and Gerard Manley Hopkins, and in many poems of the late nineteenth century (Lautréamont) and early twentieth century (Surrealism, Imagism) the author escapes from a similar dilemma, usually simply compromising with both the classic and extreme forms of a "free" verse, which is in the end a useful vehicle for new contents and metaphorical combinations, but weak in its monotony, and poorly distinguishable from common prose.

That my research in the field of "folk," or ethnomusicology, influenced the search for a stricter, more severe, and geometrically formulated versification is obvious; though I had been writing prose pieces and poems in different languages since the age of seventeen, as if testing valid new forms in every language, I did not succeed in formulating this new geometrism—even after much study of mathematics, physics, and sentence analysis—until age 28, with the opening of the first lines of the poem *La libellula* (1958). The problem seemed so complex that I had even established a correlation between the metrical question and problems in spatial photography, living the poem without writing it, and mentally and emotionally "filming" each environing reality. As if writing verse were equivalent to the sensing [*sentire*] and thinking of an environing visual-emotional space, I practically thought in forms that were approximately cubic, with sensing following seeing in terms of energy as well.[1]

My introductory argument to this essay, which is already in itself dense and difficult, because highly personal, and at the same time dogmatic, continues to be overly vague.

I had the chance to explain my intentions in poetic realization when I brought my first book *Variazioni belliche / Bellicose Variations* (1959–1963) to Pier Paolo Pasolini, already having a commitment by Vittorini and Calvino to publish 24 poems in *Il Menabò* No. 6. I remember that it proved impossible to clarify my intentions, especially those that had to do with meter. Pasolini asked me to write about what had encumbered me so in explaining. Returning home, frightened by the difficult task, I described in a way that was not overly technical what was impossible to specify in conversation. Realizing that many were indifferent to such a theme or problem, I condensed and lightened the explication in such a way as to render it accessible and incomprehensible at the same time: that is, I used a vocabulary that was in part musical, and avoided classical or scholastic terminology, seeking to express myself at a simple mathematical level, and at an average grammatical and musical level. I believe that none of the critics, literati, or poets comprehended that 1962 piece titled "Spazi metrici"; I included it at the end of the book when I had to correct the first proofs, as a brief afterword of mine. Years later, the problems described in the essay were highlighted by Mengaldo in his 1978 Mondadori anthology.[2] I note that the poetry of others is often linked

1. I have translated *sentire* as "sense" in this case in order to retain as many senses of the word as possible: hearing, feeling, and even smelling. In her "Laboratorio di poesia" conducted by Pagliarini, Rosselli describes the fourteenth-century Italian and the sixteenth-century English sonnet as "cubic," to indicate verse with "a depth and weight of energy" that wasn't classical. Rosselli, *Una scrittura plurale*, 241.

2. Pier V. Mengaldo, *Poeti italiani del Novecento*.

to the metrical system proposed there; whether consciously or not, I wouldn't know.

I think that I have hit upon something, and I believe that the text is valid and even to be expanded upon, in the case that only a few poets comprehend it. It is not a matter of graphic "systematizations" but of sensitizing the poet to other disciplines, among which stand those of the cinematographer, modern physics, and aerodynamics. I have personally never felt myself to break away from this same metrical system, and I hope that for the scholars of modern prosody, this text of mine can be of fundamental help in the future.

February 4, 1993

Metrical Spaces (1962)

Any problematic of poetic form has always been connected for me to that which is more strictly musical, and I have never in reality divided the two disciplines, considering the syllable not only an orthographic nexus but also a sound, and the sentence not only a grammatical construct but a system as well.

To define the syllable as a sound is inexact, however: there are no "sounds" in languages:—in classifications of musical acoustics the vowel or consonant is defined as "noise," and that is natural, given the complexity of our phonetic-physiological apparatus, and the variation from person to person even of the magnitude of vocal cords and oral cavities, so that a phonetic classification system other than statistical has never been reached, until now.

In speaking of vowels, in any case, generally we mean sounds, or even colors, given that we are often indebted to them for "timbric" qualities; and in speaking of consonants or groupings of consonants, we mean not only their graphic features, but also muscular movements and mental "forms."

But if when we vocalize, of all the individuable elements in music and painting, only rhythms (durations or tempos) and colors (timbres or forms) stand out, when we write and read, things go a bit differently: we think contemporaneously. In that case the word does not have merely a sound (noise); in fact, at times it does not have one at all, and it *resounds* only as an idea in the mind. The vowel and consonant, then, are not necessarily phonetic values, but simply graphic values as well, or components of the written idea, or word. We do not even hear timbre when we think or read mentally; and durations (syllables) are elastic and imprecise, according to the reader's scanning and individual dynamics, rhythmicity, and velocity of thought. In fact, at times, in reading without vocalizing, all voiced elements disappear, and even the poetic phrase is reduced to logical or associative sense, perceived with the help of a subtle graphic and spatial sensibility (spaces and forms are the mind's silences and points of reference).

And so, when faced with sonorous or logical or associative material in writing—classified until now either abstractly or fantastically, but never systematically—one speaks to me of "feet" and of phrases, without telling me what a vowel is. Not only that: the language in which I write at isolated moments is only one, while my sonorous, logical, and associative experience is certainly that of all peoples, and reflectable in all languages.

And it is with these preoccupations that I set out at a certain point in my adolescence to seek universal forms. To find these I sought from the beginning my most basic (Western and rational) organizational element in writing. And this turned out clearly to be the "letter," voiced or unvoiced, timbric or non, graphic or formal, symbolic and functional at once. This letter, sonorous but equally a "noise," created phonetic nodes (*chl, str; sta, biv*) that were not necessarily syllabic, and were in fact only functional or graphical forms, and noise. For a classification that would be neither graphic nor formal it was necessary, in seeking the reserves of poetic form, to speak of the syllable, understood not overly scholastically, but rather as a rhythmic particle. Rising out of this still-insignificant matter, I came upon the word as a whole, understood as definition and sense, idea, well of communication. Generally the word is considered the definition of a given reality, but it is viewed more as an "object" to classify and to subclassify, and not as an idea. I instead (and here perhaps I would do well to warn that since my experimentation and deduction are quite personal and in part incommunicable, every conclusion that I might have drawn from them is truly to be taken "cum grano salis"), had very different ideas in mind, and considered even *il, la*, and *come* to be "ideas," and not merely conjunctions or specifications of an argument expressing an idea.[1] I posited that the whole argument should indicate the thought

---

1. *Il*, "the," masculine; *la*, "the," feminine; *come*, "as/how." Rosselli expands upon this passage in Elio Pagliarani's 1988 poetry workshop: "I have already, by education, learned not a grammatical analysis of the word but an idea in my mind with regard to this . . . phoneme *il*. . . . Those who write must reconsider all of this again, asking themselves: why have they told me what a pronoun is? Why is it masculine? Why does it make that sound? How can I use it?" *È vostra la vita che ho perso*, 235.

itself, and thus that the phrase (with all of its functional colorings) was an idea that had become slightly more complex and manageable, and that the sentence was the logical exposition of an idea, not static like the one materialized in the word, but rather, dynamic and "becoming," and often unconscious as well. Wanting to broaden my classification, which was truly not that scientific, I inserted the Chinese ideogram between the phrase and the word, and I translated the Chinese scroll in the delirious course of Western thought.[2]

Later I took to observing the mutation of this delirium or scroll of my thought in accordance with the situation my mind confronted at each turn of life, at each spatial or temporal displacement of my daily practical experience. I noted strange thickenings in the rhythmicity of my thought, strange arrests, strange coagulations and changes of tempo, strange intervals of rest or absence of action; new sonorous and ideal fusions in accordance with the changing of practical time, graphic spaces, and the spaces surrounding me continually and materially. In conversing and in sensing other mental or psychological presences with me in a space, thinking became tenser, more fatigued, almost complementary to that of the interlocutor, even as it was renewed or destroyed in the encounter with him or her.

I tried to observe every external materiality with the most absolute meticulousness possible within an immediate period of experimental time and space. With each additional movement of my body, I would attempt a complete "picture" [*quadro*] of surrounding existence; my mind had to assimilate the picture's entire meaning within the period of time in which it remained there, merging with its own interior dynamism.[3]

2. From Rosselli's presentation of "Metrical Spaces" at Pagliarani's workshop: "Do not take the word *delirante* [delirious] as true delirium. The scroll form suggests the slow raving, the unfurling of the idea. That there is this interruption, then, between phrase and word, through the Chinese ideogram, which is neither phrase nor word alone, except in rare cases, was a need of mine for universality." Rosselli continues, "Pound suggested that we read Chinese poems. I studied various languages in my youth, if not all to the point of being able to speak them. I studied German, I studied Arabic, an easy language, Hebrew, which was quite difficult, I had studied Greek and Latin at school, and I had deduced various questions regarding form." Rosselli et al., *È vostra la vita che ho perso*, 235, 236.

3. The word Rosselli uses for "picture" here is *quadro*, which also means "square." The quotation marks surrounding it highlight the extended pun: Rosselli will later duplicate the surrounding "picture" with a "square" on paper. As she explains to Pagliarini's workshop regarding her process of writing *First Writings* and *Diary in Three Tongues* in the 1950s, "I took notes walking through Trastevere with little notebooks that I then transcribed onto paper. . . . By night, by day, walking, standing still, just to observe the shifting of my observation and of the encounter with things or people

Until that time, in writing, my complexity or completeness with respect to reality had been limited subjectively: reality was mine, not that of others as well: I wrote in free verse.

In effect, even in interrupting a long line with the termination of a phrase or an unconnected word, I isolated the phrase, rendering it meaningful and strong, and I isolated the word, rendering it its ideality, but dividing my train of thought into unequal strata and disconnected meanings. The idea was no longer in the entire poem, as a moment of reality in my mind, or as my mind's participation in a reality, but was instead torn apart into slow flights of steps, and it was traceable only at the poem's end, or from no point at all. The poem's graphic aspect influenced logical impressions more than the means or vehicle of my thought, which is to say, the word, phrase, or sentence.

As for prosody, being free, it varied courteously in accordance with association or my own pleasure. Intolerant of preestablished designs, bursting out of them, it adapted itself to a tempo that was strictly psychological, musical, and instinctual.

By chance, I resolved to reread the sonnets of the first Italian schools; fascinated by regularity, I resolved to reattempt the impossible.

I took up again in hand my five classifications: letter, syllable, word, phrase, and sentence. I framed them [*Le inquadrai*] in an absolute time-space.[4] My poetic verses could no longer escape the universality of the total space: the lengths and tempos of lines were preestablished, my organizational unity could be defined, my rhythms adapted themselves not to my will alone, but to the space that had already been determined, and this space was wholly covered by experiences, realities, objects, and sensations. Transposing the rhythmic complexity of language spoken and thought but unscanned, through abundant variation of timbric and rhythmic particles within a unified and limited typical space, my meter was, if not regular, at least total: all possible imaginable rhythms filled my square [*quadrato*] meticulously to timbric depth, my rhythmics were musical in the sense developed by the latest experiments of post-Webernism; my regularity, when it existed, came into contrast with a swarming of

---

or spaces and movement and time [*tempo*]. Then I copied it out on the typewriter because gridded paper can achieve results almost like the typewriter. I could transpose the spaces that I had swiftly seized from surrounding space." Rosselli et al., *È vostra la vita che ho perso*, 236.

4. Here the verb for "frame," *inquadrare*, contains the word *quadro*, both "picture" and "square." She continues to work with this dual meaning of the word—geometrical and conceptual—through the remainder of the essay. I include original terms at points of ambiguity.

rhythms translatable not into sentences or into long or short measures, but into microscopic durations that were only just annotatable, if desired, with pencil on graph paper in millimeter rule. The basic unity of the verse was neither the letter, disintegrative and insignificant, nor the syllable, rhythmic and cutting yet still lacking ideality, but the entire word, of whatever type, indifferently, all words being considered of equal value and weight, all to be manipulated as concrete and abstract ideas.

In laying out the first line of the poem I fixed the width of the spatial and temporal frame [*quadro*] definitively at once; subsequent lines had to be adapted to equal measure, to identical formulation.[5] In writing I moved from line to line without minding any priority of meaning in the words placed at the end of the lines as if by chance.

In reality, there was always that hidden point of the right margin of my frame [*quadro*] to aid me in measuring or ending my line; and to close the line, either the whole word, or any orthographic nexus that was meaningful insofar as it really existed as a time of "waiting" both in speaking and thinking, could fall upon it. The empty space between one word and the other was considered rather nonfunctional, and was not a unity, and if by chance it fell upon the right margin of the frame [*quadro*], it was immediately followed by another word, so as to fill the space entirely and close the verse. The square [*quadro*] was to be covered entirely, in fact, and the phrase to be enunciated in a breath and without silences and interruptions—reflecting spoken and thought reality, where in sounding we link our words and in thinking we have no interruptions but those of punctuation, which are explicative and logical. I thought in fact that the dynamic of thought and sound would generally be exhausted at the end of the phrase, sentence, or thought, and that vocal emission and writing would thus follow its being born and reborn without interruptions.

In reading aloud, each one of the lines was then to be phonetized within identical time limits, corresponding to the equal confines of graphic length or width previously formulated by drafting the first line. Even in the case that one line would contain more words, syllables, letters, and punctuation than another, the overall reading time of each line had to remain as identical as possible. Line lengths were thus approximately equal, and their reading times along with them; they had the word and orthographic nexus as metrical and spatial unity, and graphic space

5. It is notable that here and in the next paragraph Rosselli uses the term *rigo* (literally, "line") rather than the traditional poetic term *verso* ("verse") to indicate the "line." As Florinda Fusco points out, this choice underscores that traditional conceptions of verse are being overturned. See Fusco, *Amelia Rosselli*, 56.

or time as a containing form, with the latter laid out not in a mechanical or entirely visual manner, but as a presupposition in scanning, and as an agent in writing and thinking.

I would break the poem off when the psychic force and significance driving me to write—that is, the idea or experience or memory or fantasy that moved the meaning and space—were exhausted. I attributed to the empty spaces between one section of the poem and another the time elapsed, or the space mentally traversed, in drawing logical and associative conclusions to add to any of its parts. And the idea was logical, in fact; but the space, though preestablished, was not infinite, as if *it compromised* the idea, experience, or memory, transforming my syllables and timbres (which were scattered throughout the poem, like nonrhythmic rhymes) in dense and subtle associations; the sentiment momentarily relived was affirmed through some fixed rhythm. At times, however infrequently, a fixed rhythm predominated and haunted, and in the end I resolved to find the perfect rhythmic regularity of this sentiment, and being unable to, I closed the book with its single attempt at abstract order—that is, the last poem.

In writing by hand instead of on the typewriter, as I realized immediately, I could not establish perfect spaces and perfectly equal line lengths (at least by formula), having the idea or word or orthographic nexus as functional and graphic unity, unless I wanted to write on the graph paper of scholastic notebooks. Writing by hand normally, I could only attempt to seize the established space-time instinctively in the formulation of the first line, and perhaps later and artificially, I could convert the attempt to an approximate form, reproduced through mechanical print. Writing by hand, one also thinks more sluggishly; thought has to wait for the hand and it becomes interrupted, and free verse makes more sense in this form, as it reflects these interruptions, and this isolation of the word and phrase. But writing by machine I can perhaps, for a short time, follow a thought faster than light. Writing by hand perhaps I would have to write prose, so as not to return to free forms: prose is perhaps in fact the most real of all forms, and it does not pretend to define forms.

But to reattempt the equilibrium of the fourteenth-century sonnet is a real ideal as well. Reality is so heavy that the hand tires, and no form can contain it. Memory rushes thus to the most fantastic enterprises (spaces, verses, rhymes, tempos).

Extreme Facts: An Interview with Giacinto Spagnoletti

First printed in *Antologia poetica* (Milan: Garzanti, 1987)

Let's begin with the facts of your biography. You were born in Paris in 1930 to Carlo Rosselli and Marion Cave, an Englishwoman with remote Irish origins. What memories do you have of your early childhood?

My father had been an exile in Paris since 1929, after having organized the flight of Turati, together with Pertini and Adriano Olivetti.[1] Rosselli was already known as an anti-Fascist, follower of Salvemini and professor of political science.[2] From '36 forward he led the Justice and Liberty Brigade in favor of the Spanish Republic; he led the eponymous movement and its journal of resistance to Fascism, *Justice and Liberty*, having contacts in Italy, England, and elsewhere. After his assassination, along with his brother Nello, perpetrated in France by order of Mussolini and Ciano, we remained for another two or three years in the French capital.[3] I have a few images in mind. I remember my father as a serene, affectionate man, and my mother, a bit fugitive, preoccupied. Our relations with our parents—I speak of myself and Andrea, who was the younger of my two brothers—were a bit fleeting. One shouldn't upset the children, speaking of the dangers that encumbered. But at the table, when they conversed among themselves, one intuited something. Of my father, apart from the affection, there remains in me a sense of disembodiedness.

1. Filippo Turati (1857–1932), an Italian sociologist, poet, and politician—one of the intellectuals instrumental in the founding of the Italian Socialist Party in 1892—was a major opponent of Fascism who lived under surveillance and threats until this dramatic escape from Italy aided by Carlo Rosselli. Alessandro Pertini (1896–1990), an Italian socialist and key figure of the Italian anti-Fascist Resistance, was imprisoned from 1935 to 1943, during which period he served time with Gramsci and, famously, saved the latter's diaries; he eventually served as seventh president of the Italian Republic from 1978 to 1985. Adriano Olivetti (1901–1960) was an idealistic, innovative Italian entrepreneur known for his manufacture of typewriters, calculators, and computers, and also for his utopian designs in urban planning

and radical publishing activities following World War II (including *Comunità*, a journal that disseminated the philosophy of the Community Movement he advocated).

2. Gaetano Salvemini (1873–1957) was a writer, historian, and politician who fought for universal suffrage and the uplift of the Italian South; jailed for his opposition to Fascism in 1925, he continued to organize Resistance efforts in France, England, and, eventually, the United States.

3. Galeazzo Ciano (1903–1944), Mussolini's son-in-law, heralded as a hero in the Italian invasion of Ethiopia, became minister of foreign affairs in 1936 under Mussolini; in 1943 he pushed for Italy to exit from World War II and for Mussolini to be removed from power, and was executed.

When he left for Spain in '36, I had only just turned six, and so I do not remember very much.

How did you hear the news of his death?

My mother called Andrea and me. I don't know whether she had already spoken with Giovanni Giacomo (John), the eldest brother; I suppose that she had. Being about two years older than me, he was already very mature. She called us into her room. She was in bed, I remember, with a broken air, of a woman put to trial. But she was fundamentally calm. She asked us: "Do you know what the word assassination means?"

And the two of you?

We said yes, then all I remember is that we returned together to our room; we seemed almost to be twins, even if we had different characters. He was six years old, I was seven. Then I don't remember much. We couldn't see our mother for some time, since her condition had been aggravated; she suffered from heart problems from a young age.

Did you take up your studies again?

Yes, in Paris, still, from age six to ten. French was spoken at home as well, except with my father, who was faithful to Italian. When Uncle Nello arrived, we spoke Italian; I had to learn English later.

Was it in '40 that you went to England?

In '40, after the invasion of France by the Nazis, in order to be able to flee to England, all three of us siblings (Giovanni, Andrea, and me) were attached to my mother's passport, and thus naturalized as English. We spent a certain period in England, in the countryside, because London was not very safe. In London I experienced the air-raid sirens, but they had been a test. I got lost in the hotel, I found my mother and my brother in the metro, after having searched for the exit for a long time amidst the hotel corridors. I remember my mother being so relieved to see me again. Then came the decision to leave England. We embarked on a ship with a group under escort, in winter, and my grandmother (Amelia Rosselli, a Venetian), my Aunt Maria, the wife of Nello, and her four very young children, who had previously lived in Florence, caught up with us. We had to get to New York, via Canada. The trip was dangerous and stormy. We arrived in Montreal and went on to New York. Further on we settled in a town an hour away from the metropolis. I went to elementary and high school until age fifteen, taking some summer courses in the end in anticipation of my return to Italy, which took place in 1946. I saw Vermont in the summer and got to know Quaker environments (vacation and training camps); and I worked in the fields as well. In Vermont I learned to cut down trees, to construct a bridge over a river, to ride on horseback, to climb mountains with very heavy packs, to sleep in a sleeping bag. All this around age twelve-thirteen. In another place (New York State) I learned to gather hay, to clean horses, to milk cows, to paint big wooden barns, dark red with white trim. I loved the work in the fields; and I did very well in a Quaker environment such as that one. I do not remember having actual illnesses, I was strong, only thin and a bit anemic.

So you took up your studies in America, then, and at what level?

I accelerated them as much as I could, so as to graduate at age fifteen. Unfortunately my mother was struck with an embolus, and the whole family, my grandmother, my aunt, and the four cousins, then we three siblings, had to wait for her to get well or be able to walk in order to set off again for Italy. At age sixteen, then, I reached Florence, and there were some complications. The studies I had completed were not considered an equivalent qualification in Europe; it was a great disillusionment for me. They wanted me to study with thirteen-year-olds. I refused and my brother Andrea as well. I lived in Florence for some months; I moved to London to take up my studies again, which hadn't ended up being valid in Italy. I lived with friends and in furnished rooms, attending Saint Paul's Girl's School for a year, taking graduation exams at a higher level. I got to know my grandfather, the one on my mother's side, who was English, but not rich like my father's family.

Did your musical education begin during that period?

In London, exactly; in America I had only had generic training in school (solfeggio and song): then my mother, who had looked after me as she could, due to her illness, let us listen to an hour of classical music on the radio every evening. In London I began studying violin and piano, and composition. In those same years I lived through the experience of English Labourism as well, and attended a great number of concerts, and the theater. I was as passionate about literature as I was about music. I had an extraordinary literature teacher in school. Unfortunately I no longer remember her name. There was a remarkable scholastic library there; in class we read and recited Shakespeare.

You didn't make any intellectual relationships in those two years?

No, I stayed very much alone. My mother was very ill, but I practically didn't realize it; she had always been ill. When she returned to the English climate, which she had been advised against from a young age, they told me that she fell ill with ascites. I took my graduation exams with average results. Afterwards, I could have registered in political science; my mother hoped that I would, but I was aware of a certain weakening of my memory, and so I chose to study music and composition. My mother was displeased; at home we didn't have much to live on; she was incredibly worried and knew she was nearing death.

Your English period ended, if I am not mistaken, in '48.

Yes, in the spring of '48 I returned to Florence on vacation in my grandmother's house (the Rosselli home was on Via Giuseppe Giusti), and I wrote to my mother, asking her if I could remain in Italy for some time. I suffered from the English climate as well. I was still in Florence when, suddenly, wretchedly, she died. It was the month of October. I was nineteen at the time. So I had to find work. I believe it was grandmother Amelia who put me in contact with Community Editions, and I began to translate, working half-days, in Rome.[4] I found lodging in a house not far from that of Ernesto and Ada Rossi.[5] A new life began for me. But I was soon prey to a strong bout of nervous exhaustion. Perhaps because I did too much. Apart from the translations, I was taking composition lessons with Guido Turchi, recommended to me by Dallapiccola and Petrassi.[6]

4. Le Edizioni di Comunità, Adriano Olivetti's publishing venture.

5. Ernesto Rossi (1897–1967) was a journalist, politician, and anti-Fascist activist whose ideas were fundamental to the Action Party and the Radical Party that succeeded it, and a close friend of Salvemini; Ada Rossi was his wife and custodian of his papers.

6. Guido Turchi (1916–) is an Italian composer and writer interested in musics predating the nineteenth century (such as Gregorian chants and Renaissance madrigals) and in non-Italian musics of contemporary Europe. Luigi Dallapiccola (1904–1975), a composer known for his lyrical twelve-tone compositions, was the primary proponent of serialism in Italy; among his best-known compositions is a trilogy surrounding concepts of imprisonment and justice. Goffredo Petrassi (1904–2003), a classical composer, conductor, and teacher, is considered one of the most influential Italian composers of the twentieth century, who turned from a Wagnerian-style Italian revival to post-

In short, I was intensely engaged. I was visited by the psychoanalyst Perrotti, of the Freudian school. He told me that all things considered, I was well, and could go to Venice to participate in the first conference on the partisans.

Poetry didn't interest you very much at that time?

Music dominated. I studied languages, philosophy, literature, and mathematics as well on my own. The private composition lessons then fed into studies of music theory (ethnomusicology). Years afterward, I published the first essays in *Diapason* (1952–1953) and *Civiltà delle macchine* (1954), with the help of Leonardo Sinisgalli.[7] *Il verri*, through Luciano Anceschi, will publish the entire work, which cost me fourteen years of research in Italian, French, and English libraries.[8] In Darmstadt, near Frankfurt, I had also enriched my studies of composition, in the summer courses (1959–1960). I also studied electronic music at RAI, though departing from the Bartók tradition, and studying, for example, nontempered musics of the Third World and the East at the Musée de l'Homme in Paris.[9] I offered an explanation of the underpinning intuitable and analyzable "system" followed instinctively by musicians who were not influenced by the Leibnizian rationalism of the seventeenth and eighteenth centuries.

Did you have friends among Italian artists?

Naturally. Apart from Guido Turchi, Roman Vlad, and Dallapiccola; among the painters, Afro and Guttoso.[10] Rocco Scotellaro introduced me to Carlo Levi.

Webernism and experimented with a range of poetic materials from Latin hymns through Cervantes.

7. Sinisgalli (1908–1981) was an Italian poet and art critic, a close friend of Ungaretti and Scipione, who founded the journal *Civiltà delle macchine* (1953–1959).

8. Luciano Anceschi (1911–1995) was an Italian literary critic and essayist who founded the important experimental literary magazine *Il verri* in 1956; he also directed the Paravia series *La tradizione del nuovo* and the journal *Studi di estetica* from 1976 forward.

9. RAI (Radiotelevisione italiana, or Italian Broadcasting Company) hosted the Studio of Musical Phonology, a pioneering electronic music studio in Milan designed in 1955 by Luciano Berio and Bruno Maderna.

10. Roman Vlad (1919–), an eclectic Italian composer, pianist, and musicologist born in Romania, whose books include a history of twelve-tone music and biographies of Stravinsky and Luigi Dallapiccola. Afro Basaldella (1912–1976) was an important abstract painter and member of the Roman School; Renato Guttuso (1911–1987) was a Sicilian painter and politician in the Communist Party.

If I may, let's pause a minute on your relationship with Scotellaro.

I met him at that conference on the partisans to which I alluded before. I was sitting in the last rows of the hall, and at a certain moment a very friendly young man came up to me. When he learned that I was the daughter of Carlo Rosselli, he was surprised and interested, and became more and more attentive to me. We became friends, but real friends like a brother and sister. In *Diario ottuso,* a prose work I published recently in the magazine *Braci,* I speak of our meeting, evoking various moments of my youth. When I met Rocco I was twenty and he died three years later. Ours was an intense friendship, very rich and natural, not forced in the least. He invited me to his town in Lucania (Tricarico), where I was his guest for a week, and got to know his mother.[11] He had already withstood that unjust condemnation (any pretext at all to discourage him from becoming the socialist mayor).[12] He left the Socialist Party and found a post at Portici, at the Institute of Agrarian Economy [Agraria della Casa] for the South. When Rocco came through Rome, he always called me; in short he was my best friend: these are the things that happen in one's youth and are never repeated. He was a very mature man and without my realizing it, he formed me. I don't exaggerate in saying that he was an exceptional being. I had begun to write in just that period. And we spoke naturally of poetry as well. He was willing to converse about his problems, those expressed in the book *Farmworkers of the South.* And Carlo Levi, who had been a great friend of my father, was frequently with him.

What idea did you have of Scotellaro's poetry?

He rarely showed me what he was writing, but he also dedicated one or two poems to me. However, I was interested in what he was working on, *Farmworkers of the South,* a book of prose that certainly influenced me a great deal. I also got to know the poems better after his death; I read them recently. They seem rather weak to me; he had more strength in prose. After Scotellaro's friendship, I can't neglect to recall the solicitude

11. Lucania was an impoverished region in the South described by Carlo Levi in the 1945 book *Cristo si è fermato a Eboli* (*Christ Stopped at Eboli*).

12. At age twenty-three Scotellaro (1923–1953, an important poet and activist for Southern Italian agricultural laborers) became his town's mayor, and was imprisoned in 1950 for abusing his power as a public official (a sentence believed to have been issued for his socialist activities). He resigned as mayor after being acquitted and went on to study the conditions of the agrarian South in work that culminated in *Contadini del Sud* (*Farmworkers of the South,* 1954).

of Niccolò Gallo, his involvement, his interest in my being able to publish *Bellicose Variations* with Mondadori.[13] The book could have been printed, but I was asked to make a financial contribution, and I refused on principle. I couldn't permit myself to be a dilettante.

The fact of not being able to publish Bellicose Variations *didn't have consequences for you?*

I didn't care about it at all. I sent the manuscript to four editors without any biographical note, not knowing anyone. I must say that, having had many encounters with Bobi Bazlen, he—skeptical toward the "search for glory"—didn't push me at all to come forward.[14] In the end, to study, I was able to count on my work as a translator. I worked for various editors, I did a bit of consultation with Bompiani as well; I was at a school for interpreters, still continuing my musical studies.[15] But I always returned to literature, because I couldn't avoid it. Then, when I had published some of the poems from *Bellicose Variations* in *Menabò* with Vittorini, with the enthusiastic presentation of Pasolini I found work as a publicist in various journals, most of them leftist. I wrote some semi-political articles, I would say rather of a sociological nature, and apart from poetry, I published various other prose writings and some pieces of criticism.

So let's come to your poetry. What did you want to do?

What did I want to do writing poems? Why did I want to write them? One rarely knows that the writer, and above all the poet, has very precise aims in writing in one way rather than in another—and that this chosen style, being apparently only self-expression, or all "natural," is the fruit of long reasoning, of research: of ideals brooded over at times for years, which are at times ultimately realized through "inspiration" and unexpected illumination or synthesis, but also because the author had very clearly, consciously and unconsciously, preestablished the intention, the aim.

13. Gallo (1917–1971) was an important editor, translator, literary critic, and director of several series at Mondadori.

14. Roberto ("Bobi") Bazlen (1902–1965) was an important Jewish intellectual from the eclectic "MittelEuropean" culture of Trieste; he helped found the Adelphi publishing house, translated Freud's *Interpretation of Dreams* into Italian (1952), and promoted Jungian psychoanalysis in Italy, as well as the work of Kafka and Musil. He was one of Rosselli's first readers and sources of encouragement. Bazlen refused to publish his own work during his lifetime, but his writings were collected posthumously.

15. Rosselli refers to the Milanese publishing house Bompiani.

And prosody?

There are poems in so-called free verse, tending however toward closed verse, with which I occupied myself in the second part, titled *Variations.* The *Variations,* from 1960–1961, have a closed metrical system, whose birth I described in the afterword at the back of the book, an essay titled "Metrical Spaces," which is from '62. The *Poems '59* could be considered a poetic scheme: for some of them it was enough for me to play a prelude of Bach or Chopin to reinterpret it, almost immediately afterward, in poetic form. Other poems seem to remain only a scheme, nearly definitive. They also allude to a closed verse, a form used in 1958 in earlier manuscripts (*The Libellula*), rendered more dynamic in *Variations* and as if I had achieved the cube-form, not only energetically. In the first as in (especially) the second part, the poems follow one another in chronological order, in any case; they have a narrative tone, especially in the second section. The book closes upon the linguistic-formal clarification of the last pieces, as if the dangerously new and at times political thematic necessitated transparency. The implicit inspiration for the *Variations* is Kafka, and the intention is at times prosaic.

Let's pause for a moment on the theme.

I wanted to express the birth and death of a passionality that was from the first bridled and contorted, and then led into battle and denunciation; it is only toward the last pages that the book is placated and the poems become less violent, more transparent. There is also a religious problematic in the central section that, at the moment of disillusionment, leads into the freedom of passion.

And The Libellula, *now republished, that goes back to 1958? The subtitle is* Panegyric to Liberty . . .

Today I realize that the subtitle of this long poem doesn't possess the irony that I meant for it to possess. I believe however that the text is clear in this sense: I point out that some ten times there are allusions and lines from Rimbaud, Montale, Scipione, and above all Campana; that in its unfolding in perhaps baroque form, it does not make use of the lapsus, or slip. In *Bellicose Variations* there were simple bilingual (or even trilingual) inventions. Pasolini spoke first of the "lapsus," as you know. But, in my opinion, the lapsus would be a mnemonic forgetting, whereas linguistic invention is usually conscious. I must also add that I had been ruminating on a poem of that kind for five years, and for around ten years I had been racking my brains in testing out various possible metrical formulations, never rigorous enough from my point of view as to be able to be considered "systems" that were not only metrical but also, or almost, philosophical-scientific and historically "necessary," inevitable. As soon as I intuited this "system," suddenly, the flood of words flowed into song that was very natural to me, and which synthesized years of laborious and nonlaborious experiences.

Let's talk about the books that followed.

The second part of *Hospital Series,* written some years later, is very different—to be contrasted with the first part, composed of that long, fluid song that can never again be repeated. Eighty poems, of a cautious and, I believe, extremely interior tone. A grave illness that didn't seem definitively curable at the time exhausted me (it was Parkinson's, diagnosed rather late, at around age 39). Such an illness would never have allowed me to work as an organist, a post offered to me by a teacher. I could read or write, and naturally, study, only at the cost of grave efforts. What's more, to resist weakness and survive in some way creatively, I had to isolate myself and conduct a life that was systematically private, interiorized, lacking in contacts. The poems reflect this melancholic privation of life, but I believe, and hope, also a greater linguistic rigor, and a recognition with greater humility of the many cultural debts (not only toward the usual Rimbaud, Kafka, Campana, Montale), in the face of writers considered either "minor" or surpassed (Saba, the hermetics, Mallarmé, Verlaine, Rilke, et al.). The series of poems is of the order of the "hospital" insofar as it is also resigned to a critical retracing of one's own steps, insofar as it is no longer bellicose in the face of rarer or more rarefied sentiments and intuitions.

Is the landscape set into relief in this critical return of yours?

Certainly. The rediscovery of a nature (the forests and rocks of upper Abruzzo) that was, if not benign, at least protective, counted for a great deal: the recognition at the last instant that that mad dreaming with eyes open, very much the dreaming of youth, could in some way be revivified.

Which language, among those adopted, do you prefer?

In my youth, as you know, I wrote in French at times, and very often in English: that self-expression was still postromantic or methodically hallucinated even if in some way systematic, meticulous. *Document* for me meant a search—even if based as ever upon the metrical formulation defined in '58—for the courage and perhaps also the mysticism of those adolescent years: rationalizing them to their final consequences. The results are often violent, the contents are outright screams; but I believe that there is no longer desperation, and that the aim of the book (a balance between wholly controlled and willed form, and content which was never inducted and deducted automatically, through the unconscious, or for merely literary provocation) is achieved in the whole.

Did you discard poems you weren't very certain about from your books?

Naturally. Especially the ones lacking the authenticity of inspiration or impulse. For me books are in a certain sense extreme, synthetic facts.

Your relationship with Pasolini became a friendship as well, beyond literature.

I did not see him very often. He was always a bit timid, very reserved. When I would see him, we would speak at length, however. After seeing *Accattone* I was very impressed with his talent, or genius. At first, I must say, I had not even read his poetry; and furthermore he had a didactic vocation, and hearing me speak of metrical problems inherent to my work, he suggested that I write that brief essay of which I spoke, placed at the end of *Bellicose Variations.* He succeeded in inspiring a "better prose," so to speak, and I was so worried that I didn't know how to do it well that when I returned home my commitment was greater than what I would have achieved on my own. I brought him the second book as well because I wanted his opinion. For this reason I was derided by some, because at that point the Gruppo 63 had been formed, and this absurd war was going on.

How were you co-opted by the Group itself?

They invited me to participate in their meetings—I believe through Falzoni, a surrealist painter and poet. But I was worried about not entering into official or informal polemics. I was interested in them, but I also thought it through. In fact I made a light joke of it in certain allusive poems of my volume *First Writings.* The only poet with whom I felt close, and who influenced me, was Antonio Porta. I liked his first books; his elegant abstraction made me curious.

Which authors do you feel more influenced by?

In reality, by many. Among the Italians I read Dante and Michelangelo, a good deal of Leopardi. I read even the juvenilia or minor works of Dante attentively. Among the moderns, beyond the French writers I have cited and Kafka, I must mention above all Campana and Montale, Pavese and Penna. Pavese exercised an influence over me, in the sense of calling my attention to the rupture with hermetic experience. A strong influence.

How was your love for Scipione born?[16]

By pure chance. I found the edition of his writings edited by Falqui in '43 at a bookstand. And those ten poems are unforgettable. Recently I reread them in public. Even his *Diary* possesses a particular intelligence, and a great stylistic elegance. When he can no longer paint, he seeks to transmit the image through writing. Another poet whom I cannot leave out is Lorenzo Calogero, about whom no one, apart from specialists and poets, knows how to speak at all.[17]

When you settled in Rome definitively, did you begin systematic psychoanalytic therapy?

On Bazlen's suggestion, I went to Ernst Bernhard, who practiced Jungian psychotherapy in Rome. A German Jew, he had an exceptional calm in his relations with patients, relations, it must be said, not legalized by ordinary psychiatry. He succeeded in making me remember the childhood that I had forgotten, after the immediate shock of my mother's death. It must be added that he was hostile to my registration in the Communist Party. He prohibited it; he had fits of fear for me, being affectionate by character. Much later, after I dissented, I consulted with the Freudian school, with Bellanova among others.[18] Bellanova provided for an analysis

16. Scipione (1904–1933), poet and painter of the Roman School. Rosselli wrote the preface to his *Carte segrete* (Turin: Einaudi, 1982).

17. Calogero (1910–1961), a Calabrian doctor and symbolist/hermetic poet, who committed suicide in his home in Melicuccà.

18. Piero Bellanova (1917–1987), the personal physician of F. T. Marinetti, and one of the founders and leaders of the psychoanalytic movement in Italy; he was interested in creativity and had many clients who were artists, such as Federico Fellini.

of "support" for some months. In the end his diagnosis was: "You have only a slight neurosis."

Let's return to poetry. After Document *there were the* First Writings.

I published that volume, dated 1952–1963, with the idea of clarifying the trilingual formation of my youth, which from age 22 through 1963, through prose and poetic exercises, attempted to achieve certainty in stylistic and linguistic innovation. Even here the "pieces" have intentional dates, and so they recall the slow decision to use one language or another, and decisions about inspiration, as opposed to the prose pieces and poems in French and English that were Baudelairean-Rimbaudian or Joycean reechoings. I would say that *Le chinois à Rome* is a point of refusal of the exercise, however, even if Montalian and Joycean in its virtuosity, and also an aesthetic, as in fact one of its parts explains with the subtitle *Esthétique jeune.* The work is from 1955 to 1956. The book closes with a series of poems dedicated to the members of Gruppo 63, *collage* or true poems as they are, always wholly ironic and, indeed, critical. The chapbook *Impromptu,* a long poem written in December of '79—and here we are nearing the current moment—is born of my yearning, from the end of the draft of *Document* forward, for a lightening of my writing almost of a Pascolian type. Unfortunately I had to halt all creative writing nearly entirely from '73 through '79, and then again through today. You know the reasons why. I am awakened too early. And so my day begins, normally. I don't sleep enough. I usually need eight hours normally; and instead I sleep an average of five hours, at most six. I wake up at six, at seven. With the troubles I had earlier from the CIA and now, it seems also, from the Cosa Nostra (or people thrown out of the CIA), I do not manage to live as I would like.[19] I hope that one day these "troubles" will terminate. And so I am obliged to practical activities, because I can only read journal articles here and there. It has happened that I have read a book—they did everything to keep me from reading—lately it has been impossible to go on for longer than fifteen minutes. My day starts out with the house. I clean it and I try to defend myself from each attack so as not to fall into misery. And so the "readings" that bring me outside of Rome are welcome, even if they cost me physical fatigue. It isn't that I don't like it; one doesn't like to read oneself. It is interesting to read something that one has just written to test out the results on others. To read things that do

19. The "Cosa Nostra" is a common term for the Mafia.

264

not currently represent me ends up as *routine,* but one must have patience. I have done everything to defend myself from attacks; I compiled a dossier for the government and then for the UN: there are too many things that I would not even like to know. And I know horrendous things. What I try to do is preserve my good humor and friends, so as not to go crazy. This condition has lasted for almost twenty years. As soon as it ceases, I am certain to return to normal life, and my relationships will be simplified.

You published Notes Scattered and Lost *as well, put together from the years 1966–1977 . . .*

Many of the 86 poems included simply did not find a space in *Document,* and they were thus retained and published afterward in magazines. A few required revision, cuts, extrapolations. The notes were on the other hand written very quickly, by hand, or else they were in and of themselves what remained of a poem thrown away. There's perhaps a depressive tonality to be noted in the collection.

Has your opinion of intellectual Italian society changed with respect to that of yesterday?

Around age thirty I decided not to frequent artistic and literary circles very much, in fact not at all. I had, as I have said, certain socialist principles that were quite precise. I needed to get to know Italy better, and the literary salons didn't serve me so much in this. But there is no doubt that the society of today has changed. I have problems quite different from those that are discussed in the salons or among the young people; and, yes, it pleases me that young writers come to me, that they send me their books; it helps me stay in contact with the reality of others; but it always ends up that at a certain point one loses patience, not with friends but reflecting upon my personal situation, and I begin to recount it. And that's what I would rather not do; therefore I avoid people somewhat, except if they are very strong, and know how to joke and appease me. It is not that I do not have a circle around me, but I find it difficult to describe it objectively for the reasons I have discussed.

I was referring as well to the difference between a past and a present subject to the abuses of commercialization, of obsessive advertisement.

I find the imposed mass media a bit ridiculous; I try not to let it make a fool of me. Beyond this situation, I see a constant enlargement of culture, it is expanding; the gross bourgeoisie no longer commands culturally, at least not as much as before; and there are people who are interested in good books. I am not displeased by the attempt to popularize that has gotten underway; this is the positive side of mass media. I do not believe that one can go back, in any case. Fashion or foreign impositions will change, because Italy sucks up fashion. But we cannot return to a cultural world that is only for the use and consumption of the elite.

And what do you think of current interests around poetry?

Even some pop songs are better than those of yesterday. I also observe a spontaneous adhesion to poetry today, in the sense that, beyond editorial publishing, one can count on the attention of some people. I have usually lived in the historic center, and I am able to note something happening. I see, for example, artisans and bartenders who read poems, who are interested in our questions. You can have some interesting conversations with them.

Hasn't your falling by parachute to find yourself in a country that was utterly new to you, like Italy, been a way of reconquering your father?

In fact, it was from the beginning an unconscious labor. Then, in the libraries, I read in order to reconstruct the figure of my father, almost totally forgotten by me. The first eight months of my first analysis session helped me to reconstruct my childhood and remember my father. Even my adolescence, because my mother's death had crushed me.

So, has your poetry then served you in this way as well?

Perhaps.

266

From the Correspondence

To John Rosselli

12 Febr.
1951

DEAR JOHN,

HERE SPRING IS BURSTING OUT ALL OVER THE PLACE,
AND ALTHOUGH I'VE REALLY NOTHING NEW TO WRITE TO
YOU ABOUT, HERE'S A BIT OF WRITING ABOUT NOTHING.
YOU WHO ARE IS [*sic*] SO GOOD ABOUT DOING FAVOURS FOR
PEOPLE: I AM IN NEED OF THIS: CAMPBELL'S COMMENTARY
TO FINNEGAN'S WAKE, AND IF YOU GO TO PARIS, THE FRENCH
EDITION OF ULISSE, WITH THE FRENCH COMMENTARY, FOR
A FRIEND WHO CANNOT READ ENGLISH WELL-ENOUGH.
IS IT VERY TROUBLESOME? MONEY WOULD SOMEHOW BE
REFUNDED.

NEWS AS TO MY COURTSHIP: I HAVE WELL DONE TO
COURT. NEWS AS TO WORK: DILUTED FOR THE TIME BEING.
NEWS AS TO FINANCIAL SITUATION: DISASTROUS, BUT UNCLE
R. WRITES THAT IF I "COOPERATE" 60,00 [*sic*] POUNDS SHOULD
BE ARRIVING. THANK GOD. TID BITS: MUCH HEAVY READING,
MOSTLY FROM THE EINAUDI COLLECTIONS. IMPROVED
PIANO TECHNICHE. DO YOU THINK YOU'LL BE COMING TO
EINAUDI (FATHER)'S COMMEMORATION IN MARCH, OF BABBO
E ZIO NELLO? NONNA WRITES THAT SHE EXPEXTS YOU. WE'D
BE SEEING EACH OTHER THEN. PERHAPS THIS WILL BE THE
LAST OF THEM. [*Written in blue pencil:* I mean the commemorations]

AWFUL THE NEWS YOU GIVE ME OF HAVING TO DO
ANOTHER MILITARY COURSE. I CAN WELL UNDERSTAND
YOUR BEING SHAKEN BY ALL'S QUIET ON THE WESTERN
FRONT: [*Handwritten:* I] READ THE BOOK WHILE IN AMERICA,
BLESSED THE SKIES, FOR BEING A WOMAN—AT LEAST. HERE
IN IRRATIONAL ITALY THAT SEX HAS NOT BEEN RATIONED!
IN FACT AFTER FORTHCOMING 21ST BIRTHDAY, THINK I'LL BE
TAKING ON DOUBLE NATIONALITY—THAT IS AFTER HAVING
MADE NEW PASSPORT, [*Crossed out and handwritten:* ~~WHICH~~ the
last] WAS STOLEN IN THE HOTEL AT VENICE [*Crossed out and*

Both letters to John Rosselli were origi-
nally written in English. They have not
been published in their entirety before, and
are transcribed here as they appear in the
sizeable folders of correspondence between
the siblings at the Fondo Rosselli, housed
at the Archive of Modern and Contempo-
rary Authors at the University of Pavia. My
thanks go to the director, Professor Maria
Antonietta Grignani, for her kind permis-
sion to print them.

handwritten: ~~LAST~~ this] SUMMER. NOT A WORD OF THIS TO NONNA—I'LL MANAGE WITH THE CONSULATE BY MY SELF.

[*Written*] Ti abbraccio
Melina

To John Rosselli

9 November 1952

Dear John,

Really i <u>must</u> let off steam with you as to our dear Uncle Roger: pest of a man!!!! If only to grab that ~~income~~ [*replaced with* capital] out of his hands i shall marry prestissimo. I'd like to twirk his nose, crib his knees, reduce him to a/cauliflower, nothing more—let him watch out: good thing i'm not in contact by letter with him: might pulverize him— . . . . .

Let him find a daughter someplace else, of a more regimental character than I. Send him my love, though.

Madame Magda, with her Chinese cards, had warned me money affairs would be settling down as you yourself explained. If U. R. wants to know how i spend money, tell him, please, most blandly, that I've spent 5000 lire already, going five times to see/this most precious lady: he'll have a fit.

Seriously—I assure you you need have no qualms as to my "blowing" money, except for this detail. It's quite an expense putting up a whole wardrobe, beginning from literally nothing, as I had nothing but Mamma's clothing, which I have managed to sell only in small part. And though others may not know it, my health is filthy just now, what with the ending of this famosa nevrosi,—the headaches are recurrent, strong enough almost to make me faint: am in constant state of tension: having punture [*sic*] right into the head, top-middle part; this takes money, and so do the visits to dentists, which i had avoided the past four years, not being able to pay for them. Sounds all very dramatic: are you not just a <u>little</u> scosso? Pray be so, —not overly, a teensy bit: am really on the famosa via della guarigione: my room is now a palace, am almost all equipped for the BATTLE OF LIFE!!!!!!!!!!!!!!!!!!!!

This letter to John in London appears amid a series of letters written in a far more fluid and contemporary-sounding English idiom; I include it here because it shows how Rosselli wields language performatively, so as to take up personas, in her correspondence as well as in her verse.

Poor John, at the incrocio della vie, fra U.R. and I, both grabbing for his own. We are turning you into an office clerk, what with our letters, money affairs, demands, ecc., and Andrea too, I imagine. Is there some manner you could suggest in which I might take some of the weight off your hands? As to practical things, I mean.

Crossways are on hand for me too just now; though feeling a little better all around, than is usual, am most perplexed as to a good many questions: the political ritornello keeps popping into my mind—hereditary, I suppose: I am slowly but surely being attracted by Marxist ideals and non-socialist (socialism as defined by Carlo Rosselli, Labour Party, PSLI, ecc.) methods: your hair is sure, at this point, to raise on end: and so does mine, that's the fix. But now what with Stevenson licked, Bevan [*Written:* and Attlie] unconvincing and caged in, Pinay throning, italian socialists floundering, i am beginning to think they'd attempted something too partial: the "base" has turned against them: you yourself in your acceptation of English life and tradition are justified, perfectly so, in accepting such a draw-back to democratic, gradual revolution,—I myself am not, for reasons which are none too clear as yet: must get to know italy and italian political life a little better; economics and politics in general a little better, too.

Digging hard into the piano: got hold of a grand piano at an English friend's house: playing early clavicembalo music, and Bach. The [*Handwritten:* Ancona] instrument I have not as yet seen, not a crumb of it: wrote to have the whole thing speeded up: got an offer to experiment the new system of notation which I had worked out while in Paris; 150 folk songs from Lucania, recorded, but not transcribed, as finally, to my surprise, I must say, other musicians seem to realize it is rovinoso for the understanding of popular music to transcribe it with normal notation and on the basis of classical musical systems and scales. It's too risky for me to do the thing till the instrument is fra le mani: however if the transcription will eventually come to be done, it will serve excellently as exercise, practice, study; Madame Magda says I shall be very very rich through this instrument and new system!

Bored?

Please tell me all about your taking of the degree at Cambridge, and your writing; also some news of Andrea, if you've got time.

    all fagged out

                        love,
              [*Written*] Melina

To Pier Paolo Pasolini

(505169)

Dear PierPaolo,

Imagining that you were quite busy and unreachable by telephone, I thought I would do well to send you the essay on meter that you had proposed I write as an addition to the book of poems probably to be published in September.

It's a bit long; but I find it impossible to abbreviate it without rendering it incomprehensible. If it should be added to the book I would give it the title "Metrical Spaces"; if instead it isn't possible to publish it as a whole (at the end of the book, by way of an appendix, I think, and not together with the preface), or if it were to be published separately in a journal, or if you would simply like to extract some phrase or paragraph to refer to in the preface, I would instead call it "Transpositions."

You will see that it's a bit technical, and at the same time a bit fantastic, a bit mad. It could be that it isn't at all appropriate to add explanations to a book of verse, whose inspiration could very well remain secret in the end, as is the case anyhow in nearly all publications. But if someone should think that the explication of formal and metrical concepts would be useful, or that the poems included in the collection "Variations 123" require clarification of that sort—it's the best that I can do.

As for the title of the book itself:—

I would like for every group of poems to have the original title, that is: "Poems 33," "Variations 123," and "Fragments 44." For the title of the whole book I would suggest the following for now:

BLUE

INCORONATIONS

THE MIRRORS

CONFINES

IMPROBABILITIES

MECROPOLIS

in order of preference. The title "Blue" doesn't displease me at all, and it's certainly the least literary, even if perhaps too eccentric. "Incoronations" is nice, but suggests something vaguely mystical, which I would like to avoid at least in the title. "The Mirrors" is a little bit banal, "Confines" not very original. "Improbabilities" too reasoned, intellectual; and moreover I intend it as a plural, not in its singular form.[1] "Mecropolis" is a mixed form, that is, a fusion, of Necropolis and Metropolis; but as a whole it seems forced to me, even if expressive. I am not really happy with any of these titles; if others come to my mind, so much the better. Then from the commercial point of view they could be unsuitable; I am not a good judge of that, truly. I would however like to avoid the typical literary title, for example "The Widowed World," "Ancient Seraphim," "Rattles," "An Anonymous Illness," etc., etc.

This should be all: you wanted me to speak with Pietro Citati after he had read the poems (and the essay, I suppose). Your mother told me over the phone that you are always out due to the films, and so I imagine that it's better for me to wait for you to call? If not I could come look for you where you go, during breaks, but I am afraid of taking you away from work. So perhaps I will wait for a sign from you.

Thanks again.

Another thing: I believe that I gave you not 123 "Variations" but some other number of those. The same for "Poems 33" and "Fragments 44." Certainly it would be better to try including exactly those original numbers; I have the discarded poems at home, perhaps among those there are a few that are good enough to include in order to obtain that exact numbering.

ciao and cheers and best wishes,

Amelia
(Amelia Rosselli)

P.S. Perhaps instead of "Poems 33" and "Variations 123" etc. placing simply "Poems," "Variations" and "Fragments" as the titles of the various sections?

If it were possible to speak with Citati in not too long I would also mention to him the idea of a series of texts on music, or else of anthologies of essays on folk, contemporary, or other music. Around the eleventh of May I must go to Milan and Turin for twenty days, and so I would also meet those in charge of publishing houses, to explain the proposal in detail. It would be better if I could speak about it with someone from Garzanti before leaving.

For "The Libellula":—if it should be of interest for an eventual publication I would like to mention again that that book is entirely to be redone, that is, I think that the parts that I have signaled out in pencil

---

1. In Italian, without the article, it is impossible to tell whether *Improbabilità* is singular or plural, and Rosselli notes that this is undesirable.

in the margins of the text ought to be cut, and for that reason entire paragraphs to be reformulated as well. So, if it should be of interest, it would be a good idea for me to take up the work again in order to revise it: I don't have another copy with the correction marks. But if the work doesn't interest at all I would need it again for revision in any case.

To Pier Paolo Pasolini

21 June 1962

LungoTevere Sanzio 5

Roma

Dear Pasolini:

two words to ask for your advice about various matters, and so:

I sent Silvio Bernardini (of "Garzanti"), who had asked for it, a proposal for the publication of texts concerning modern music. I suggested an anthology of writings that had appeared in foreign and Italian magazines over these last twenty years; I also drafted a list of the books that were in my opinion marketable and urgent both for the public and for musicians themselves, which concern contemporary music, in its popularizing-technical or historical aspects. The proposal is a good six pages long: I wanted to explain my reasons in depth, and to give very detailed information about the texts and articles.

Bernardini liked the proposal very much, and would support it; unfortunately Citati is not of the same opinion, it seems, and would prefer, like Garzanti itself, that books such as "How to Pay Less in Taxes" be purveyed instead. That is it seems that Garzanti is worried, and has asked for greater marketability. Bernardini advises me to ask you to recommend the proposal to Citati, if it interests you, and finds that the idea of an anthology in particular is practical and marketable. I do not know Citati, nor have I had occasion to meet him: my idea seemed to interest you, and perhaps it wouldn't be disagreeable to speak about it with Citati, if it is to him that one must recur. In fact it isn't that Citati has rejected the proposal entirely; it is now with Silvio Bernardini at Garzanti (670267): if you have time to read it it's better, in any case I hope that you can do something! In my view the proposal regarding the publication of actual volumes is the more serious one: the anthology could however serve to take the pulse of the public: but in reality the texts in their entirety are of broader interest, more useful and essential:

the articles require a public that is already cultivated, and more literary than musical. Musicians would be interested (without a doubt) in the complete texts rather than the articles, which they already know in part. I will phone you in a few days if you would like, asking for your opinion: I wanted to write to explain myself better.

As for my poems. I imagine that by now Vittorini has written to you; in any case I know that he intends to do so. Looking over the discarded poems from "Variations 123" and "Poems 33" again (which he intends to use for the selection in *Menabò*) I noted that some are good, and perhaps publishable along with the rest of the book. In all it's a matter of some fifty poems; I sent them to Vittorini for his final selection. Would you like me to deliver them to you, or for me to send or hand them over to Bertolucci when it's time to eliminate some of them? In effect the selections that I made were not the same that you, Vittorini or others did: so I wouldn't know very precisely how to judge as to the opportunity to exclude these poems as well: then I like the number 123 for "Variations 123" and I'd like to keep it; in the package that I sent you there were other ones, it's true: but choosing attentively it would be possible to reduce the total number (151) (discards included) to 123, preferably. In the text "Poems 33" fewer were included: with the discarded ones they come to be 33 exactly. The same goes for "Fragments 44."

Vittorini seemed so embarrassed by my linguistic "ductility" or anarchy ("fused," invented or deformed, or archaizing words) that as you know he asked me to correct the "jarring notes" [*stonature*] as much as possible.[1] I wrote to him communicating my decision (and your advice) not to change that language—which was spoken, and at times resonating as low or deformed—at all (only here and there, where it was a matter of a typing error). Marco Forti, who works at Mondadori, and with whom I attempted some corrections upon Vittorini's suggestion in Milan, then recommended that I formulate a glossary of the words that weren't "pure" or "correct," explaining their formation. I did this for "Poems 33" and "Variations 123" (including the discarded ones); and I sent the glossaries to Vittorini, for clarification.

Personally I would prefer that this glossary, done "on the surface," a bit carelessly, not be included in the completed book and that it be asystematic, since the jarring notes [*stonature*] were as well. But in rethinking I believe that I ought to expect, upon publication, quite a number of criticisms and quite a number of uncertainties or

1. The word used to describe the jarring linguistic features of Rosselli's text is "stonature," a musical term for notes out of tune.

incomprehensions as far as linguistic fact is concerned: perhaps these glossaries should be included anyway? What do you recommend? It's true that the essay "Metrical Spaces" is placed there entirely and only in the formal and abstract sense: but I would have thought that the language in its violence should remain quite obvious in its intentions, and that the way those fusions and improprieties and concoctions were formed would be crystal clear. And it would be if you mention it in the preface: so perhaps there is no need to publish glossaries (which would lead away from an immediate and empirical comprehension). I am sending you however [?] the glossaries: without the texts at hand they will tell you little; but at the right moment they could be of use to you. Then if you would like to advise me on this question as well, I would be grateful.

I believe that's it; so I'll telephone to ask you 1) about the proposal for Garzanti (music) 2) if you want to see the eliminated pieces (maybe later) 3) if you think it would be better to publish the glossaries and if it's appropriate to speak about it with Bertolucci.

All my best wishes for your film that I hope will be as beautiful as the first, which I found stupendous.[2]

Ciao

Amelia Rosselli

P.S. In case it is desirable to publish glossaries, I would like to redo these, obviously: since they are drafted in a personal and loose way.

2. Rosselli had seen *Accattone* and notes in later interviews that she was astonished by Pasolini's ability to link soundtrack with imagery. See P. Perilli, "L'ultima intervista," in *Poesia* 93 (March 1996): 13.

On Amelia Rosselli

A Note on Amelia Rosselli, by Pier Paolo Pasolini

One of the most clamorous cases of Amelia Rosselli's linguistic connectives is the lapsus, or slip. At times feigned, at times true: but when it is feigned, it is probably so in the sense that, having been formed spontaneously, it is immediately accepted, adopted, fixed by the author under the aesthetic species of an "invention that makes itself." It is thus inserted into the series of studs that this language—born as if outside the mind, almost the physical projection of a rationally inexpressible spiritual sheath—needs to constellate in order to present itself as a recognizable, legible cultural product.

In reality this language—I repeat—is dominated by something mechanical: an emulsion that takes form on its own, nonmastered,[1] as one imagines coming about through the most terrible laboratory experiments, tumors, atomic blasts, dominated only scientifically, yet not in the symptoms of their terribleness, in their by now objective happening. So that the magma—the terribleness—is fixed in strophic forms as closed and absolute as they are arbitrary.

The slip—strange to say—is in the end the only thing that renders this language historically, or at least currently, determined. It is the only fact that is in some way shared—upon reasonable analysis—with the great texts that it presupposes (it must be noted that Rosselli read these texts in their original languages, in school and at home, as a matter of course). Feigned slips are characteristic of the language of linguist poets[2] (a category to which Rosselli is not reducible, however) and they are also one of the most common elements of surrealistic poetry (but Rosselli is not related to that). I mean that Rosselli certainly knows she is conducting linguistic experiments out in the open, in a public laboratory—and that, in fact, the public character of those experiments is a formal fact of her poetry. Rosselli certainly knows, furthermore, that there are analogies between her nexes and those of the surrealists, of itinerant mystics—alliterant, etymological, anaphoric, artificers of *reminders*.[3] And she knows

1. Here Pasolini invents the term *imposseduta* (literally "nonpossessed" or "nonmastered") to describe Rosselli's linguistic emulsions.

2. Pasolini uses this term, presumably, to refer to contemporary poets who experiment with language such as the Novissimi, of whom both he and Rosselli were critical. Pasolini refers to their "inane and a prioriistic search for novelties to try out." See Pasolini, "Libertà stilistica," reprinted in *Saggi sulla letteratura e sull'arte* (Milan: Mondadori, 1999), 1237.

3. I italicize this word to mark that Pasolini uses the English term "reminder" in his text.

that she has some relationship to Pound, that Pound who in Milanese transcriptions is so literary and provincial.

In any case, I would say that more than being cultural (and they are), the slips of Rosselli are of an ideological type.

Through these studs—which ensure historicity, continuity, and stability to texts that are in reality spiritual murmurs I would call epileptic, ideographs in which a soul projects itself to the letter, and not without being literary—the world presents itself as typically liberal and irrational.

One could say that the poet's self-criticism—in a relationship similar to her relationship with the real—takes place almost solely through the slip: that is through the fabulation . . . a phocomelic fabulation . . . of its own institutional filiations, which thereby, due to social obligation and consecration, remain intact.

Rosselli, therefore, crushes her own language. Yet she does not do so with the violence of another rival language—"other" ideologically and historically—, but with the violence of that very same language alienated from itself through a process of disintegration (musical, the author would call it) that, in reality, she represents as abnormal, yes, but still identical to itself.

Slips, taking on the form of lexical and grammatical error, as is the case here, leave the word as is: they simply reveal it under a horrendous aspect of putrefied or ridiculous objectivity. Agony or death do not change the world.

All the "esprit"[4] of liberal society is in fact founded on the slip as linguistic deformation. The comedy of the period of literature created by capitalism, of the great bourgeoisie, is founded on a pure and simple deformation of the institution, which excludes every real possibility of reform or linguistic (and institutional) revolution. I would even say that a deformed word is more resistant to the corrosives of a revolutionary ideology than a normal word is. Deformity bears a more integral capacity for resistance if it creates an indomitable sphere of death and sacrality around itself. The whole liberal spirit lives on witticisms that deride institutions without eating into them, contented simply to inoculate them with the illness of mystery, in an unconscious reification. (I have at hand a book that has been successful in France, *La foire de cancres,* errors of jackass scholars: "Who are the prophets? The inhabitants of prophecy, a small, very industrious nation," "he killed his enemies in refineries of

4. I use the French term for Pasolini's "spirito" here because this translation for "spirit," unlike the English term, can allude both to wit and to the Hegelian sense of a spirit of the age.

cruelty." And I could cite as well all the witty sayings attributed mainly to a collective center of production, the world of jargon of the Via Veneto's lay elite.)

The slip offers a profound liberation: it allows one, at long last, to be liberated from the weight of institutions—which burden the whole length of the soul—and, at the same time, to respect them. There is no saying in the form of a slip that is so cynical, ferocious, ironic, contemptuous that does not comprise a fundamental respect for the language and institution in use. It is the typical negativity that affirms, if ever there was one. The basis of Rosselli's book—I have managed to say it in spite of its total rejection, its crazy coherence, which welds it from all directions like a frail fortress—is the great European liberal culture of the twentieth century. And it is so with a wholly exceptional splendor. I would say that I have never in these years come across a product of this sort, so potently amorphous, so objectively superb.

The Myth of Irrationality (let's capitalize it) has, with the poetry of Rosselli, in the 1960s, its best product: a luxuriant, floral oasis with the stupefying and random violence of the fait accompli,[5] at the margins of dominion. And the avant-garde revival—so tetric in the work of the eternal apprentices of Milan and Turin—has found in this sort of stateless person [apolide] from the great familial traditions of Cosmopolis, a terrain in which to explode with the fatal and marvelous fecundity of mushroom clouds in the act of their becoming forms, etc., etc. I will not go beyond the limits of the flyleaf. And I will add that the theme of the slip is small, secondary and trifling with respect to the great themes of Neurosis and Mystery that pervade the corpus of these poems: it is only a thread I have followed so as to devise some christening [effato] of this splendid text that proposes itself as ineffabling.[6]

(1963)

5. The term Pasolini uses is "dato di fatto," but I use the French term (common in British usage) as the English approximation, since "given" does not quite render the force of this phrase.

6. Here Pasolini's language plays on speakability, or "effability": the effato is a prayer said to consecrate a temple or place, from the Latin effatum, past participle of effor/ecfor (ex + for, to say, express, determine, fix); the essay's last word, ineffando, is the gerund for a verb, ineffare, related to the term "ineffable," which also echoes the "fabulation" of the argument above.

Amelia Rosselli: *Documento*, by Andrea Zanzotto

"I am not what I appear to be / and in the cattle / of a cattlish day chilled I call / on you all to recite." In these lines (from "Snow 1973") Amelia Rosselli presents, almost brutally, that which constitutes her distance and her presence today—while she summarizes in the most charged and nevertheless necessarily "incomplete," unspoken, way some of the reasons for her writing as ever. If one can call this merely "writing"; if poetry is, in general, merely writing. Amelia Rosselli was born inside this "writing," and cannot escape from it; and at the same time she is outside of it, and has always contested it. In each of her books, from *Variazioni belliche* to *Serie ospedaliera* to the current *Documento,* which brings together verse of hers from 1966 to 1973, she continues to charge the same terrain upon which the poetic act can constitute itself; she repels whoever comes near her toward a "before"—tough even in its charms—where what will coagulate swarms, always reluctant, as a fact of words; and, on the other hand, she calls one to recite with her, "in the chill."

One senses how inappropriate, not to say indecent, terms such as "enjoyment," and even "reading," are in the face of how much Rosselli gives to us. And then how improbable or inexistent are her effective relations with schools or groups. Rare are the analogies with the circumstances of other authors, and possible analogies serve only as preambles to the clearer individuation of constitutive differences (the most distant Celan and Calogero could in this sense be closest to her). There is no "will" toward experimentation here, because the very breathing-surviving of the person, of the burden of her from whom this speech comes, is an uninterrupted, harsh trial—is experimentation. And yet, in so much seizure of physical and corporeal darkness there is a maximum of conscience, so much more lucid, exhaustive, advancing, than it is capable of expressing itself in conciliatory spirals of justification.

In the past Amelia Rosselli consisted entirely in those clots of matter of hers in which ashes and incandescence coexisted, though always crossed by some strain toward the abstract. In these clots language cracked into distortions, slips [*lapsus*], "digressions" [*diverticoli*] of phonic gravitation and even in grammatical and orthographical errors, which were perfectly functional within a maximum of coagulation, producing quick edges and reliefs, clawed little monsters of light, chills by gusts: neologisms, solecisms, "barbarisms" upon leaden depths. All of this in a situation tranquilly blasphemous with regard to "communicativeness," and not only in that word's more careless accepted meaning.

Musicologist of a music (muse) particularly averse to accepting compromises with the semantic and grammatical constraints of a language, or rather, of language *itself,* seduced but also alarmed by the rampant fraying of signification, by the effects of dress that accompany true music, Amelia Rosselli had sought, even in confronting the dangerous fundamental nature of this, directions for ascertaining those zones where the authority of a different logos shows itself, presses in vain, or springs violently. The result had been a language of pure loss-necessity, involved in the admirable strabismus of those who look "well beyond": a language heeded as a direct emanation, or halo, of "something," and which hovered between so-called lunacy and so-called oracularity, an oracularity moreover repressed, stripped away immediately, forbidden in its possible presumptions.

In this more recent period Amelia Rosselli says: "I have / seen with my eyes my language / become low to the earth and decipherable: but no / it is so often that it moves—the earth— / with its unscathed wheels." In reality, even in changing she does not contradict herself, and assails the now better glimpsable lines of a personal history or of history itself with her "mysteries." Thus, the poetry's primary monologue facing the void, colloquy with a presumably inaccessible "you," and upsetting sortie on public terrain (in which everything, as a rule, appears to be known, while instead an emergency seethes which exceeds every plan or perspective) are brusquely related along a single axis. Connection to the "obscure" and an expression of faith in its power of estrangement and therefore of illumination do not give way, however. Even in components such as "General Strike 1969" or "I try one market / then I try another" or "Christ (Easter 1971)" the themes of an evident unequivocalness, brought to irregular intersections, grow and become real as they flee toward the most intense polysemy.

Revolt is relearned in the initial alpha, sealed unjustly as static; "sibylline" words, as always for those who have the right ear and faith in Delphi, literally explode in vital directions, mobilize to every praxis. Even if understanding them, which involves understanding one another, is a maximal risk, even if the part one is called to recite might continue to lack any ultimate meaning, and the speaker retreat into the double depths of an ultimate irony. But she will still have heaved afloat a reality—and a "good"—which must not be resisted: "Good the fir, even better the hanging / branch: kilos of fruit and flower weigh / upon it: and still you do not remember / that other name it has."

(1976, 1994)

Acknowledgments

This book would have been impossible to pull together without the guidance, debate, and good humor of a host of colleagues and friends over the course of the past decade. I would like to thank above all Barbara Spackman, who led me to Rosselli's poetry, and Anne Carson, without whose initial inspiration, example, and encouragement at the turn of the millennium this project would never have taken wing so curiously. I am immeasurably grateful to the teachers and comrades who have read from the manuscript in part or in its entirety and supported me through the daunting labor of getting Rosselli's Italian into English: Robert Hass, Joshua Clover, Carla Billitteri, Heather McHugh, Norma Cole, Michael Palmer, Lyn Hejinian, Giorgio Agamben, Paolo Valesio, Chris Chen, Leslie Scalapino, Susan Stewart, Simon Pettet, Pierre Joris, and Jerome Rothenberg. Andrea Raos, Marco Giovenale, Gherardo Bortolotti, Marinella Caputo, and Maurizio Vito have been phenomenally generous in discussing the finer points of Rosselli's choices and potential translation strategies with me. Andrea Cortellessa, Alessandro Baldacci, Florinda Fusco, Michele Zaffarano, and Valdo Spini provided precious materials, both bound and broadcast. Guglielmina Otter kindly shared her personal archive of photographs, including those she had taken of Amelia and her loft on the Via del Corallo. I would also like to thank Silvia Rosselli, David Rosselli, Maria Attanasio, Daniela Rampa, Marisa di Iorio, Simon Pettet, and Nelson Moe for sharing with me their memories of and correspondence with Amelia. It goes without saying that I am deeply indebted to the gamut of scholars and translators who have contributed to an understanding of this complex body of work, and that I am the sole person responsible for any errors or infelicities contained herein.

My grateful acknowledgment goes to Dr. Nicoletta Trotta for her initial permission to access the Rosselli archive when it was still in the process of being indexed, as well as to Dr. Jader Bosi for help navigating the mass of materials at the Centro di ricerca sulla tradizione manoscritta di autori moderni e contemporanei—Fondo Manoscritti at the Università degli Studi di Pavia. Special thanks go to the archive director, Professor Maria Antonietta Grignani, who provided kind permission to publish these materials. I am also grateful to Director Mariano Rapisarda and the staff at the Biblioteca della Facoltà di Lingue e Letterature Straniere Moderne, Università degli Studi della Tuscia, for their help in consulting the Fondo Amelia Rosselli. And I thank Andrea Zanzotto for permission to translate and print his short essay, "Amelia Rosselli: *Documento*," from *Le poesie e prose scelte* (Milan: Mondadori, 2000) (© Andrea Zanzotto, all rights reserved; handled by Agenzia Letteraria Internazionale, Milan, Italy); and the Estate of Pier Paolo Pasolini to translate and print "A Note on Amelia Rosselli" from *La libellula* (Milan: Studio Editoriale, 1996), as well as two letters that Rosselli wrote to Pasolini dated 19 April and 21 June 1962 (© The Estate of Pier Paolo Pasolini; all rights reserved).

Versions of translations from the manuscript have appeared in *Satellite* (Fall 2000); *The American Poetry Review* 31, no. 4 (Summer 2002); *Circumference* 1, no. 2 (Fall 2004); *Bombay Gin* 32 (2006); *The Brooklyn Rail* (September 2006); *Zoland Annual*, vol. 1 (Random House, 2007); *GAMMM* (2007); *Aufgabe* 7 (2008); *Washington Square* 24 (Summer–Fall 2009); and *The FSG Book of 20th-Century Italian Poetry* (2012). A bilingual chapbook including a critical introduction and eleven poems appeared as *In the Suburbs of Illusions: Selections from the Poetry of Amelia Rosselli* in *Mid-American Review* 24, no. 1 (Fall 2003). "Metrical Spaces" and accompanying poems will appear in *Chicago Review* 56:4. I am grateful to the editors for their support, and above all to Randy Petilos, Carol Saller, and the entire editorial staff at the University of Chicago Press for taking on this demanding project.

This project was supported by a Katherine E. Sherston Memorial Fellowship at the University of California, Berkeley, and sustained by the bequest of Josephine Miles to the Berkeley English Department for shelter to poets. The manuscript's completion and ongoing research on Rosselli were generously supported by the American Academy in Rome.

Thanks as ever to my beloved parents and to my grandfather, Angelo "Frank" Sirico (December 7, 1904–July 17, 2000).

Notes to Poems in Translation

These notes provide springboards for interpretation of Rosselli's Italian poems and insight into finer points of the translation process. They are not—nor could they hope to be—exhaustive. At the time of writing, no annotated scholarly edition of Rosselli's poetry exists in Italian. Such an edition, prepared by a team of scholars and culling the results of collective work with a considerable amount of archival material that remains unpublished, is in the final stages of completion for Mondadori, and is eagerly awaited. We must remain mindful nevertheless that Rosselli herself resisted being pinned down by explication, providing her glossary to Pasolini on the condition that it not be published alongside the poems of *Bellicose Variations,* and occasionally contradicting her own glosses. Interpretation of these texts, like their translation, is potentially infinite.

Da *Primi scritti* (1952–1963) / From *First Writings* (1952–1963)

Prime prose italiane (1954) / *First Italian Prose* (1954) (pages 50–54)

Rosselli later wrote of this piece: "*First Italian Prose* is a brief piece from 1954, and it has a slightly ironic title. But it was really the first time that I had written in Italian, in prose that wasn't scholastic or simply essayistic and rational. There was also in it an aim to evade prose poetry, and the influence of Dino Campana and many others was strong. The piece is short, inspired, in some fashion; it is inspired, in fact, by the Tiber, along which I lived. It was written partly outside my home, walking, and thus by hand; or I took notes mentally and then transcribed that mental writing once at home. I do believe though that I succeeded, as long ago as 1954, in avoiding (as if it were a plague) 'prose poetry,' which was very common in that period. The text longs to possess the softness of the poems of Scipione, and thus to evade the dramatic Campana" (*Diario ottuso,* 53).

Da *Palermo '63* (1963) / From *Palermo '63* (1963)

The series of barbed lyrics from which these poems are drawn follows Rosselli's participation in a conference, held in Palermo, of the circle of authors from the nascent Neoavanguardia movement called Gruppo 63. These lyrics bring out Rosselli's ambivalence surrounding the group's experiments: she characterized their techniques as "second-hand" assimilations of French and Anglo-Saxon modernism (see *Dossier Amelia Rosselli,* in *Il Caffè illustrato* 13/14 [2003]: 47) that focused on form at the expense of "semanticity," and also expressed impatience with the male-dominated dynamics of the group.

Poesia dedicata a Gozzi / Poem dedicated to Gozzi (pages 54–55)

This short lyric to the dramatist Luigi Gozzi—composed as if for a thriller script—contains a series of textual ruptures and innovations that provide a useful introduction to Rosselli's poetic. *Assassinatore* and *sperdere* are archaic and courtly. *Traumaturgo* is a neologism amalgamating "trauma" or "trama" (texture; plot) and "dramatist"; it also echoes the term *taumaturgo,* miraculous or godlike healer. *Grigione* is a pivot point or punctum of the lyric, given that it refers to *testi* and *testa:* it indexes most immediately a small, ferocious, rodent-hunting mammal allied to the glutton and marten, invoking its etymology in the gray color of the animal's coat. The English "Grison" (like *grigione,* taken from the French) can also refer to a grison stone or to a servant dressed in gray so as to perform secret errands. The Grisons are, moreover, the largest and easternmost canton of Switzerland, a trilingual canton mirroring Rosselli's own trilingualism; *grigionaccio* is an archaic Italian pejorative of *grigione* meaning "rebel against authority," derived from the fifteenth-century Swiss Protestant sect of *Grigioni* (in English, the Grey League) founded to resist the bishop of Chur. The penultimate line plays with the gender of *testo*—aptly, as the speaker's gender has been suspended from the start: the juxtaposition of *testo* and *testa* underscores that texts are masculine, the head, beheaded, feminine. This play culminates in the last line: *manoscritta* may be a feminization of "manuscript" or an adjective qualifying *testa,* meaning "handwritten" or "in manuscript." The young Rosselli could also be plumbing the English "man" in *mano,* since she has used the English term for "suspense," newly incorporated at the time into Italian, and translated here as "suspence" (as the term is sometimes spelled by Italians) to maintain the estrangement of the foreign term. Suspense invokes a cliffhanger brought to fruition in the last line's *scoglie,* a term for shedding skin or archaic feminine form of "cliffs" or "setbacks." The poem's end finally rivals the head, "straightaway / manuscripted," as it harbors an echo of "man-written.'"

Poesia dedicata a Spatola / *Poem dedicated to Spatola* (pages 54–57)

This poem is dedicated to Adriano Spatola, an important experimental poet associated with the Gruppo 63 with whom Rosselli felt the most affinity.

1: *Il tempo* signifies both "time" and "weather," as well as "pace"; I chose the cognate in this case, as it carries the meaning of pace (and its musical connotations) along with a semantic kinship to weather.

6: *Veraconda* and *scematura* are unusual terms. *Veraconda* is a botanical term, but seems to function here as a variation of *verace*, or "authentic." It also recalls an adjective dear to Giacomo Leopardi, *verecondo* ("modest; bashful"). *Scematura* modifies *scemamento* or "diminution."

6–7: Since *belle dolci signore* takes a moment to parse—as *signore* could mean either "ladies" or "mister"—I have opted for the more expansive route, rather than translating the phrase as "beautiful sweet ladies."

Da *La libellula: Panegirico della libertà* (1958) / From *The Libellula: Panegyric to Liberty* (1958)

The title of this early Italian poem (pages 58–67), written in what Rosselli called a state of inspiration, is teeming with puns. The term "libellula," for the genus of insect commonly called the skimmer, dragonfly, or adderfly, plays on what Rosselli identified as a central theme—"liberty" (*la libertà*)—but also on "libel" (*libello*) and "libellate" (from *libellare*, Latin for "to put in writing, convey by charter," and *libellus*, diminutive form of *liber*, or book, meaning "pamphlet" or "tract," a document used to certify performance of a pagan sacrifice, thereby demonstrating loyalty to the authority of the Roman Empire). Both *La libellula* and *Variazioni belliche* contain the "war" of the Latin term *bellum*, as well as the sound of the English *bell*. An additional association with the body arises from the cognate "belly"—*bellico* being an archaic form of *ombelico*, as noted by Andrea Cortellessa and expanded upon by Gian-Maria Annovi in "*Time can stop (and it does)*: 'un inedito da SLEEP,'" in *È vostra la vita che ho perso*, 190. Rosselli used both "bell" and "belly" in unexpected ways in her English verse. The insect itself never appears in the work; instead, the title means to evoke its motion, "the almost rotary movement of the libellula's wings, . . . in reference to the rather volatile tone of the poem," as Rosselli wrote in her own annotations, reproduced in the 1996 Studio Editoriale edition of *La libellula e altre poesie* (31). "Panegyric," besides perhaps being used ironically to refer to an overly complicated story or discourse, also puns on the "giro del pane," or the circuit of daily bread, as Rosselli specifies in the interview "Paesaggio con figure" (*È vostra la vita che ho perso*, 297)—thereby bringing the classical form of eulogy down to earth. Choosing not to sacrifice the richness of these linguistic associations, I have used cognates in translating.

Rosselli explained in her notes that "the poem is conceived as well in the form of a dragon that eats its own tail; end and beginning should in fact link up, if the poem is read with agility, intuitively" (*La libellula,* 31). She traced the origins of her new metrical system to *La libellula,* identifying this as the moment at which she "inserted the Chinese ideogram between the phrase and the word, and . . . translated the Chinese scroll in the delirious course of Western thought" before moving on to the cube-form ("Metrical Spaces"). In her annotations to *La libellula,* Rosselli refers to this poem as a "scroll" that is instead "inspired by the Jewish notion of justice" (31). I have attempted to achieve a regular line duration and length wherever possible, without compromising the image sequencing or the destabilizing semantic currents of the poem. *La furia dei venti contrari* contains a facsimile of the poem as printed in monospaced font in addition to an excellent set of critical interventions: see pages 1–108.

Rosselli identifies 1958 as the date of this poem's composition, but Stefano Giovannuzzi details the lengthy process of revision that occurred thereafter in "Come lavorava Amelia Rosselli," *La furia dei venti contrari,* 20–35. Though *La libellula* was begun before *Variazioni belliche,* it was finally published alongside the later poems of *Serie ospedaliera* in 1969.

FIRST EXCERPT (pages 58–63)

1: "The holiness of the holy fathers . . .": Stefano Giovannuzzi argues that this poem, like Pasolini's verse polemic "A un papa," was triggered by the death of Pope Pius XII. See "*La libellula:* Amelia Rosselli e il poemetto," in "Amelia Rosselli: Un'apolide alla ricerca del linguaggio universale. Atti della giornata di studio. Firenze, Gabinetto Vieusseux, 29 maggio 1998" Special Issue, *Quaderni del Circolo Rosselli* 17 (1999), 45–57.

28–32: With regard to the faintly negative and critical relationship to the sea present here and elsewhere in her poetry, Rosselli explains, "I felt like protesting, but perhaps in an ironic way, against a tranquilizing vision of the sea ever at the disposal of painters and poets. . . . The sea can be beautiful and of help but can also be disagreeable and repetitive." See the tracts of conversation transcribed by the actor Ulderico Pesce, who performed *La libellula,* in his essay "La donna che vola," in "Amelia Rosselli: Un'apolide alla ricerca del linguaggio universale," 44.

49: Rosselli seems to have Italianized the French word *penible,* which means "burdensome" or "annoying." It seems to mean "punishable," but the effect is ambiguous. As such, I have altered the word "onerous."

52: Rosselli's *pegna* seems to stand between the words *pegno* (pledge; pawn; token), *pregna,* (pregnant), and *pena* (punishment; pain). As such, I have used the word "pawning," so as to hover between pawn, pawing, and pain.

65–68: "Nel mezzo. . . . / Nel mezzo d'un . . . cammino": these phrases strongly recall the first line of Dante's *Inferno.*

81: The word *pietà* recurs throughout this poem, and may be translated as "pity" or as "piety." While this presents obvious interpretative challenges, I have attempted to choose the most fitting term in each instance, here and elsewhere, according to context.

SECOND EXCERPT (pages 62–65)
This section addresses the figure of Hortense that appears in section H of Rimbaud's *Illuminations*. Rosselli also notes that its deployment of the verbs *cercare* (to seek) and *trovare* (to find) plays on Picasso's rejection of the word *recherché* in modern painting, in which he counters, "Ce qui compte, c'est trouver." See "Paesaggio con figure," in *È vostra la vita che ho perso*, 298.

THIRD EXCERPT (pages 64–67)
This section addresses the figure of Esterina, who appears as the first defined feminine personage within Eugenio Montale's work in *Ossi di seppia / Cuttlefish Bones* (1925). Rosselli begins by citing the celebrated first line of "Falsetto," in which Esterina is threatened by the approach of twenty years of age. In a conversation transcribed by the actor Ulderisco Pesce, Rosselli says that in this section, "I try to collapse the division between a writing I and an imagined you. I wanted to create a full identification of the writing I, which is also a you that I address, with the you of Esterina, who becomes another I. The sharp division between an I and a you, present in Montale as it is in other poets, is perhaps a typical feature of masculine language. . . . My passion for [Montale] was so strong in a certain moment of my life that I sought in every way to contradict him. . . . It was a way of discovering myself." See "La donna che vola," in "Amelia Rosselli: Un'apolide alla ricerca del linguaggio universale," 42.

5: Rosselli uses enjambment cuttingly when she turns the vision of a seascape through which Montale's Esterina cavorts into an economic one: *banco* can refer to both a geological reef or bank, or an economic institution. In line 25, it is clear that *banchi* refers most immediately to "counters" behind which tired girls "serve," but I have opted to retain the word "bank" here for textual consistency.

38: *Tromba delle scale* is a means of saying "stairwell" in architectural discourse (likely due to the horn-like shape of spiraling stairs), but its musical connotations could not have escaped Rosselli, for *tromba* means "trumpet," and *scale* means both "steps" and "scales." This expression is used more than once, and perhaps recalls the trumpets of Joshua before the walls of Jericho—given the walls of the Holy See that open the poem—and the theme of "Jewish justice." My translation tries to invoke both the image of the stairwell and its musical connotations.

60–61: The *angioli* here (departing from the more familiar *angeli*) echo Scipione's "Sento gli strilli degli angioli" ("I hear the shrieking of the seraphim"). Scipione, alias of Gino Bonichi, a Scuola Romana painter, was a dear friend to the Rosselli family and is echoed in various poems by Amelia, who also composed the preface for an edition of his poetry: *Carte segrete* (Einaudi, 1982). The scene with which *The Libellula* begins perhaps recalls Rome's Castel Sant'Angelo, which functioned as a papal fortress and prison complex surrounded by a moat, and was depicted in Scipione's somber 1930 oil painting, *Il ponte degli angeli.*

Da *Variazioni belliche* (1964) / From *Bellicose Variations* (1964)

I have chosen to translate this title with the adjective "bellicose" in order to retain the associations with "bellum," "bell," and "belly" discussed above in relation to *La libellula.* While *Bellic Variations* would be slightly closer to the original in literal terms, the two-syllable word would have compromised the beat of Rosselli's *belliche.*

Da *Poesie* (1959) / From *Poems* (1959)

Roberto, chiama la mamma, trastullantesi nel canapé / *Roberto, mum calls out, amusing herself in the white* (pages 68–69)

1–8: This opening poem of *Variazioni belliche* features a number of intriguing irruptions of standard Italian. *Babelare* is an inventive extrapolation of *Babele,* or "Babel." *Car* acts as the French term "because" here, and reappears frequently in the series of poems from which this hails, identified by Rosselli in her glossary as a key word. It could also be an elided form of *care,* or "dear," modifying the *foglie* or "leaves." I have therefore retained the original term in italicized form. The *per lo più* ("mostly") in a later line appears in the place of the *per i più* ("for the most") expected by the reader, effecting a startling contraction of two distinct phrasings. Rosselli's *vetra* is an inventive plural form of the masculine *vetri,* calling up plural constructions such as *le mura,* or the walls of a city as opposed to those of a room or building—thereby extending the perceived dominion of the glass. In her brief 1964 "Glossarietto," Rosselli called *le riverberate mura* an "obvious archaism for closure," though it is actually a pseudoarchaism, as Bisanti points out (*Una scrittura plurale,* 69; Bisanti, *L'opera plurilingue di Amelia Rosselli* [Pisa: Edizioni ETS, 2007], 132).

Non da vicino ti guarderò in faccia, né da / *Not from close up will I look you in the face, nor from* (pages 70–71)

8: *i valli:* Rosselli marks her departure from the standard form *le valli* here, in the "Glossarietto," as an "interchange of gender, frequent in the entirety of *Variazioni belliche,* and frequent, I believe, in spoken discourse, in literary use and probably in the dialects. I accentuate poetic license, and uncertainty that is fundamentally grammatical, not just my own (Latin *vallis* or *valles*)" (*Una scrittura plurale,* 69). *Vallo* is the Latin verb for fortifying with a rampart.

nullo / *null* (pages 70–71)

I translate *nullo* as "null" rather than "nothing," partially for sound and partially because this English word was dear to Rosselli; see "O Null is the World,

& Null am I / who do Skamper after It, . . ." in *October Elizabethans,* printed in Rosselli, *Le poesie* (Milan: Garzanti, 2004), 65.

Certe mie scarpe strette, sì vilmente mi causano torture / Certain tight shoes of mine, so contemptibly cause me agony (pages 72–73)
Rosselli indexes for Pasolini various features of this poem—grammatical involution ("son paragonabili / così come . . . "); poetic abbreviation (*rubi* for *rubini; pò'* for *posso); wild enjambment (i/O!)*—which are "archaic forms brought back in a grotesque sense: wholly invented even if they have a quasi-precise resonance." *Lettere a Pasolini,* 23. The typescript of the *glossarietto esplicativo* held at the Fondo Rosselli in Pavia and reproduced in *Una scrittura plurale* deviates from this account. Here Rosselli glosses "non i rubi / li . . . " as a poetic (pseudoarchaic or Provençalizing) abbreviation for "non li rubi i sentimentali cori, essi si rubano da sé" / "you don't rob the sentimental hearts, they are robbed on their own." She identifies "pò i / O!" as an abbreviation for "possa io" in an "allusively secret, phonetically reductive language: linguistic disgregation not necessarily only Poundian." *Una scrittura plurale,* 69.

Cos'ha il mio cuore che batte sì soavemente / What ails my heart which beats so suavely (pages 74–75)
See my introduction for an extended discussion of this poem.

i rapporti più armoniosi e i rapporti più dissonanti, tu povero / the most harmonious and the most dissonant relations, poor you (pages 76–77)
In the glossary provided to Pasolini, Rosselli notes that this poem alludes to the Romantic tradition of Italian poetry, specifically that of Leopardi. She also notes that the neologism *sgragnatiture* means to place together *graffiature* (scratches), *sgraffiature* (a more familiar term: scrapes), *sgranare* (to shell, hull, say the rosary; crumble), *sgrammaticato* (ungrammatical), *sgranocchiare* (to munch), *sgraziato* (clumsy, ungraceful), and *gragnolare* (the falling of *gragnola,* a popular term for *grandine,* or hail). *Lettere a Pasolini,* 25.

tu rubi da anni l'antico ereditaggio / for years you've robbed the antique hereditage (pages 78–79)
  1: Rosselli explains in the Glossarietto that *ereditaggio* is a combination of *eredità* (inheritance; heredity) and *retaggio* (heritage). *Lettere a Pasolini,* 25.

  8–9: *Rotta* means both "rout" or "tumult" and "route" as a noun; as an adjective it modifies a feminine noun as "broken." Another translation could be "you'll iron yourself / a route among pity's rags."

o dio che ciangelli / oh god may you chancel (pages 78–79)
  1: Rosselli explains to Pasolini that *ciangelli* recalls the English term "to chancel" as well as *cangiare,* a poetic term for change, or *cambiare,* and *cianciare* (to chatter), with reference to *cancello* (gate), *augelli* (poetic term for

uccelli, or birds), or *angeli* (angels), as well as *cancellare* (to erase). *Lettere a Pasolini,* 25. *Ciangelli* also recalls a notorious shrew, Cianghella della Tosa, cited as an example of dissoluteness in Dante's *Paradiso* 15.128. I have retained the term "chancel" as it contains "chance" with echoes of "change," "cancel," and "angels."

9: Rosselli notes that she had originally written *barbàre* in place of *barbare.* I keep the accent to place the emphasis on cross-lingual play. The use of *un' / auto* between lines 2 and 3, as Rosselli explains to Pasolini, is also meant to perform as a Greek poetic form of *tenere,* or "to keep" (*Lettere a Pasolini,* 25).

Da *Variazioni* (1960–1961) / From *Variations* (1960–1961)

Per le cantate che si svolgevano nell'aria io rimavo / For the singing that unwound in the air I rhymed (pages 80–81)

2ff: *sinistra:* I have retained the cognate "sinister," though the Italian word also provides a pun on the (political) "left."

Contiamo infiniti morti! la danza è quasi finita! la morte / We count infinite dead! the dance is almost done for! death (pages 80–81)

2: As Tatiana Bisanti points out in *L'opera plurilingue di Amelia Rosselli,* the swallow, an allegorical figure for freedom, is a recurrent topos in Rosselli's work.

4: Rosselli glossed "tarda giacevo fra / dei conti in tasca" as a "clumsiness typical of common speech, illiterate-archaic" (*Una scrittura plurale,* 70). I have preserved Rosselli's unusual use of "late" early in the phrase and chosen the more folksy, old-fashioned "amongst" in the place of "among."

17: *Congenitale* is an Anglicizing deviation from the standard Italian *congenital:* Rosselli's glossary refers to it as a "fusion . . . in a grotesque-allusive sense" of *congenita* (the standard Italian for "congenital"), "'congenital,' English for *congenita,*" and *genitale* ("genital") (*Una scrittura plurale,* 70). As Emmanuela Tandello points out, this term echoes the "generation" of line 11 and thus emphasizes the poem's intermingling of personal (including sexual) and public history. See "Doing the Splits: Language(s) in the Poetry of Amelia Rosselli," *Journal of the Institute of Romance Studies* 1 (1992), 372.

Dopo il dono di Dio vi fu la rinascita. Dopo la pazienza / After the gift of God was the rebirth. After the patience (pages 82–83)

Rosselli notes in her glossary that throughout this poem the construction "Dopo *della* gioia; dopo *della* fame; *della* noia" (afterwards *of the* joy; afterwards *of the* hunger; *of the* struggle) and so on alternates with the standard "dopo *il* dono; dopo *la* pazienza" (after *the* gift; after *the* patience), etc. I have maintained this effect by alternating between "afterwards of" and "after."

6: The term "refocillate," from the Latin *focillare, focillatum* (*focus:* hearth) means literally to warm into life (*re,* again). Deployed in the seventeenth and eighteenth centuries in English—in Donne's *Sermons,* for example—it means to refresh, reanimate, comfort.

In preda ad uno shock violentissimo, nella miseria / *Prey to a most violent shock, wretched* (pages 82–85)
This poem cites the massacre at the Ardeatine Caves of June 1944 in which, following a partisan attack, 335 Italian prisoners were killed by German occupation troops in retaliation (theoretically avenging every German killed with ten Italian men). Taken to the sand caves among the catacombs on the outskirts of Rome, they were murdered one by one before the entrance to the caves was blown up with dynamite. A plaque placed at Rome's Passetto di Borgo crowned with the Justice and Liberty emblem now remembers the thirty members of the Action Party who were murdered during this event. Lucia Re provides a reading of the poem in *War Variations* (16–17) and a robust account of Rosselli's weaving of personal with public history and war in her essay "Amelia Rosselli: Poesia e guerra." *Carte italiane* 3 (January 2007): 71–104.

Ma in me coinvenivano montagne. Nella cella di tutte / *But in me mountains coinvened. In the cell of all* (pages 84–85)
    1: "Coinvened" is a literal rendering of Rosselli's inventive *coinvenire.*
    11: Rosselli notes that her use of the term *le castelle,* which displaces the standard masculine *i castelli,* is part of a strategy that occurs throughout the whole of *Variazioni belliche:* "Usual inversion to the feminine gender, often for reasons that are phonetic as well, if not ironic" ("Glossarietto," in *Una scrittura plurale,* 71). We accept these deviations and their conceptual effects because the poem builds its own digressive logic through assonance—*nelle castelle* rhymes with *nella cella,* as *malizia* does with *milizia,* and narrative rhetoric gives way to the proliferation of staccato terms beginning with *p* and what Rosselli called "phonetic nodes" in her theoretical work: *pre* and *po.* Repetition produces a proliferation of cells, acts of waiting, prohibitions, and fires. The 16-line poem itself, as a shape and set of more or less regular lines, also resembles a ruptured cell.

Il Cristo trainava (sotto della sua ombrella) (la sua croce) un / *Christ hauled (below his parasol) (his cross) a* (pages 86–89)
    3: Within a single line Rosselli uses two words that potentially refer to a cloister: *chiostro,* the more common term, and the more literary *chiostra,* which can denote "cloister" but may also mean "ring," "circle," or "enclosure." Dante uses the term *chiostra* in Canto 29 of *Hell* to describe the circle of Malebolge, and in *Paradiso,* Canto 3 ("fuor mi rapiron de la dolce chiostra" [line 107]). Many translators, including Longfellow and Mandelbaum, have used the term "cloister" here rather than "ring," and I have chosen to keep to this term rather than shifting to "ring" or "circle" so as to retain the poem's strong echoing from

phrase to phrase. However, I have elected to use "clauster," a more archaic spelling for "cloister," which refers to a shut-up place, cell, or cloister; the term has the added advantages of replacing the masculine "o" with "a" as Rosselli does, and of potentially sounding like "cluster."

I quattro contadini spostavano la rete, depositavano nella / *The four farmers were shifting the net, depositing their* (pages 88–89)
In her "Glossarietto" (*Una scrittura plurale*, 71–2), Rosselli notes that this poem alludes to Campana's "Ho scritto. Si chiuse in una grotta / Arsenio fortissimo disegnatore / dipinse quadri piccoli e grotteschi" (from his *Quaderno*, in *Opere e contributi*, vol. 2 [Florence: Vallecchi, 1973], 334).

Nell'elefantiasi della giornata si conduceva un rapido / *In the elephantiasis of the day one conducted a rapid* (pages 88–89)
This poem contains a range of Rosselli's inventions: unusual terms (*elefantiasi*); substitution of expected terms with terms that are sonically related, but slightly altered, resulting in semantic divergence from the norm, as in *sbaraglio* (risk; rout) instead of *sbaglio* (mistake; wrong), *perdonare la gara* (to pardon the race) instead of the anticipated *perdere* (to lose the race), *condonare la folla* rather than "to condemn the crowd"; paranomasia (*affetti* following *effetti*, *cellula* following *cella*, *condonare* following *condizionata*); hapax ("magniloquacious"); Latinisms ("pulchritude"); departures from expected articles (*gli* instead of *i* for *ricchi*). I attempt to maintain these effects where possible; for example, I render *sbaraglio* as "wrout" to make way for the possibility of reading as both "rout" and "wrong."

Cercatemi e fuoriuscite. / *Seek me & banish.* (pages 88–89)
This seemingly simple one-line poem plays upon the ambiguity between the verb *fuoriuscire* (to leak, discharge, abandon, or escape) and its passive form, *essere fuoriuscito* (to be exiled, banished, expelled from one's native land for political reasons, or to willingly expatriate oneself—used most frequently to refer to anti-Fascists such as Carlo Rosselli). I use "banish" because, in rhyming with "vanish," it invites both a transitive and an active yet intransitive reading.

Il tuo sorriso ambiguo curvava ogni mia speranza / *Your equivocal smile curved every hope of mine* (pages 90–91)
6: In this poem, Rosselli uses the word *sparimenti* instead of *sparizioni* (disappearances)—to rhyme with *fallimenti* (bankruptcies, failures, flops).

La farfalla che nei tuoi occhi si schiuse / *The butterfly disclosed in your* eyes (pages 92–93)
6: *Ritrassi* can mean either to depict, as in a portrait, or to withdraw, *ritirare;* I have tried to preserve both possibilities by splitting the English word between two lines.

Il corso del mio cammino era una delicata fiamma / *The course of my journey was a delicate flame* (pages 92–93)

1: The word *cammino* that haunts this work inevitably summons the "mezzo del cammin di nostra vita" ("midway through the journey of our life") with which Dante's *Divine Comedy* begins.

Da *Serie ospedaliera* (1963–1965) / From *Hospital Series* (1963–1965)

settanta pezzenti e una camicia che si rompeva / *seventy destitutes and a shirt that ripped itself up* (pages 94–95)

This poem was first published in 1964 in an anthology of writings by the Gruppo 63—*Gruppo 63: La nuova letteratura, 34 scrittori,* ed. Nanni Balestrini and A. Giuliani (Milan: Feltrinelli, 1964).

The "shirt" in the poem ineluctably echoes the black and red shirts of an epoch just past.

15: With *le ciglie* Rosselli has resisted the standard plural form for parts of the body, in this case "[eye]lashes," *le ciglia;* I thereby eliminate the definite article that would allow the phrase to read more clearly as a part of the body and delimit its plural character.

Severe le condanne a tre. In rotta con l'arcipelago fummo / *Severe the threefold sentences. En route with the archipelago we were* (pages 96–97)

9: *Vinto* can be a highly ambiguous word: though "that has been won" is its most obvious translation, especially when linked to *battaglia,* it can also mean "defeated."

Le tue acquerelle scomponevano la mia mente / *Your aquarelles discomposed my* (pages 96–99)

Lucia Re points out that this poem is built of "a reticulation of meaning radiating from the associative chain *'scomponevano'-'scompiglio'-'scalinavo'- 'scomposto'-'scostarsi'-'s'accostava'-'scomponendosi'-'stornavi.'*" See "Poetry and Madness," 148. I have done my best to echo such effects of the original.

1: The first phrase recalls the beginning of a poem from *Variazioni belliche:* "I bambini d'inferno crescevano sporadicamente, le / tue acquerella scomponevano la mia mente." *Acquerello* is the standard, masculine term for watercolor; Rosselli has feminized it, and in the earlier poem treated its plural state like a member of the body or foundation of a city. In the "Glossarietto esplicativo" to *Variazioni belliche,* she marked this move as "literary/popular/archaic distortion" (see *Una scrittura plurale,* 71), though in fact there is no documented instance of such a usage (see Bisanti, *L'opera plurilingue di Amelia Rosselli,* 130).

2: *Invernizio* is a brilliant neologism: a wintry inversion of *primizie,* or the first produce and fruits of the season, or latest news, fusing the terms for winter (*inverno*) and solstice (*solstizio*). My literalizing "winterice" also tries to accommodate the ice cliff implicit in the verb *scalinare,* which appears in the following line and designates the act of cutting footholds in Alpine climbing.

Facce appese, bronzi al muro, facce di bronzo, santi appesi / *Faces hung, bronze to the wall, brazen faces, saints hung* (pages 98–101)

1: *La faccia di bronzo* or "bronze face" is a slang term for a person with nerve, a brazen-faced person.

4: The verb *trombare* ("to trumpet") also means both to flunk (in an exam) or reject and to screw, etc., in Italian slang. I have chosen to remain true to the literal sense of the term, as it proves the most generative of possible figurative permutations.

5 poesie per una poetica / *5 Poems for a Poetic*

PART I (pages 100–101)

13: The idiom *farmi fuori,* which means "to kill," literally means "to make me outside."

16: Rosselli has Italianized the English word "refrigerator," rather than using the standard Italian *frigorifero.*

PART 5 (pages 102–105)

21–22: Here, *l'ingaggio* / *di vostra madre* ("the engagement / of your mother") is certainly a pun on *linguaggio,* or "language," and therefore harbors an echo of "mother tongue." I borrow from the French to translate *l'ingaggio* or "engagement" while preserving the specter of "language."

Sollevamento di peso e particolarità della sorte / *Weight heaving and oddities of fate* (pages 104–105)

13: *La mitra,* here *mitre,* is haunted by *il mitra* or *la mitraglia:* submachine gun in Italian. The term *mitra* appears throughout Rosselli's oeuvre. She would have cherished the possible rhyme with the English term "meter," while being drawn to its religious implications (the cult of Mitra, or Mithras, a mystery religion with origins in the Zoroastrian deity of contracts popular among members of the military during the Roman empire, which strongly impacted Christianity; the ceremonial headdress of Catholic bishops and ancient divinities; also, in ancient Greek, an armor belt, possibly cognate with "contract," "friend," from the Indo-European root meaning "to bind") and its common military use (*il mitra* is short for *pistola mitragliatrice,* or machine gun pistol). I have opted to add a word here, "submachinic," so as not to lose this crucial effect entirely, which preserves the "miter" without naming any gun definitively.

la vita è un largo esperimento per alcuni, troppo / *life's an experiment agape for some, too* (pages 106–107)

9: "To bend" or "to fold"—*piegarsi*—is a key term in Rosselli's poetry, not only because of the meningitis from which she suffered physically, but because she is highly suspicious of the narcissism of the figure of the artist "piegata su se stessa" ("folded in on herself" or retreated into herself, wrapped up in herself). Rosselli praises the Mozambique poet José Craveirinha as a figure who has lived through so much that he "would seem to laugh at our being wrapped up in ourselves ["questo nostro piegarsi su noi stessi"]: he has seen everything, misery and depravation and degradation—what need is there to be wrapped up in oneself any longer?" ("José Craveirinha: Poeta Politico," never published, reproduced in *Lettere a Pasolini*, 63).

"Lentement, et tres tendrement, quoy que mesuré" (pages 108–111)
This poem takes for a title the section of François Couperin's *Pièces de clavecin* (14th order, book 3) called "Le rossignol en amour" ("The nightingale in love"), which leads to an ornamented variation, or "Double de rossignol." The composer's directions—"Slowly, and very tenderly, but measured/in time"—would have interested the poet as she explored closed poetic forms. The archaic spelling suggests that Rosselli transcribed directly from a score. Couperin (1668–1733) was the harpsichordist under Louis XIV.

Risposta / Response (pages 110–111)
    10–11: *Sampietrini* refers to the cobblestones pervasive in Rome and used to pave St. Peter's Square (literally "saintpeterstones," from the apostle taking the name Rock who vowed to build Christ's church); it can also refer to the caretakers of the Basilica itself. Rosselli echoes Petrarch's "Chiare, fresche e dolci acque" with *chiare acque / e fresche ombre*. With *rivoltàme* and *mangiame* she creates new forms: ambiguous truncations of *rivoltamento* (literally, "revoltment") and *mangiamento* ("feeding") that recall the elisions of dialect.

Le sentinelle al di là dei ponti, i sacro santi / The sentinels beyond the bridges, the sacro sanct (pages 110–113)
This poem is a variant (presumably a revision) of a poem written in pencil on the last page of Rosselli's copy of Ludovico Geymonat's *Storia del pensiero filosofico e scientifico* (Garzanti, 1964).

Carta da bollo per gli incendiati un papavero / Legal paper for the victims of fire a red (pages 112–113)
    9: The term *verecondia* has a strong Christian-moral cast. See the first lines of Leopardi's "Ultimo canto di Saffo" (1822): "Placida notte, e verecondo raggio / della cadente luna . . ."

Dolce caos, un addolcimento visionario / Sweet chaos, a visionary sweetening (pages 116–117)
Critics have noted resonances between this poem and Petrarch's lyric 35 from *Il canzoniere* (with its "passi tardi et lenti") as well as D'Annunzio's *La pioggia*

nel pineto, contained in Rosselli's library now held at the Università della Tuscia. Regarding Rosselli's yoking of a traditional lyric idiom to poetically blasphemous signifiers of banal quotidian life, see Niva Lorenzini, "Memoria testuale e parola 'inaudita': Amelia e Gabriele," in *Trasparenze* 17–19 (2003): 155–71.

Questo giardino che nella mia figurata / This garden that in my figurate (pages 116–119)
 17: In this instance, *annunciare* contains distinct echoes of the Annunciation of the Virgin Mary.

E accomodandosi tutto lei piangeva, disperatina / And with all made at home she wept, little wretch (pages 118–119)
The *tutto* in this poem's first line is seemingly unresolvable, as it cannot refer to the "her" who cries. This provides a fitting introduction to a scene of traumatic ambiguity, in which a horrific event, described in nearly surgical detail, never becomes localized in a specified body. Éanna Ó Ceallacháin writes persuasively of the way this poem's confusion of subjectivity and tonal clashes demonstrate Mengaldo's point that Rosselli offers us a sense of the normality of horror. *Twentieth-Century Italian Poetry: A Critical Anthology (1900 to the Neo-Avantgarde)* (Leicester, UK: Troubador, 2007), 341.

Attenta alla medusa: un bianco un po' livido, la Giulietta / Look out for the medusa: a white a bit livid, the Juliette (pages 118–119)
 4 and 7: Musical cadences in this poem, as well as the ongoing reciprocity between music and verse in Rosselli's oeuvre, have led me to retain the terms *castrati* and *adagio* in the poem, rather than translating them more conventionally as "castrated" and "sinks" respectively.

tuo motivo non urlare, dinnanzi alla / your motive not to scream, facing the (pages 126–129)
This poem's opening stanza encapsulates Rosselli's poetic, insofar as exile and modernist/experiential *chance* (appearing in its English form) hover over and determine—or "motivate"—her entire oeuvre. The poet deviates from the standard *locomotiva* ("locomotive") with the Latinizing term for an electric train, *locomotrice*—a vehicle that, she notes, is not "pardoned" by prevailing conditions of displacement and chance. Throughout, the "locomotrix" (recalling a mobilized feminine *matrice,* or "matrix; mother; mold") haunts the "motive" being exchanged between the speaker and the unidentified *tu.*
 11: Rosselli's use of the word *impara* is unexpected in this context and could be translated as the command "learn," though it is syntactically somewhat awkward, or as an alteration of the term "uneven; odd" (*impari*). I have chosen an English rendering of the latter, because it echoes the poem's tendency to feminize unfeminine forms while offering richer possibilities for construing the relationship between the poem's speaker and addressee. "Unpaired" is meant to echo "impaired," with a difference.

Di sera il cielo spazia, povera / *At evening the sky ranges, poor* (pages 130–131)

7: In Italian, *salmo* means "psalm," while the feminine noun that haunts it, *salma,* means "corpse, remains." Rosselli uses *salmo* in the plural while allowing the feminine noun to hover over the lyric.

10: *I labbri* refers to the lips of a wound, unlike *le labbra,* which would refer to the lips of the mouth; I have therefore employed the more abstract "the lips" in place of the possessive here (still ambiguous, as it can be linked either to *chi scuce* or to *il cuore*).

C'è vento ancora e tutti gli sforzi / *There is wind still and all efforts* (pages 132–133)

4: *Tintinnire* is a modification of *tintinnare,* to tinkle or clink, and was a verb beloved of Giovanni Pascoli and Gabriele D'Annunzio.

Cercare nel rompersi della sera un nascondiglio / *To seek in the breaking of the evening a hiding place* (pages 136–137)

3: *Nappa* is a fringe or tuft, but Rosselli's heightened sense of sonic associations across languages must have made her mindful of the English "nap," whose more common usage suits the sleeping in fits and starts of this volume ("formerly frequent in renderings of Biblical passages," as the *OED* informs us), and which, in less frequent usage, also designates a rough type of pile.

Da *Diario ottuso: Nota* (1967–1968) / From *Obtuse Diary: Note* (1967–1968)

In his preface to *Diario ottuso,* Alfonso Berardinelli characterizes the entire work with skill: "Serious, grave and totally demanding like a children's game, like a tragedy whose precedent is obscure and which lacks final scenes, the writing of Amelia Rosselli does not have the happy instability of flux, but is alarming and intermittent" (7).

Stanza 1 (pages 138–139): Here a favored pun is employed again; *mitra* refers to a submachine gun, but in its feminine form, it would refer to a miter. The rhyme with "meter" is clear.

Stanza 3 (pages 138–139): "Storia di Ada" is a 1967 narrative by the neo-realist novelist Carlo Cassola about the suffering of a young woman who, losing her hand in an accident, is obliged to take a job as a postal worker in Tuscany and to marry unhappily. Rosselli's piece seems to provide a metacommentary on the deterministic tendency of realist literature.

Da *Documento* (1966–1973) / From *Document* (1966–1973)

In a 1977 interview with Gabriella Sica, Rosselli said of this book, "The title is ironic. Poetry has never been a precise document of what is lived, but instead a sublimation; poetry attempts not to be sublimated. Because of this I can lose control: my life has taken a turn toward discouragement, I therefore document what happens, in life and in poetry: I have no choice. I abandon the scheme of a single/whole [*unico*] verse, I insert free verse, I abandon the idea of always providing a philosophical synthesis of the contrast of each poem, I accept impressionistic passages. I record what happens to me: poetry is not, as some think, pure spirit, but records unexpected events, the exhaustion of quotidian life." *È vostra la vita che ho perso*, 16.

Uno strepitare svelto di ali smorzate / A swift uproar of muffled wings (pages 142–143)
    8: With *fanciulla senza colomba*, Rosselli invokes (and inverts) the genre of classical statuary depicting girls or young women with doves.

a Shubert / to Shubert (pages 142–143)
This spelling of Schubert appears in the original.

Quanti rami hanno gli oliveti che tu / How many boughs fill the olive groves that you (pages 146–149)
    11–13: *Ricercare* means to search for again, to hunt, to investigate, to seek after or seek out; I have chosen to translate the term as "researched" so as to retain Rosselli's play on *cercare* ("to search") and *ricercare* ("to re-search") present in the final stanza. Rosselli defined herself as a *poeta della ricerca* ("poet of research"). A more colloquial translation could read "You've poisoned your existence seeking / the comfort of prose while poetry / sought out your glory."

E veleno forzarsi per nervi occulti / And venom to force its way through occult nerves (pages 148–149)
    12: The Italian word for room, *stanza*, accentuates the textual overtones of this poem on the architectonics of the body, civilization, and nature, emphasized by *invariabile*, which, as applied to grammar, means "uninflected."

Mentre mi avvicinai alle pareti odoravano / As I came closer to the walls these walls were odorous (pages 150–151)
In translating this highly sonorous poem (which depends on rhymes between *odore, ardore, amore*), I have tried to maintain the echo-chamber effect, though it means using the archaizing "amour" (often used in Rosselli's English verse).

Un orrore di bombe che cadono tremanti / A horror of bombs that fall trembling (pages 152–153)
Tatiana Bisanti notes that the manuscript for this poem dates it to Rosselli's thirty-seventh birthday (*L'opera plurilingue di Amelia Rosselli*, 179). Such is the impulse of *Documento* to "express problems and solutions to problems that are collective," even when the I is present, rather than to focus on the self. See "Il

dolore in una stanza," a 1984 interview with Renato Minore," in *È vostra la vita che ho perso,* 64.

3: "Sommossa contadina" could refer either to a peasant uprising or to a farmer or peasant-girl who is troubled or excited—in the first case *sommossa* is a noun and *contadina* an adjective; in the latter, the roles are reversed.

5: Here the Italian *Vittoria armata* rhymes ironically with the famous Greek statue of Winged Victory in the Louvre, *la Vittoria alata.*

6: Here as elsewhere in Rosselli's poetry *sinistra* can mean either "sinister" or "left" as in "leftist."

Dialogo con i Morti / *Dialogue with the Dead* (pages 152–157)
5: Here Rosselli plays on the idiom *fallire il colpo,* which means "to miss the mark" or to fall short, to go wrong.

Vento d'Oriente e libeccio di malavita / *Orient wind and southwesterly wind of a life of crime* (pages 156–157)
1: The Italian word *libeccio* for the southwest wind refers particularly to that which blows throughout the year in Corsica.

4, 9, 12: Rosselli plays on the rhyme between "disarm" (*disarmare*) and "unlove" (*disamare*). I have had to stretch English to recreate the echo.

18: *Imbandire* is to lay out a table sumptuously; this verb contrasts with the timetable, schedule, or *orario,* at the beginning of the last line—with an implicit cross-lingual pun on "table."

Rimai, verso una proda / *I rhymed, versus a shore* (pages 158–161)
1: Substitution is in play here as often in Rosselli's lyrics to confuse a landscape with a textual scene. "Remai, verso una proda" ("I rowed, versus a shore") would be the standard phrase; Rosselli has displaced the action of rowing with that of rhyming by changing the *e* to an *i.*

Hanno fuso l'ordigno di guerra con le / *They have fused the war device with* (pages 164–167)
1: *Ordigno* is a term that recurs in the oeuvre of Montale, a poet dear to Rosselli; it appears as *ordegno* (a Florentine form) in *Ventaglio, Mediterraneo,* and in the eleventh motet of *I motetti.* The term denotes a complex, unstoppable mechanism.

Continenza europea, semmai venne / *European continence, if ever it came* (pages 174–177)
Stanzas 3–4: As *stanza* means both "stanza" and "room," *canto* in the original poem's last line—*non volge in canto forte*—also means "corner" in Italian; this entire poem thereby straddles two strata of meaning—those of architecture and poetry. Through such veritably untranslatable puns, the poem echoes

adjoining poems in *Documento* such as "And venom to force its way through occult nerves" and "C'è come un dolore nella stanza," which I have translated as "There is something like pain in this chamber," so that the architectonic meaning remains intact while the self-referential quality of the poem is simultaneously stressed.

nel nordico / *in the nordic* (pages 176–177)
This poem echoes futurism's imperatives: "Vengano dunque, gli allegri incendiarii dalle dita carbonizzate!" was one of the rallying cries of the first futurist manifesto published in 1909. Aldo Palazzeschi's *L'incendiario* (*The Arsonist*) was published with Marinetti's press in 1910.

E nell'acquedotto / *And in the aqueduct* (pages 178–179)
5: *Divorazione* is an archaic noun related to the act of devouring, with usages hearkening back to a fourteenth-century Italian-language Bible, and to fourteenth-century commentary on Dante's *Inferno* and on sacred texts. I have thus used a rare word in translation.

Da *Appunti sparse e persi: Poesie* (1966–1977) / From *Notes Scattered and Lost: Poems* (1966–1977)

Benediva la casa il tepore finto / *Fake lukewarmth blessed the home* (pages 188–189)
6: *Paraffinato,* which contains the word *raffinato,* or "refined," means to wax or waterproof.

Il colore che torna dal nero / *The color that returns from black* (pages 188–191)
6: An alternate translation of this line could be "through the streets white at times." In this context, *volta* is placed so as to signify "time," in the sense of "occasion" (*a volte bianche*—"at times white" or more improbably "white times"), yet, once the adjective is encountered, also "vault" (*a volte bianche*—"to white vaults"). *Strade bianche* or "white roads" are unpaved roads that one encounters in the plains, lining ridges or brooks; *volte bianche* makes for a much more architectonic image, albeit so fantastic as to suggest the structure of an afterlife.

Pel cielo che /*Across the sky that* (pages 190–191)
5: By using the word *esterefatte,* Rosselli taps a common misspelling for *esterrefatto,* perhaps taking advantage of the *estero* ("abroad") within the error. "Aghast" is a common misspelling for "agast," or "struck with amazement," probably due to an incorporation of echoes of "ghost." The "friendship" that ends this poem echoes the author's given name, and contains within it the *amor* of the penultimate line; I have thus translated it as "amity."

Da *Impromptu* (1981) / From *Impromptu* (1981)

1: As Nelson Moe notes, this opening statement is not lacking in self-irony, due to Rosselli's origins in the Italian bourgeoisie—and it can be read productively as a rejoinder to the charges against the "liberal" character of Rosselli's work that Pasolini expressed in his introductory "Note on Amelia Rosselli," delivered nearly two decades after the fact. See Moe, "At the Margins of Dominion: The Poetry of Amelia Rosselli," *Italica* 69, no. 2 (Summer 1992), 192. The phrase *in borghese* (plainclothes; in street clothes; in disguise) is deployed throughout the poem.

2: *Tralappio* is a neologism that contains within it the terms *tralasciare* (to interrupt; omit, fail, neglect; skip; miss) and *acchiappo* (seize) and *cappio* (a taking). In this context one also intuits a kind of literal skipping or hopping in the term. Moreover, the word could well be a homophonic translation of the English "trollop," a somewhat outmoded term for a slovenly or "loose" person, especially a woman, possibly deriving from the term "troll." Rosselli makes the noun into a verb, and her transference of *o* to the feminine *a*, while retaining the sound of the English word, could also be read as a feminine appropriation of a derogatory term—introducing into it as well the *tra* of "transit" and "betweenness." I have therefore created my own neologism, "trallops," which contains within it the *tra* and the terms "trollops," "trolls," "trumps," "wallops," and "traps."

15: Rosselli's interest in the term *par terre* dates back to her work with it in the 1955–1956 *Diario in tre lingue:* "se poussent loin au plus loin des souris des sous-terres / (partenaires) // par-terre // par t(e) de l'air / pact en terre / (packaboat) / (nickerbocker) // une part (ie!) en terre / l'autre aux cieux vagabonds d'un seul bond / par terre / (voici le packboat le pack hound voici le moment s'en aller / sous-terre / sur la terre / trainant ses longs pieds par une chemise étroite / . . . / pas en air (le ciel velouté exceptionel / plomb / aux ramages / rapprochés / approché(s) / (c'est un parterre / parte-guère / partenaire" (*Le poesie,* 85–86).

24: I use the term "unmoved" in translating *fermo* in order to retain the implications of stability and firmness in addition to motionlessness that are contained in the Italian term; the issuance of judgments regarding those who were stable and those who were not would have been of prime concern to Rosselli, given her long history with a range of psychological institutions and the polemic issued in "Storia di una malattia" (reprinted in *Una scrittura plurale,* 317–26). The resultant double negative is also in keeping with this poem's strategies.

32: Throughout this poem, Rosselli addresses a "you" that is at times identifiable as plural, and can at times be read as an old-fashioned form of formal address to the second person singular. For example, in part 6, line 14, the *mancerie* ("seductions" or "come-ons") usually associated with a single male subject are attributed to the *voi* who are found several lines later *tutti stesi / in un grano di turco,* hence plural. This ambiguity is highly generative, as it has identifiable political implications at times. I have used the word "all" here to indicate the shift from the second person singular (*tu*) in the third and fourth stanzas to the *voi.*

PART 2 (pages 196–199)

1: Rosselli uses the English term "tank," which I have retained in italics.

15: This line is a quiet, nearly secret, tour de force of cross-lingual play. Rosselli uses the word *frassine,* an archaic version of *frassino,* or ash tree (*fraxinus* in Latin), to address Pasolini. She thus compares the author of *Le ceneri di Gramsci,* or *The Ashes of Gramsci,* to a tree whose common English name is Ash. Both the English and Italian words derive from terms for "spear": the ash is known for its combination of great strength and resilience. This term would have been particularly important to Amelia as it was the name of the Rosselli home in Florence. The first syllable of *frassine* also anticipates the word *fratello* ("brother") on the next line. Due to this partial rhyme and above all to keep the intimate encoding of associations intact, I have used the Latin nomenclature in translating.

PART 3 (pages 198–199)

The "indifference" that pervades this section seems inflected by Alberto Moravia's 1929 novel, *Gli indifferenti.* Moravia was a cousin from the Pincherle side of the family, though tensions arose between the Rossellis and Moravia in the postwar period.

16: "Mistinguett" (birth name Jeanne Bourgeois, 1875–1956) was an actress, showgirl, and singer, the most popular French entertainer of her time.

PART 6 (pages 200–203)

18: "in un grano di turco": *granoturco* is a word for "corn," but because Rosselli has used this term instead of *mais,* it is likely that she wanted the term to echo "Gran Turco," or "Great Turk" (the Ottoman emperor).

PART 8 (pages 202–205)

This is a highly sonorous section of the poem, and paradoxically so, given the dark and contemporary subject matter, which is emphasized in Rosselli's own performance of the poem first issued by Carlo Mancosu on cassette for the 1993 edition of *Impromptu,* then by San Marco dei Giustiniani on DVD, now available at http://www.youtube.com/watch?v=vSwjx-s8DQ8. I have had to move rhymes from one place in the poem to another at points in order to maintain semantic fidelity.

14: Rosselli returns to the word *mitra* (miter or submachine gun); here it clearly refers to the latter, but I have retained a word that could pertain to meter as well.

25: See Dante's *Inferno,* 21: "Quale nell'arzanà de'Veneziani / Bolle l'inverno la tenace pece, / A rimpalmare i legni lor non sani. . . ." *Rimpalmare* is interpreted by scholars as restoration through caulking, using the boiling pitch of the Arsenal. The "filth" that first emerges in the sweat *concimato* ("fertilized"; "manured") of the poem's first stanza thereby rearises here, implicitly. While she does not specify which canto she was reading, Rosselli notes in a 1987 interview that she had been studying a canto of the *Inferno* in depth (as well as a bilingual edition of the poems of Ingeborg Bachmann) in the days preceding the composition of *Impromptu*. See *È vostra la vita che ho perso,* 209.

PART 13 (pages 204–207)
The images beginning this section appear to refer to Sandro Botticelli's *Primavera:* they could be a loose rendering of Botticelli's representation of the nymph Chloris (with "curled stalk" in her mouth) being pursued by the gray and cloudlike Zephyr.

7–8: The idiom *per altri versi* (in other directions, ways, places, lines) could be translated literally as "for other verses," with the reference to lines of poetry; I have therefore translated it with the term "versus" so as to include the echo of "verse."

Uncollected

In its use of the terms *seppia* and *gioconda* (pages 212–213), this poem invokes two canonical works of Italian art: Eugenio Montale's 1925 *Ossi di seppia,* or *Cuttlefish Bones,* which had exerted a strong influence upon Rosselli as a girl, and *La Gioconda,* the common epithet for Leonardo da Vinci's *Mona Lisa.* I use the term "sepia" to invoke both the genus of cuttlefish and the ink that it releases, as both are certainly in play in this self-reflexive late piece, and the cognate "jocund."

Selected Bibliography

Books by Amelia Rosselli

Note: A new critical edition of Rosselli's collected works edited by Emmanuela Tandello, Laura Barile, Chiara Carpita, and others is forthcoming with Mondadori's I Meridiani series.

Antologia poetica. Edited by Giacinto Spagnoletti. With an essay by Giovanni Giudici. Milan: Garzanti, 1987. Won the 1987 Premio Cittadella, the 1988 Premio Fondi, and the 1988 Premio Chianciano.

Appunti sparsi e persi (1966–1977). Reggio Emilia: Aelia Laelia, 1983. 2nd ed., Rome: Empirìa, 1997.

Diario ottuso: 1954–1968. With a preface by A. Berardinelli. Rome: Istituto Bibliografico Napoleone, 1990. 2nd ed., with an essay by Daniela Attanasio. Rome: Empirìa, 1996.

Documento (1966–1973). Milan: Garzanti, 1976. Won the 1977 Premio Indizi and the 1980 Premio Pier Paolo Pasolini.

Impromptu. With a preface by Giovanni Giudici. Genoa: San Marco dei Giustiniani, 1981. 2nd ed., with preface by Antonella Anedda and recording of Rosselli reading on audio cassette. Rome: Carlo Mancosu Editore, 1993. 3rd ed., with preface by Giovanni Giudici, an unpublished letter by Rosselli to the editor, and recording on CD. Genoa: San Marco dei Giustiniani, 2003.

La libellula, e altri scritti. With "Una notizia su Amelia Rosselli" by Pier Paolo Pasolini. Milan: Studio Editoriale, 1985. Reprinted, 2010.

Le poesie. Edited by Emmanuela Tandello. With a preface by Giovanni Giudici. Milan: Garzanti, 1997. Reprinted with corrections in 2004.

Primi scritti: 1952–1963. Milan: Guanda, 1980. Won the 1981 Premio Luigi Rosso.

Serie ospedaliera (1963–1965), including *La libellula (1958).* Milan: Mondadori, 1969. Unanimously won the 1969 Premio Argentario.

Sleep: Poesie in inglese (1953–1966). Translated into Italian and with a postface by Emmanuela Tandello. Milan: Garzanti, 1992.

Sonno—Sleep (1953–1966). Translated into Italian by Antonio Porta. Rome:

Rossi e Spera, 1981. 2nd ed., with a preface by Niva Lorenzini. Genova: San Marco dei Giustiniani, 2003.

Variazioni belliche. With an afterword by Pier Paolo Pasolini. Milan: Garzanti, 1964. 2nd ed., with reprinted 1963 essay by Pier Paolo Pasolini. Rome: Fondazione Piazzolla, 1995. Contains the essay "Metrical Spaces."

Translations by Amelia Rosselli

Dickinson, Emily. Poems 430, 443, 505, 520, 601, 632, 945, 963, 1651, 1705. In *Emily Dickinson: Tutte le poesie.* Milan: Mondadori, 1997.

Evans, Paul. *Dialogo tra un poeta e una musa.* Rome: Fondazione Piazzolla, 1991.

Plath, Sylvia. In *Le muse inquietanti e altre poesie.* Milan: Guanda, 1965. Reprinted by Garzanti in 1985.

Collections of Related Correspondence

Lettere a Pasolini, 1962 – 1969. Edited and with a postface by Stefano Giovannuzzi. Quaderni del Tempo. Genoa: San Marco dei Giustiniani, 2008. Includes full text of glossary Rosselli provided to Pasolini for *Variazioni belliche* as well as heretofore unpublished essays on the Gruppo 63 conference and José Craveirinha.

Politica e affetti familiari: Lettere di Amelia [Pincherle], Carlo e Nello Rosselli a Guglielmo, Leo e Nina Ferrero e Gina Lombroso Ferrero (1917 – 1943). Edited by Marina Calloni and Lorella Cedroni. With a preface by Giulio Sapelli. Transcribed and translated by Paola Ranzini. Milan: Feltrinelli, 1997.

Rosselli, Carlo, Nello Rosselli, Amelia Pincherle Rosselli, and Zeffiro Ciuffoletti. *Epistolario familiare: Carlo, Nello Rosselli, e la madre (1914 – 1937).* Milan: SugarCo, 1979.

Prose

Rosselli, Amelia. *È vostra la vita che ho perso: Conversazioni e interviste, 1964 – 1995.* Edited by Monica Venturini and Silvia De March, with a preface by Laura Barile. Florence: Le Lettere, 2010. Interviews that appeared in print as well as transcribed radio broadcasts.

———. *La furia dei venti contrari: Variazioni Amelia Rosselli. Con testi inediti e dispersi dell'autrice.* Edited by Andrea Cortellessa. Includes a DVD of the documentary film *Amelia Rosselli . . . e l'assillo è rima* by Rosaria Lo Russo and Stella Savino, and a CD featuring Rosaria Lo Russo reading *La libellula.* Florence: Le Lettere, 2007.

————. *Una scrittura plurale: saggi e interventi critici.* Edited by Francesca Caputo. Novara: Interlinea, 2004. Rosselli's essays range from musicological studies to articles on conflicts between avant-garde and mainstream magazines, the working conditions of screenwriters, radical black poetics, and individual authors, such as Pasternak, Kydd, Bazlen, Barth, Berryman, Pavese, Porta, Penna, Eliot, Hemingway, Kerouac, Corso, Woolf, Joyce, Scipione, Plath, and Sara Zanghì. Collection also includes key materials on Rosselli's own poetics such as the "Glossarietto esplicativo" to *Variazioni belliche* that she prepared, "La serie degli armonici," and "Storia di una malattia."

Monographs and Edited Collections on Amelia Rosselli

Baldacci, Alessandro. *Amelia Rosselli.* Universale Laterza. Rome: Laterza, 2007.
————. *Fra tragico e assurdo: Benn, Beckett e Celan nella poetica di Amelia Rosselli.* Cassino: Edizioni dell'Università degli studi di Cassino, 2006.
Bisanti, Tatiana. *L'opera plurilingue di Amelia Rosselli: Un "distorto, inesperto, espertissimo linguaggio."* Letteratura Italiana. Pisa: Edizioni ETS, 2007.
Carbognin, Francesco. *Le armoniose dissonanze: "Spazio metrico" e intertestualità nella poesia di Amelia Rosselli.* Bologna: Gedit Edizioni, 2008.
De March, Silvia. *Amelia Rosselli tra poesia e storia.* Naples: L'Ancora del Mediterraneo, 2006.
Fiori, Giuseppe. *Casa Rosselli: Vita di Carlo e Nello, Amelia, Marion e Maria.* Turin: Einaudi, 1999.
Fusco, Florinda. *Amelia Rosselli.* La scrittura e l'interpretazione. Palermo: Palumbo, 2008.
La Penna, Daniela. *"La promessa di un semplice linguaggio": La dinamica delle fonti nell'opera trilingue di Amelia Rosselli.* Rome: Carocci, 2009.
Limone, Giuseppe, and Simone Visciola, eds. *I Rosselli: Eresia creativa, eredità originale.* Naples: Guida, 2005.
Sannelli, Massimo. *Il prâgma: Testi per Amelia Rosselli (1999–2000).* Naples: Dedalus, 2000. E-book at http://www.vicoacitillo.net/led/rosses.pdf.
Savino, Stella, and Rosaria Lo Russo. *Amelia Rosselli . . . e l'assillo è rima.* In *La furia dei venti contrari.* Florence: Le Lettere, 2007. A documentary film.
Snodgrass, Ann. *Knowing Noise: The English Poems of Amelia Rosselli.* Studies in Italian Culture: Literature in History. New York: Peter Lang, 2001.
Tandello, Emmanuela. *Amelia Rosselli: La fanciulla e l'infinito.* Rome: Donzelli, 2007.

Journal Issues Devoted to Amelia Rosselli

Attanasio, Daniela, and Emmanuela Tandello, eds. "Amelia Rosselli." Special Issue, *Galleria: Rassegna quadrimestrale di cultura* 48, nos. 1–2 (January–August 1997). Caltanissetta: S. Sciascia, 1997.

Devoto, Giorgio, and Emmanuela Tandello, eds. *Trasparenze* 17–19 (2003). Triple issue dedicated to Amelia Rosselli.

Giovannuzzi, Stefano, ed. "'Se / dalle tue labbra uscisse la verità.' Amelia Rosselli a dieci anni dalla scomparsa. Atti del Convegno del Circolo Rosselli, 8–9 June 2006." Special Issue, *Quaderni del Circolo Rosselli* 27 (March 2007).

———. "Amelia Rosselli: Un'apolide alla ricerca del linguaggio universale. Atti della Giornata di Studio, Florence, Gabinetto Vieusseux, 29 May 1998." Special Issue, *Quaderni del Circolo Rosselli* 17 (1999).

———. "Se dalle tue labbra uscisse la verità: Amelia Rosselli a dieci anni dalla scomparsa. Atti del convegno del Circolo Rosselli, 8–9 June 2006." Special Issue, *Quaderni del Circolo Rosselli* 3 (2007).

Sgavicchia, Siriana, ed. Dossier on Amelia Rosselli. Special Issue, *Il caffè illustrato* 3, nos. 13/14 (July–October 2003).

Verbaro, Caterina, ed., *"Scrivere è chiedersi come è fatto il mondo." Per Amelia Rosselli.* Atti del Convegno, Università della Calabria, 13 December 2006. Soveria Mannelli: Rubbettino, 2008.

Representative Anthologies and Collections

Allen, Beverly, Muriel Kittel, and Kealla Jane Jewell, eds. *The Defiant Muse: Italian Feminist Poets from the Middle Ages to the Present. A Bilingual Anthology.* New York: Feminist Press at the City University of New York, 1986.

Ballerini, Luigi, Paul Vangelisti, and Paolo Barlera, eds. "Shearsmen of Sorts: Italian Poetry 1975–1993." *Forum Italicum*, Italian Poetry Supplement (1992).

Blum, Cinzia Sartini, and Lara Trubowitz, eds. *Contemporary Italian Women Poets: A Bilingual Anthology.* New York: Italica Press, 2001.

Butcher, John, and Mario Moroni, eds. *From Eugenio Montale to Amelia Rosselli: Italian Poetry in the Sixties and Seventies.* Leicester, UK: Troubador, 2004.

Davico Bonino, Guido, and Paola Mastrocola, eds. *L'altro sguardo: Antologia delle poetesse del Novecento.* Milan: Mondadori, 1999.

Frabotta, Biancamaria, ed. *Donne in poesia: Antologia della poesia femminile in Italia dal dopoguerra ad oggi.* Rome: Savelli, 1976.

Luperini, Romano, and Pietro Cataldi, eds. *Neoavanguardia e dintorni: Edoardo Sanguineti, Elio Pagliarani, Amelia Rosselli.* Palermo: G. B. Palumbo & Co., 2004. Videocassette containing interview with Rosselli and critical commentary.

Mengaldo, Pier Vincenzo, ed. *Poeti italiani del Novecento*. Milan: Mondadori, 1978.

O'Brien, Catherine. *Italian Women Poets of the Twentieth Century*. Dublin: Irish Academic Press, 1996.

Ó Ceallacháin, Éanna. *Twentieth-Century Italian Poetry: A Critical Anthology (1900 to the Neo-Avantgarde)*. Leicester, UK: Troubador, 2007.

Picchione, John, and Lawrence R. Smith, eds. *Twentieth-Century Italian Poetry: An Anthology*. Toronto: University of Toronto Press, 1993.

Rothenberg, Jerome, and Pierre Joris, eds. *Poems for the Millennium: The University of California Book of Modern & Postmodern Poetry*. 2 vols. Berkeley: University of California Press, 1995.

Smith, Lawrence R., ed. *The New Italian Poetry, 1945 to the Present: A Bilingual Anthology*. Berkeley: University of California Press, 1981.

Vegliante, Jean-Charles. *Poésie entre les langues*. Paris: Université de Paris III, 1994.

Venturini, Monica, ed. *Dove il tempo è un altro. Scrittrici del Novecento: Gianna Manzini, Anna Maria Ortese, Amelia Rosselli, Jolanda Insana*. Rome: Aracne, 2008.

Book-Length Translations of Amelia Rosselli

The Dragonfly: A Selection of Poems, 1953–1981. Translated into English by Deborah Woodard and Giuseppe Leporace. With a preface by Deborah Woodard. New York: Chelsea Editions, 2009.

Impromptu. Translated into French by Jean-Charles Vegliante. Paris: Tour de Babel, 1987.

Poesías. Translated into Spanish by Alessandra Merlo, with the collaboration of Juan Pablo Roa and Roberta Raffetto. With a prologue by Pier Paolo Pasolini. Montblanc, Tarragona: Igitur, 2004.

Tatakai no vuarieshon. Translated into Japanese by Tadahiko Wada. Tokyo: Shoshi Yamada, 1993.

War Variations: A Bilingual Edition. Translated into English by Lucia Re and Paul Vangelisti. With an introduction and notes by Lucia Re and an afterword by Pier Paolo Pasolini. Los Angeles: Green Integer, 2005.

Selected Critical Articles on Amelia Rosselli

Anedda, Antonella. "Lampi di pena in gelide atmosfere." Review of *Diario ottuso*. *Il manifesto*, 4 January 1991.

Annovi, Gian Maria. "Una libellula da combattimento: lingua, corpo, genere nella poesia di Amelia Rosselli." In *Altri corpi. Poesie e corporalità negli anni Sessanta*, 93–192. Bologna: Gedit, 2008.

Barile, Laura. "Due parole-tema in *Sleep* di Amelia Rosselli." *Mosaici: St. Andrews Journal of Italian Poetry* 1 (April 2011). http://www.mosaici.org.uk/index.php?p=show_item_home&ID=94.

Berardinelli, Alfonso. "Le poesie di Giovanni Giudici e Amelia Rosselli." *Quaderni Piacentini* 16, no. 64 (July 1977): 153–56.

Carbognin, Francesco. "Amelia Rosselli: Prove d'autore." *Strumenti critici* 19, no. 105 (2004): 245–71.

Carpita, Chiara. "'At the 4 Pts. of the Turning World': Dialogo e conflitto con l'opera di T. S. Eliot nella poesia di Amelia Rosselli." *Mosaici: St. Andrews Journal of Italian Poetry* 1 (April 2011). http://www.mosaici.org.uk/index.php?p=show_item_home&ID=99.

Centanin, A. Satta. "Per Amelia." *Poesia* 11, no. 113 (March 1998): 47–49.

Coletta, Cristina Della. "Amelia Rosselli." In *Italian Women Writers, A Bio-Bibliographical Sourcebook*, edited by R. Russel, 360–67. London: Greenwood Press, 1994.

Cortellessa, Andrea. "Amelia Rosselli, una vicinanza al Tremendo." In *La fisica del senso: Saggi e interventi su poeti italiani dal 1940 a oggi*, edited by Andrea Cortellessa, 317–39. Rome: Fazi, 2006.

———, ed. "Con l'ascia dietro le spalle: 10 anni senza Amelia Rosselli." 5 RAI Radio broadcasts, 6–11 February 2006. Now available at http://www.radiotresuite.rai/radio3.

D'Elia, Gianni. "Lo spazio sonoro del verso." *Il manifesto*, July 31, 1987.

Di Cinque, Carmen. "Amelia Rosselli and Exile in the *Serie ospedaliera*." *Carte italiane* 1, no. 14 (1994): 22–29.

Forti, Marco. "La poetica del lapsus." Review of *Variazioni belliche*. *Corriere della sera*, 21 October 1964.

Fortini, Franco. "Amelia Rosselli." *Breve secondo Novecento*. Lecce: Manni, 1996. Reprinted in Franco, *Saggi ed epigrammi*, 1171–72. Milan: Mondadori, 2003.

Frabotta, Biancamaria. "Lingua di molte madri." Review of *Sleep*. *L'indice dei libri del mese* 6 (June 1992): 9.

———. "'Lo sai, debbo riperderti e non posso': Le terribili guerre delle parole nei primi scritti di Amelia Rosselli." *Il manifesto*, 18 October 1980.

Giovannuzzi, Stefano. "*La libellula*: Amelia Rosselli e il poemetto," in "Amelia Rosselli: Un'apolide alla ricerca del linguaggio universale; Atti della giornata di studio. Firenze, Gabinetto Vieusseux, 29 maggio 1998." Special Issue, *Quaderni del Circolo Rosselli* 17 (1999), 45–57.

La Penna, Daniela. "Aspetti stilistici e linguistici della poesia italiana di Amelia Rosselli." *Stilistica e metrica italiana* 2 (2002): 235–72.

Leake, Elizabeth. "'Nor Do I Want Your Interpretation': Suicide, Surrealism, and the Site of Illegibility in Amelia Rosselli's *Sleep*." *Romanic Review* 97, nos. 3–4 (May 2006): 445–59.

Loi, Franco. "Poesie italiesi senza peccato." Review of *Sleep*. *Il Sole-24 Ore*, 26 April 1992.

Lorenzini, Niva. "Memoria testuale e parola 'inaudita': Amelia e Gabriele," in *Trasparenze* 17–19 (2003): 155–71.

Maraini, Dacia. "Sola contro il mondo." *Paese sera*, 2 July 1976.

Mengaldo, Pier V. "Amelia Rosselli." In *Poeti italiani del Novecento*, edited by Pier V. Mengaldo, 993–97. Milan: Mondadori, 1978.

Moe, Nelson. "At the Margins of Dominion: The Poetry of Amelia Rosselli." *Italica* 69, no. 2 (Summer 1992): 177–97.

Moroni, Mario. "Desinenze differenti: L'io poetico al femminile." In Moroni, *La presenza complessa: Identità e soggettività nelle poetiche del Novecento*, 129–44. Ravenna: Longo, 1998.

Parzen, Jeremy. "Amelia Rosselli's *Sleep (Sonno)*: Beyond the Double Margin." *Carte italiane* 1, no. 14 (1994): 31–39.

Pasolini, Pier Paolo. "Notizia su Amelia Rosselli." *Il Menabò* 6 (1963): 66–69. Reprinted as preface to A. Rosselli, *Variazioni belliche*, edited by P. Perilli, 7–10. Rome: Fondazione Piazzolla, 1995. Reprinted in A. Rosselli, *La libellula*, 101–5. Milan: Studio Editoriale, 1996.

Passannanti, Erminia. "Logos e spazio nella poesia di Amelia Rosselli: *La libellula* e *Serie ospedaliera*." In *Spazio e spazialità poetica nella poesia del Novecento: Saggi su Fortini, Montale, Rosselli, Ungaretti*, edited by Laura Incalcaterra McLoughlin, 67–88. Leicester, UK: Troubador Publishing, 2005.

Pedullà, Walter. "Meglio i poeti." Review of *Serie ospedaliera*. *Avanti!* 6 September 1969. Reprinted in Pedullà, *Letteratura del benessere*, 576–79. Rome: Bulzoni, 1973.

Peleggi, Valentina. "Amelia Rosselli: Musica in poesia." *Quaderni del Circolo Rosselli* 30, no. 107 (February 2010): 67–104.

Perrella, Silvio. "Per Amelia Rosselli." *Nuovi argomenti* 12 (1997).

Porta, Adriano. "Il linguaggio come storia." *Il Giorno*, 21 July 1976.

Re, Lucia. "Amelia Rosselli and the Esthetics of Experimental Music." In "Amelia Rosselli," edited by Daniela Attanasio and Emmanuela Tandello. Special Issue, *Galleria: Rassegna quadrimestrale di cultura* 48, nos. 1–2 (January–August 1997): 35–46.

———. "Amelia Rosselli: Poesia e guerra." *Carte italiane* 3 (2007): 71–104.

———. "Poetry and Madness." In "Shearsmen of Sorts: Italian Poetry, 1975–1993," edited by Luigi Ballerini, Paul Vangelisti, and Paolo Barlera. *Forum Italicum*, Italian Poetry Supplement (1992): 132–52.

———. "Variazioni su Amelia Rosselli." *Il verri* 374 (September–December 1993): 131–50.

Rosselli, Aldo. "Amelia, Sibilla e Gorgone." Special Issue, *Galleria: Rassegna quadrimestrale di cultura* 48, nos. 1–2 (January–August 1997): 155–63.

Schwabsky, Barry. "No Mother Tongue." Review of *The Dragonfly. Times Literary Supplement*, July 2, 2010.

Snodgrass, Ann. "Rosselli's 'Nouvelle symphonie litteraire': Erasure and Intertext, 'Her Sense of Distances.'" *South Atlantic Review* 63, no. 4 (Fall 1998): 1–10.

Spatola, Adriano. Review of *Variazioni belliche*. *Il verri* 16 (August 1964): 121–22.

Tandello, Emmanuela. "Doing the Splits: Language(s) in the Poetry of Amelia Rosselli." *Journal of the Institute of Romance Studies* 1 (1992): 363–73.

———. "Il volo della 'Libellula.'" In "Amelia Rosselli," edited by Daniela Attanasio and Emmanuela Tandello. Special Issue, *Galleria. Rassegna Quadrimestrale di Cultura* 48, nos. 1–2 (January–August, 1997): 47–57.

Veschi, Gabriella. "Innovazione e tradizione nella poesia di Amelia Rosselli." In *Incontri transnazionali: Modernità, poesia, sperimentazione, polilinguismo*, edited by Marina Camboni and Renata Morresi, 129–45. Florence: Le Monnier, 2005.

Zanzotto, Andrea. "Care, rischiose parole sibilline." *Corriere della sera*, July 18, 1976. Reprinted as "Amelia Rosselli: Documento." In A. Zanzotto, *Aure e disincanti nel Novecento letterario*. Milan: Mondadori, 1994. Reprinted again in A. Zanzotto, *Scritti sulla letteratura*, 127–29. Milan: Mondadori, 2001.

Note: For a more exhaustive bibliography, see Francesco Carbognin, "Bibliografia rosselliana," *Trasparenze* 17–19 (2003): 361–81; and the thesis by C. Princiotta, "Una lettura di *Impromptu* di Amelia Rosselli" (2006–2007, University "La Sapienza" of Rome, directed by Biancamaria Frabotta).

Other Works Cited

Adorno, Theodor W., and Max Horkheimer. *Dialectic of Enlightenment*. Translated by John Cumming. New York: Continuum, 1999.

Brathwaite, Kamau. *History of the Voice: The Development of Nation Language in Anglophone Caribbean Poetry*. London: New Beacon Books, 1984.

Deleuze, Gilles, and Félix Guattari. *Kafka: Toward a Minor Literature*. Translated by Dana Polan. Theory and History of Literature. Minneapolis: University of Minnesota Press, 1986.

Eliot, T. S. *The Complete Poems and Plays 1909–1950*. New York: Harcourt, Brace and Co., 1952.

Fortini, Franco. *I poeti del Novecento*. Rome: Laterza, 1977.

Foucault, Michel. "Of Other Spaces." *Diacritics* 16, no.1 (Spring 1986): 22–27.

Gabaccia, Donna R. *Italy's Many Diasporas*. Global Diasporas. Seattle: University of Washington Press, 2000.

Moravia, Alberto. *Lettere ad Amelia Rosselli: Con altre lettere familiari e prime poesie (1915–1951)*. Milan: Bompiani, 2010.

Parati, Graziella. *Mediterranean Crossroads: Migration Literature in Italy*. Madison, NJ: Fairleigh Dickinson University Press, 1999.

Pasolini, Pier Paolo. *Empirismo eretico*. Milan: Garzanti, 1995.

Pugliese, Stanislao G. *Carlo Rosselli: Socialist Heretic and Antifascist Exile*. Cambridge, MA: Harvard University Press, 1999.

Rosselli, Aldo. *La famiglia Rosselli: Una tragedia Italiana*. With a foreword by Sandro Pertini and preface by Alberto Moravia. Milan: Leonardo, 1992.

Rosselli, Amelia Pincherle. *Gente oscura*. Turin: Roux e Viarengo, 1903.

———. *Memorie*. Ed. Marina Calloni. Bologna: Il Mulino, 2001.

Rosselli, Silvia. *Gli otto venti*. Ed. Cristina Zaremba. La Nuova Diagonale. Palermo: Sellerio, 2008.

Sgavicchia, Siriana. "In principio era la musica: Da Bartok a Cage passando per l'oriente." *Il caffè illustrato* 3, nos. 13–14 (2003): 54–58.

Venuti, Lawrence. *The Translator's Invisibility: A History of Translation*. 2nd ed. London and New York: Routledge, 2008.

Verdicchio, Pasquale. *Bound by Distance: Rethinking Nationalism through the Italian Diaspora*. Madison, NJ: Fairleigh Dickinson University Press, 1997.

Index of Poem Titles and First Lines

Note: Titles appear in **boldface**.